THE TROUT
FISHERMAN'S
BIBLE

REVISED EDITION

Dan Holland

THE TROUT FISHERMAN'S BIBLE

REVISED EDITION

DOUBLEDAY & COMPANY, INC./GARDEN CITY, NEW YORK

Library of Congress Cataloging in Publication Data

Holland, Daniel John.
  The trout fisherman's bible.

  1. Trout fishing—United States.   I. Title.
SH687.H75   1979   799.1′7′55
ISBN 0-385-14406-7
Library of Congress Catalog Card Number 78–55853
9

CONTENTS

THE TROUT FISHERMAN'S BIBLE

REVISED EDITION

Chapter 1

CHARS

When man first took trout seriously—fifty thousand or so years ago—fishing was pretty good. We've all heard how good it was yesterday, or last week, or last year; and the old-timer tells us that when he was a boy—well, son, the water was stiff with trout, simply stiff with 'em, that's what. So it's reasonable to assume that the Neanderthal man packed a heavy creel.

Both man and trout are the latest things in their lines. Each is of recent origin, geologically speaking, and each has risen to occupy the top rung of his respective evolutionary ladder. Obviously, the good Lord knew that the world wouldn't be a fit place for a man without trout; so He laid His plans accordingly.

Far back in those misty beginnings of things, the ancient forerunner of trout ventured out of the life-giving sea and made a home in the cold, rushing waters of the North. He gradually developed to conform with this new environment, and by the time of that last cold spell known as the Ice Age, a trout was a trout; that is, he was much the same in appearance as the trout we know today and he was an inhabitant of cold, clean water only. As the glaciers of this period pushed south, these ancestral trout gradually moved down the coasts of America, Europe, and Asia, entering each available river once it had cooled sufficiently for their tastes.

The earth was completely formed when all this took place; therefore the spread of trout up such coastal rivers was blocked by waterfalls. Beyond these waterfalls, and in the interior of America behind the mountains, were hundreds of miles of beautiful streams as well as great expanses of clear, cold lakes which trout could not reach. Then, to make matters worse, along came civilization to this continent; man cleared the timber, tilled the land, dumped his pollution into the most convenient river, and added even more obstacles for trout by constructing dams. The sparkling waters so necessary for a trout's existence turned silty, dirty, and uninhabitable; and, in other places, the flow of migratory trout from the seas was cut off by the dams. Although trout were still fabulously abundant in the untouched back country sixty and seventy years ago, a good many trout and trout fishermen were in a bad way. So the facts don't always bear out the old-timer's memory.

But about this time the man known as the fish culturist was making himself felt. He and ambitious sportsmen packed trout fry many miles to formerly barren water, thereby extending the natural range of trout considerably. During subsequent years, biological studies have expanded even further the areas that are suitable for fishing; hatchery operations have maintained populations in places where wild trout cannot reproduce; and, most important, there is the ever-increasing bounty resulting from today's concern with purifying our water supplies. Over the nation as a whole there are undoubtedly far more trout available to the man with the rod and reel today than ever before. In fact, fishing is pretty good—maybe no better than fifty thousand years ago, but pretty good.

Varieties

All the many trout, salmon, grayling, and whitefish belong to one big family, and the branch of this family known as trout is divided by scientists into two distinct groups. Those in one group are known technically as chars. All the trout native to eastern America and the Arctic are chars, while most of those native to western America belong to the second group, the true trout. The best known of the chars is the eastern brook trout, and another member of this branch of the family is that inhabitant of the cool, green depths, the lake trout. In Alaska a well-known char is the Dolly Varden trout. The rainbow, cutthroat, and golden, along with the introduced European brown, belong to the true-trout group.

Scientists have devised this classification on the basis of the arrangement of the bones and teeth of the mouth and the finer scales of the chars; however, there are apparent differences which mean more to us fishermen. In general appearance, all true trout are black spotted on a lighter background, while the chars have light markings, sometimes red, against a darker body color. The chars demand colder water than do true trout and become increasingly abundant toward arctic regions. They are the most northerly of fish, some living on the very edge of the polar icecap. The chars are all fall spawners, while the true trout of America spawn in the spring. The brown, however, although it belongs to the true-trout group, is a fall spawner.

This division of the trout tribe into two general groups is of academic interest only. It means little or nothing to the fisherman. The general appearance and habits of trout and chars are essentially the same. They occupy the same niche in the natural scheme of things, but the anatomical differences indicate to the scientifically minded person that these are two distinct racial divisions of the trout family. For convenience, the trout falling in the char group are discussed in this chapter, those belonging to the true-trout group in the next.

Eastern Brook Trout (*Salvelinus fontinalis*)

The eastern brook trout is the first trout of America. He was the only trout known to the fishermen of this continent for several generations. Early writings on American trout fishing were confined solely to this one species and volumes have been devoted to the praise and glory of the spirited little fish. His love of the purest spring-fed waters and his shy and inscrutable ways have been an endless source of inspiration to trout fishermen.

The brook trout is not so particular about his diet as are most other trout. He is a guileless, shy little fellow and when he is on the feed he is agreeable to almost any kind of natural bait or natural-appearing bait. He feeds quite readily in the coldest of water, so he is a favorite with early spring fishermen. Since he is generally more easily caught and also demands the coldest and purest of water, the brook trout has disappeared from many of his native streams while the introduced brown and rainbow remain.

No black-and-white illustration can do justice to the beauty of a prime Eastern brook trout: the scarlet fins and tail rimmed with ivory, the green back, the red sides, the white belly edged with charcoal, and the fiery pinpoints of red in a blue setting.

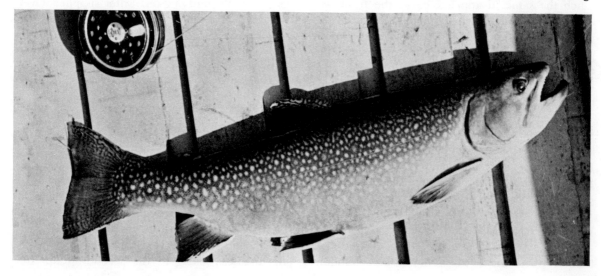

The original range of the eastern brook trout extended along the Atlantic watershed of the United States and Canada as far north as Labrador and into Hudson Bay, south through the Appalachians to northern Georgia, and west along the Great Lakes watershed to Minnesota. During the glacial epoch mentioned earlier, the brook trout entered coastal streams as far south as Georgia, but as the earth warmed gradually to the temperate climate we know today, he was forced out of the lowland rivers of the South into the tiniest of mountain brooks. Farther north, where climatic conditions were still suitable, cultivation of the land drove him back into the mountains. Therefore, he was well-named—"brook" trout. Only in the northeastern states and Canada could he exist in the main streams and rivers of the valleys. But this has not detracted from him since he has an ability to flourish in confined waters. One of the best brookies it has been my fortune to take in the States came from a meadow spring hole no bigger than an ordinary room.

I have taken many larger eastern brook trout than this from deep lakes in Maine, along St. Ignace Island in Lake Superior, in salmon rivers of the Maritime Provinces, and in the mighty Nipigon and other big Canadian rivers farther north, but these seem like different fish somehow. The brook trout has his greatest appeal in small waters. The size of trout is entirely relative to the surroundings and conditions anyway, and a twelve-incher in a meadow brook or in a dark-bottomed New England beaver pond can cause more internal combustion within me than can a four-pounder in a big northern river.

The eastern brook trout is identified immediately by the pale, wormlike mottlings on his back, known as vermiculations. No other trout has these marks. Also, when looking down on the backs of trout in the water, the fisherman can pick out the brook trout by the conspicuous white rims on the pectoral, or foremost, fins.

This is the southernmost and also the finest of the many trout in the group known as chars. He is certainly the best known and best loved by sportsmen, although he has some far northern relatives which have great sporting possibilities.

The brook trout was transplanted years ago to the waters of western states and can be found today in many of the small streams and lakes of the Rocky Mountains and Sierras. Years ago when I first had the chance to fish in the Rockies I was all excited about the prospect of catching a cutthroat, the native western trout. We first fished at the foot of the Grand Mesa in Colorado in a little creek whose ambitions to become a river were soon thwarted by irrigation ditches. The first trout I caught instead of being the expected cutthroat was an eastern brook trout. That's the one and only time I've ever been disappointed in landing a brookie.

The brook trout has done well in the creeks and high mountain lakes of many western states, but nowhere has he proven as fine a game fish as in his native waters. In many places in the Northeast, especially Maine, and in eastern Canada brook trout can still be found at their primitive best.

Dolly Varden Trout (*Salvelinus malma*)

As far as I know, Charles Dickens was not a trout fisherman, and he certainly knew nothing of the existence of the Dolly Varden trout; yet he gave this fish its name. In his novel, *Barnaby Rudge*, Dickens described the character Dolly Varden so vividly and delightfully that the colorful attire she wore set a style among the ladies of the 1840s. About this time the Dolly Varden trout of our West was discovered, described, and given this name which carried its own compliment.

Some years ago commercial salmon interests discovered that Dolly Varden trout, from which they could make no money, ate salmon eggs. It is the horrible truth. Dolly Vardens do eat salmon eggs. All trout eat salmon eggs. Even salmon eat salmon eggs. It's the nature of the beasts. But the chances are that most free-floating eggs so eaten are not fertilized and little actual harm is done. Bullheads and sticklebacks, however, do get down among the crevices in the gravel and gorge on fertilized spawn. These are the culprits, but they are kept under control by trout, including Dollies, since these little fish constitute a major source of trout food the year round. But, in the innocence of ignorance, a bounty was actually placed on the Dolly Varden. Trout tails (bounty hunters weren't too careful to distinguish the Dolly from the rainbow and cutthroat—or even salmon) were strung forty to a wire, such wires bringing one dollar in barter as well as bounty in Alaska at the time. The bounty didn't last long, but its educational effect has.

The natural range of the Dolly Varden extends from California and Wyoming north through the Pacific drainage to the edge of the

Trout are divided into two distinct groups, true trout and chars. As this photograph of an Idaho Dolly Varden shows, all chars have light spots against a darker background as distinguished from true trout which are marked in the opposite fashion, dark spots over a lighter background.

Arctic Ocean in Alaska. He is not as plentiful as he once was. Every effort was made to destroy him and none to preserve him.

I have caught many Dolly Varden trout, or bull trout, as they are usually called in the West. Some have been little mountain trout caught on a fly; others silvery ten-pound seagoing specimens on a casting rod and a pike spoon. I have enjoyed every one I ever hooked. Anyone who runs down the Dolly Varden either has been spoiled by too many rainbows and cutthroat, as can be the case in Alaska, or he is the unknowing victim of the prejudice established by the one-time bounty. The latter fisherman has probably never been lucky enough to see a Dolly Varden trout in his life.

Sea Trout (*Salvelinus fontinalis*)

The term "sea trout" in America refers strictly to the wandering eastern brook trout. In Europe a sea trout is a migratory brown, but here the name refers to an eastern brook trout which has been to salt water, somewhat in the fashion of a salmon or steelhead, and has acquired a silvery coat of mail and an extra charge of energy. Although he is a fall spawner, the sea trout enters the rivers in the greatest numbers in June, and when he arrives he is plumb full of that vim and vinegar that makes the world go round. All brook trout are dogged, tireless fighters, but the seagoing variety adds to this determination a lot of speed and high-flying tactics. He's an eastern brook trout that can't get out of high gear.

Any species of trout with direct access to the sea is inclined to take advantage of the bountiful nature of salt water and become migratory to a degree. At sea he is silvery, but after some time in fresh water he looks like any other nonmigratory trout of the same species. The best-known example of this inclination to return to the ancient ancestral home, the ocean, is the seagoing rainbow, or steelhead. In northwestern America there are seagoing cutthroat and Dolly Varden as well as steelhead, and in the Arctic the arctic char and even the lake trout go to salt water. We do not have any sea-run brown trout in America, although I have caught them in South America, where they were also introduced, of course. This big brown trout and our steelhead lead lives almost identical to that of the Atlantic salmon, journeying far to sea and returning to their parent streams only on the spawning migration. Judging by their size, I assume this is true of the arctic char as well. The sea-run eastern brook trout, as well as the cutthroat and Dolly, lead a less involved migratory existence. After spawning they return to salt water to take advantage of the more abundant food, but it is doubtful if they ever leave the influence of their parent stream. They are commonly found in brackish water off the stream's mouth, and often wander in and out of fresh water regardless of the spawning urge.

Sea trout were once plentiful throughout the coastal streams of our northeastern states, but pollution and dams put an end to that. Maine alone has maintained a limited amount of sea-trout fishing, but today the sea trout is primarily a Canadian fish. The sea trout demands much the same conditions as the Atlantic salmon and is found in the same waters, although his range extends north of the salmon's.

Lake Trout (*Salvelinus namaycush*)

The lake trout is the largest of the many varieties of trout. He is a lover of the cool, shadowy depths of our northern lakes. He lives so deep—often more than two hundred feet—that at times it is impractical to fish for him other than by trolling with heavy tackle and a wire line; which means that he hardly belongs in the same category with stream trout. His appeal lies in the mystery of probing the unknown depths and in his great size.

There are indications that in years past the lake trout grew to the huge size of over one hundred pounds. The largest officially recorded, however, was an eighty-pounder. The average today is from five to twelve pounds, depending on the waters fished, and a specimen over twenty-five pounds is unusual.

In the winter the lake trout can sometimes be taken through the ice in from twenty to forty feet of water, and in the spring just after ice is out he is found in sufficiently shoal water to be taken on a casting rod and spoon. I have caught lake trout on a fly, but only to prove to myself that it could be done. Fly fishing for lake trout is like undoing backlashes while wearing mittens—it's the hard way. He's a bottom feeder and a meat eater.

The laker, the giant of the trout tribe, is at his best in northern waters. This big fellow from Waterbury Lake, Saskatchewan, was hooked in less than thirty feet of water by casting and jigging a Dardevle even though the time of year was late July.

Since this is strictly a northerly species, we are acquainted with him principally along the southern limits of his range. This extends from northern New England through the Great Lakes drainage and west to Vancouver Island. He has been introduced south of this natural range into some large western lakes. In the most suitable lake-trout waters available to sportsmen—the Great Lakes—there is heavy competition from commercial interests. This is the only fresh-water game fish whose commercial value exceeds its sporting value. Over ten million pounds of lake trout are taken annually by commercial fishermen. This intense commercial fishing in the larger lake-trout waters accounts for the fact that the huge fish of days past are no longer seen.

On the whole this fork-tailed giant is not to be compared as a game fish with other trout. There are exceptions to every rule, however, especially fishing rules. The man who is lucky enough to go sufficiently far north will find the laker an entirely different creature from the one to which he is accustomed. In these colder waters the lake trout doesn't seclude himself in the deepest hole of the deepest lake. In the great splash of lakes which extends across northern Manitoba and Saskatchewan he is at his best from the sporting viewpoint. He is big and he is available to the man who wishes to cast rather than troll. From there north to the Arctic Ocean, where surface waters are cold enough to suit him, he may be found living habitually in shallow water and even in rivers and streams. Standing at one spot along the Newalen River in Alaska, I have caught a rainbow, a Dolly Varden, a sockeye salmon, and a lake trout on consecutive casts, all living side by side in the same type water. In the icy little streams of the arctic tundra, he actually wanders in and out of salt water and acquires a silvery sheen. Those I have seen so far north have been quite small as lake trout go, but there's a lot of room up there and a lot I don't know.

Arctic Char (*Salvelinus alpinus*)

This is something a person has to see to believe. As his name implies, the arctic char lives only in the Far North, America's last frontier. The region is imposing, but it does have something to offer the fisherman. Since this final wilderness has become more accessible, something should be said of the fabulous trout which lives there. Actually little is known of him as yet.

The name "arctic char" was first applied only to a local variety of trout found in one lake in Greenland; however, my assumption is that the arctic char is circumpolar in distribution and probably has several variations, such as this particular Greenland char. The name more aptly applies to the entire tribe.

I had the good fortune to see my first arctic char years ago. At the time, I had been the fishing editor of America's leading sporting magazine for five years, and I had grown up with an all-absorbing interest in trout; yet, until I saw this first one, I had no idea that such a fish existed. And all I know for certain today is what I have seen with my own eyes on that occasion and on a subsequent trip to the arctic coast of America.

In size and actions, this fish is like a salmon; in distinguishing characteristics, he is definitely a char; in spawning coloration, he is unlike anything any trout fisherman ever saw. The most convenient place I have seen them, and the first, is the Pilgrim River north of Nome, close to the Arctic Circle. This apparently is the southern limit of the range of this trout, and also is just about the northern limit of the range of the Dolly Varden.

The back and sides of the male chars I have seen are a rich green, dark on top and somewhat lighter on the sides. Along the sides are scattered fingernail-sized spots which are either round or peanut-shaped. In sharp contrast to the green background, these spots, the lower sides, and the entire belly are a brilliant orange-red. The lower fins are a bright red, with a broad, white leading edge, like those of a brook trout. The head is charcoal black and the snout and part of the mouth yellow.

This male fish is actually gaudy. Unlike other trout, there is nothing delicate nor pleasing about the green-orange-red-yellow combination of colors. He is stockily built with a heavy head

Grant Jackson of Nome, Alaska, had a creel made which was intended to be large enough for arctic char. The only solution, he found, was to turn back the big ones and keep the little fellows.

and jaws. The female, on the other hand, is a trim-built blue fish with white spots and a white belly and just a touch of yellow on the nose.

From a comparison of his size with the size of his stream, this fish obviously gets his growth in the sea, but whether he is sea-run in the true sense, like the salmon, or whether he merely wanders in and out of salt water, like the sea trout, I can't say. Nor do I know how big he grows. From my own experience I know that this fish attains a weight of twelve-and-one-half pounds, but my experience with this particular trout has been very limited.

Other Chars

Several other unusual trout belonging to the char family exist in America, such as the Sunapee Lake golden trout, the blue-back or oquassa trout of Maine, and the Canadian red trout, but these are of limited interest to sportsmen.

The Sunapee golden is a beautifully colored, slim trout of large size—up to twenty pounds—which was found in the deep waters of only a few lakes and ponds of New Hampshire and Vermont. Although once extremely abundant in Sunapee Lake, the ill-advised stocking of land-locked salmon and lake trout proved to be too much competition for this unique fish. This golden trout has no relation and little similarity to the famed golden trout of California which is not a char but an offshoot of the rainbow tribe.

The oquassa trout, once plentiful in the Rangeley Lakes, was a small but colorful trout; however, he too has decreased in numbers to the point that he is of little importance to fishermen today. There is likely still some good fishing for the Canadian red trout. Canada has been more conservative and wise with such unique resources than we have been. Like all chars it is very colorful, but, like the Sunapee golden and the oquassa trout, it is of limited distribution. It is found in only a few lakes in the Laurentians.

All three of these unusual trout are arctic chars left behind by the receding glaciers several thousand years ago. As the Ice Age came to an end and the glaciers slowly receded to the north, the arctic char was undoubtedly land-locked in many places. In a few of these he found water deep enough and cold enough for survival, and through the countless generations he changed color to conform with that particular environment, the result being the unusual trout mentioned here.

Exhausted and ready for the net—a fine Eastern brook trout.

Chapter 2

TRUE TROUT

At one time a fisherman could identify a species of trout merely by the area in which he was fishing. This is no longer true in America. Our diffusion of species by stocking and transplanting has been almost complete. Only in a relatively few areas south of the Canadian line does the native species still retain undisputed claim to his home waters. In the East a fisherman is far more likely to get a rainbow rather than the native eastern brook trout; and, in general in the West, his chances of happening on an eastern brook trout are as good or better than those of coming up with a native cutthroat.

The rainbow is by far the most prevalent trout in America today. He has been introduced far and wide. There are rainbows in almost all trout waters, and our hatcheries are concentrating more and more on this one species. The next most widely distributed trout in the United States is the brown trout, which was brought here from Europe.

Since this diffusion—or confusion—of trout is so thorough, a fisherman should know how to identify each trout as he sees it. This is a simple key: All the trout discussed in this chapter, the so-called true trout, are spotted black. The chars never have black spots. The eastern brook trout can be distinguished from all other species the world over by the presence of the wormlike, marbled mottlings on the back. Of course it is a char, with no black spots, but usually with tiny red spots bordered by pale blue. The brown, rainbow, and cutthroat are all black spotted, but the brown alone of the black-spotted trout may also have red or a combination of red-and-black spots. His spots are large, usually with a pale border. He has few if any spots on the tail. The rainbow and cutthroat are heavily spotted on the tail, but the cutthroat can always be identified

by the pair of red slashes under the jaw, from which he gets his name.

All the trout described here belong to the same genus, *Salmo,* as the Atlantic salmon. Anyone who has fished for both Atlantic salmon and steelhead—the seagoing rainbow—will have no-

America's only imported trout, the brown, is a native of Europe and Asia. He is considered by many to be our finest game fish today.

Anyone can tell at a glance that this old boy was king of the pool. From the Madison River of Montana, he is typical of the Loch Leven strain of brown trout: long snout, heavy black spotting, and no red spots.

ticed a marked resemblance between the two in appearance, habits and inclinations. This salmon, like his trout cousins, is black spotted.

Brown Trout (*Salmo trutta*)

This was the first and only trout known to fishermen for many hundreds of years. It is the trout of literature, dating all the way back to the ancient Persians and Greeks. It is the graceful and fleet-finned trout which was the inspiration of poets and musicians; the trout of Dame Juliana Berners, Izaak Walton, and Charles Cotton.

Even in America his history is relatively old. In 1883 a German by the name of von Behr brought a shipment of several hundred eggs of his native brown trout to this country. The trout hatched from these eggs were planted in the East. Shortly after this, in 1885, the first shipment of brown-trout eggs from Great Britain arrived, this one from Loch Leven, Scotland. These were first planted in California and later through many sections of the West.

In deference to the gentleman who started it all, the brown was immediately dubbed von Behr trout or German brown trout in the East. In the West all brown trout were called Loch Leven trout. These names still persist to some extent. While they are not wrong, neither are they exactly correct. The brown trout is the native trout of most of Europe and part of Asia, and those hatched from the original shipment of eggs from Germany were little different from the trout of Persia, England, or Norway. And there were several subsequent shipments of eggs from different areas.

Due to the environment in a few isolated spots in Europe, though, local strains of brown trout did develop. The Loch Leven was such a trout. He was typically smaller, more slender, and less inclined to have red or a combination of red-and-black spots than other browns. Occasionally in the West we still run across what appears to be a typical long-snouted Loch Leven trout, but of course browns have been so widely distributed and transplanted here that such individual characteristics have almost entirely disappeared through interbreeding. In fact, the brown was fairly well spread across the United States from coast to coast by 1900.

We are lucky to have this trout in America. Not only has he added variety to our already abundant species of native trout, but he has some outstanding characteristics of his own. One of these attributes which grows constantly more important is the fact that he can thrive in water which is slightly too warm or sluggish for any of our native species. The other is that he knows how to take care of himself. He can survive and reproduce under the most concentrated fishing conditions; that is, he provides highly interesting fishing where otherwise we might have to depend entirely on an artificial hatchery-to-fisherman situation. This is one of the many things I like about the brown. He is wise enough and wary enough to grow up, no matter where he lives. Any trout is shy and cautious, but the brown has a slight edge on our native species on this score. He has been pitted against the fishermen of Europe, then America, for untold generations; and as the fisherman learns the ways of trout, so the trout learns the ways of fishermen.

As with the Dolly Varden a misconception is that the brown trout is a "cannibal" and therefore detrimental to a stream. Any large trout will eat smaller fish when he has the opportunity, but he can catch bullheads, darters, and the young of chubs, suckers, and whitefish easier than he can small trout; so it's a good idea to have a few "cannibals" around to keep a stream clean. However, the brown is no better at this, nor any more so inclined, than a large trout of any species. In fact, the reason he is held in such high esteem by most fine-tackle fly fishermen is that he is predominantly an insect eater.

Another favorable characteristic is that he is not much of a wanderer. He will stay put and grow up as long as there is enough food. He will do well in either lake or stream. In a stream he seems to show some preference for the slower-moving water. A deep hole close against the bank is a favorite spot. He'll wax fat in the big pools and the meandering meadow sections, but don't overlook the dark, slick holes in fast waters.

The brown trout is a cunning, demanding game fish. Although not so colorful as the eastern brook trout nor so spectacular as the rainbow, he has many fine attributes, including a fighting heart which won't allow him to give up until his eyes turn in and his white belly rolls up.

Rainbow Trout (*Salmo gairdneri*)

The identity of the long-forgotten fisherman who first gave the rainbow his name has always intrigued me. There was a man with vision and imagination! No fish was ever more appropriately named. The rainbow of the heavens is a beautiful, arching, graceful thing with all the colors of the spectrum, and so it is, too, with the rainbow trout. Most species of trout have numerous local names, but no one has ever attempted to improve on the name rainbow. Fish scientists from time to time have given the rainbow at least a dozen different Latin names, but the fishermen give him just one.

This trout is America's greatest contribution to the sport-fishing world. Just as we brought brown trout here from Europe, other countries the world over have introduced rainbows. Everywhere that there are fishermen and fast water, there are rainbow trout. Excellent rainbow fishing is found today even in the Southern Hemisphere in such far-off places as South Africa, Chile, India, Australia, and New Zealand.

The native home of the rainbow trout was the Pacific watershed of North America from California to Bristol Bay in Alaska. Several individual species from different watersheds were originally classified, but the intermingling of these in fish-culture operations has eliminated any possible distinction. Most rainbows transplanted to other sections of the United States came from California stock. They were introduced into waters of the Ozarks, Michigan, and the Alleghenies as early as 1880. The rainbow and the brown have taken the place of the native eastern brook trout in many waters that have become too warm for the delicate brookie.

The biggest difficulty in stocking rainbows is the tendency of this trout to wander. Whereas browns and brookies seek the secluded spots, the rainbow prefers open water and big water. As a species, rainbow trout are inclined to work downstream toward larger water; or, if planted where water conditions or food do not suit them, they will make tracks immediately for greener fields.

The rainbow is famed as a fast-water fish, and in mountain streams he will often make his home in small, sheltered pockets right in the white water. But in spite of this he takes readily to lake life, especially if the food is plentiful. Where reservoirs have been built on rainbow streams, as is the case so often in the West, the rainbow tends to drop down into these artificial

Corey Ford (left) and Alastair MacBain exhibit a couple of Alaskan rainbows of a size to put both tackle and nerves to a strain.

A well-conditioned rainbow.

lakes and returns upstream only during the spring spawning run, much as does the steelhead from the sea.

There is no need to emphasize the sporting qualities of this trout. Wherever found, he is generally accepted as the gamest and most spectacular of all trout. He is predominantly an insect feeder and will rise readily to a small fly, either dry or wet. He will also strike willingly at a spinner or other flashy minnow imitation. Rainbow flies and lures can be somewhat brighter and less deceptive than those ordinarily used for brown trout. With a big brown the biggest part of the battle is getting him hooked, with a rainbow it is keeping him hooked. This is a fish which enhances his already great reputation each and every time he takes a fly or hits a lure.

Cutthroat trout (*Salmo clarki*)

One day on the eastern slope of the Sierra Nevadas, in California, I set out to catch five species of trout. I succeeded in getting a golden, an eastern brook, and several browns and rainbows, but I failed to complete the list with a cutthroat.

The ironical part is that the cutthroat was the only trout native to any of the waters of the area. Now, as a whole, he is the least common.

The natural range of the cutthroat is enormous, greater than that of any other American trout. He is native all the way from Mexico to Prince William Sound in Alaska; then after a gap of several thousand miles he reappears in the western Aleutians and along the northern Asiatic coast. The cutthroat was found in major watersheds on both sides of the Continental Divide, whereas other western trout were native only to the Pacific drainage.

This is the ancestral trout of the West, obviously the progenitor of the rainbow trout. He was on hand even before the Rocky Mountains had completely calmed down—or at least while they were still occasionally shrugging their mighty shoulders. Yellowstone Lake, for instance, once flowed through the Snake River into the Pacific; then the land shifted causing the lake to seek a new outlet to the Missouri River and the Atlantic. The cutthroat trout which had already occupied Yellowstone from the Pacific then had access to the eastern slope of the Rockies.

Due to earthquakes, slides, and the like, segments of these early cutthroat trout were separated from one another and isolated for thousands of generations—until man arrived. Subject to the influences of these individual bodies of water, these trout developed obvious and peculiar characteristics of their own. Originally about fifteen individual species of cutthroat were classified. Man, however, has had the opposite effect from nature. He not only has moved some of the cutthroat around, but he has introduced rainbows into most cutthroat waters. The rainbow quite apparently developed from the cutthroat, mainly as a large salmonlike member of the family in the form of the steelhead. Where introduced to cutthroat waters, it interbreeds freely and is the dominant strain. Hybrids rarely occur in the natural state, but in this man-made situation all manner of rainbow-cutthroat hybrids are evident for a few years. Finally the cutthroat vanishes entirely.

There are still some individual strains of cutthroat remaining, and each is quite distinctive. No matter where he is found, or how different he may appear from one of his cousins, he always bears the infallible red slashes under his chin, the identification marks from which he takes his name. This is his trade mark. Even when he gives way to the introduced rainbow, this is the last characteristic to disappear.

From time to time I have had the opportunity of catching cutthroat trout throughout most of their range, from the Rio Grande to the Aleutians, on many types of tackle and under all conditions. They are fine game fish everywhere, and they provide an amazing variety, from the little buzz-tail mountain trout of Colorado to the giant cutthroats of the lakes of Nevada and their silvery, seagoing cousins of northern waters. I cannot but regret to see this colorful native trout give way to outlanders in so many places, even in exchange for so fine a game fish as the rainbow.

The most plentiful strain of pure cutthroat trout remaining today lives in Yellowstone Lake

The cutthroat, once one of the most abundant trout species, is rapidly becoming rare. The thin dark stripes along the underside of the lower jaws of the Yellowstone trout below are the distinctive red marks which give the cutthroat his name.

and the Yellowstone River above the falls. The millions who have caught "black-spotted natives" there know that the cutthroat is generally willing to strike almost any properly presented lure or bait. In fact, during the many years when fishing was permitted from Fishing Bridge at the lake's outlet, cutthroat were hauled out on every conceivable type of tackle and lure. It made little difference if the fisherman had good trout sense or merely good intentions, the trout accommodated—until a heavy hatch came on, that is. Then those trout want small caddis flies and nothing else. I've seen the slick surface of the river dimpled with rising fish almost like a gentle rain. A dry-fly fisherman could slip down along the shore at such a time and make a killing, while the spinners, spoons, and bait of the bridge fishermen were ignored.

And that goes for trout anywhere, any time. When there is a very heavy concentration of any one type of food on hand, whether it's minnows, May-fly nymphs, or willow flies, the trout are inclined to feed on that food alone to the exclusion of all else.

Golden Trout (*Salmo aquabonita*)

The golden trout has inspired many writers to poetic heights. I'll try to control myself, although having just taken a pretty mess of goldens from a beautiful little Sierra lake, I find it a bit difficult to do. I will merely say that the golden is one of the most brilliantly colored trout, that he lives among some of the grandest scenery ever laid before man's eyes, and that with a mind of his own and a fighting spirit he is the match for any fisherman.

The story of the golden is pretty well known, but still interesting. Until discovered by man the golden lived only in small headwater creeks of the Kern River on the western slope of towering Mount Whitney, the highest peak in the United States excluding Alaska. These tiny streams in which he made his home ran through a light-colored volcanic sand, and the theory is that through endless generations of living in the crystal-clear water of this peculiar environment, an offshoot of the Kern River rainbow became the exceedingly brilliant golden trout.

No trout living at a very high altitude will attain large size because the summer growing season is too short, and this was true of the golden. In their native waters they seldom if ever grew to a length of ten inches.

Due to the precipitous nature of the streams which tumble down out of the Sierra Nevadas, most of the headwaters were barren of trout. Falls and cascades prevented trout from inhabiting them naturally. Most of these beautiful but

Golden trout from their native Sierra Nevada creeks. Only where transplanted to lakes with a more abundant food supply do they grow larger, but such goldens often lose the typical parr marks (blotches on sides) and are never as strikingly and delicately colored as these.

barren lakes and streams were ideal for golden trout. By dint of mules and strong backs and a sheer love of their sport, Californians packed golden-trout fry into these new waters. One of the first such places to be stocked was the Cottonwood Lakes system on the eastern slope of the Sierras. In these larger bodies of water at a lower altitude, the golden did surprisingly well. Some grew to an enormous size, as much as eight pounds.

Many other gemlike mountain lakes nestled high among the jagged Sierra Nevada peaks have been stocked with the golden trout, stemming mostly from fry from the Cottonwood Lakes golden. In most of these new waters he retains his brilliancy of color and his dashing nature; however, when introduced into unsuitable water he loses some of his characteristic color. The golden will also interbreed with the rainbow and give way to the latter fish if the two become mixed in the same water.

Purposely or not, goldens have been planted only in mountain waters unattainable by automobile. The fisherman must either hike or pack in by horse to the golden-trout country. Their value, like that of a rare gem, is only enhanced by their inaccessibility.

Steelhead (*Salmo gairdneri*)

A steelhead is a rainbow trout with the habits of a salmon. He has the size and enormous vitality of a salmon and the cunning of a trout. He has about everything that could be desired: speed, stamina, and acrobatic tendencies. He's as fine a game fish as ever took a pass at a Royal Coachman.

Like the salmon he is hatched in fresh water, then migrates to the sea where he spends most of his life. When mature he returns to his parent stream to spawn. Pacific salmon die after spawning, but the steelhead is like the Atlantic salmon: he may return from the sea two or three times on spawning migrations. The steelhead and Atlantic salmon also have much the same

stream tactics and sporting qualities; and, when fresh run, the two fish even have a marked resemblance in appearance. The man who knows how and where to fish for Atlantic salmon is well qualified to take on steelhead.

After a steelhead has been in fresh water for some time, he loses his sea-given metallic sheen and takes on the characteristic rainbow colors, complete with the cherry-red gill plates and the rainbow stripe down the side. From this time on, no one but a scientist could tell the difference between a steelhead and a nonmigratory rainbow, although in coastal waters the chances are that any large trout of the rainbow tribe has been to sea and is thus technically a steelhead.

In the strict sense of the word, we don't have steelhead anywhere in America other than their natural range from northern California to Bristol

Some fellows have all the luck! And it is a lucky young fisherman who can tie into a fresh-run Eel River (California) steelhead. After a steelhead has been in fresh water for a long enough period, his silvery sheen will give way to typical rainbow coloration.

Bay in Alaska, because by definition a steelhead is a sea-run trout. However, many of the rainbows planted throughout the interior have come from migratory stock. These trout tend to move downstream and, if they have the opportunity, will eventually wind up in a lake or reservoir. Here they live and return to the stream only on their spring spawning run. Therefore we have spring rainbow runs out of many large lakes, such as the Great Lakes, the Finger Lakes, and numerous western lakes and reservoirs, which are very similar to the steelhead runs from the sea. There are no steelhead runs out of the Atlantic.

The steelhead is generally an early-spring spawner, but the time of the spawning run varies with the particular river. It depends somewhat on the distance to the spawning grounds, but many rivers have two runs, a spring and a fall run. The spring-run fish spend most of the year in the river, while the fall- or winter-run fish may be in fresh water only a month or two. The very largest steelhead are generally those in the late runs, simply because they have remained in salt water the longest and it is in the sea where they attain most of their growth.

This is undoubtedly one of the finest of all game fish. You know you've been somewhere when you finish one of these customers—or he finishes you.

Grayling (*Thymallus arcticus*)

The grayling is not a trout, but he is almost the essence of a trout in his actions and habits. By nature he is all but strictly an insect eater, more so than any trout, and if given his head when hooked he will outdo a trout at his own game of jumping. There is grace and rhythm in his every movement, from the moment he splits the stream's surface to take a dry fly until he lies exhausted at the angler's feet. A grayling performing on light tackle is a beautiful thing to behold.

He lacks certain trout characteristics, however, most important of which are hardiness and caution. I have seen a grayling caught, released, and caught again on the same dry fly within a matter of minutes. This would never happen to a trout. He is unable to cope with concentrated

The most distinctive physical characteristic of the grayling is his large, colorful dorsal fin. Also evident in this illustration is the black stripe under the chin where the cutthroat trout carries his red emblem. Today this is primarily a fish of northern waters, this large individual coming from the Clearwater River, Careen Lake, Saskatchewan.

fishing and also is susceptible to the least unfavorable change in water conditions. Moreover, he doesn't respond favorably to hatchery rearing. He grows more slowly and is more delicate than a trout. The fry demand food two days after hatching—food so fine that it must first be passed through cheesecloth or a sieve—and they must be fed as often as every twenty minutes at first and watched carefully. They must be given an infant's care for three months, which is too much bother for most hatcheries. So the dainty grayling, once very numerous in two distinct areas south of Canada, is little more than a curiosity today. Only in Alaska and parts of Canada —notably, northern Saskatchewan—are these delicately colored, sweet-meated fish found in abundance.

Frank Dufresne once told me that he considers the most beautiful of all fish the arctic grayling in its spring spawning colors, and so it has been throughout the angler's history. Everywhere that man has associated with grayling, he has praised him.

Izaak Walton wrote, "And some think he feeds on water-thyme, for he smells of it when first taken out of the water." The French, in turn, once believed that the grayling fed on gold, so highly was he valued. In the Middle Ages Dame Juliana Berners said, "The grayling is a delicious fish to many's mouths." St. Ambrose, the Bishop of Milan, who lived in the fourth century, spoke of the grayling as the "flower of fishes." And, even before his time, Aelian, the Roman rhetorician who wrote in Greek and was the first ever to mention an artificial fly in writing, significantly spoke of the fly in connection with the grayling.

Chapter 3

LIFE HISTORY

It's a sad fact that 10 per cent of the fishermen catch 90 per cent of the trout. There are many reasons for this; each page of this book attempts to explain these reasons in part. The purpose of the book as a whole is to make better fishermen of those who read it, and to this end no one phase of the sport can be neglected. If any one section of it is more important than any other, however, it is these beginning chapters concerning the nature of the trout. If a man thoroughly understands a trout's character, he could find and kill them with his bare hands; if he fails to comprehend the wheres, whys, and hows of a trout's existence, he could use the finest tackle in the world all day long and not get the first strike. Read this and apply it when you are on the stream: move slowly, be aware, observe. With the knowledge you acquire in this manner you can put tackle to the purpose for which it was designed.

From the very start, for instance, a trout is a fast-water fish. His first voluntary move is to orient himself to the current which surrounds him, the current which will be his home for at least a year and probably for a lifetime. He first sees the light of day in the headwaters of brooks and creeks, sometimes many miles from the home of his parents. As he grows, he gradually moves downstream to larger water, and by the time he arrives in the neighborhood of the parent trout he is big enough to fend for himself— and take care of himself he must, for even his own kind is ready and willing to make a meal of him. A trout's existence is hazardous from the moment he first wriggles out of the gravel. He is shy and cautious. If he weren't, he would never live long enough to take a hook.

Spawning

When the spawning season approaches, trout commence an annual migration, the extent of which depends upon the distance to suitable grounds for depositing their eggs. Sometimes the journey is quite prolonged, on the order of the salmon run from the sea. For certain trout it is a trip of many miles all the way to the headwaters of their river, while others may be so situated that they must travel but a few hundred yards to a nearby tributary.

Some eastern brook trout are said to spawn successfully in the lake or pond in which they live by taking advantage of the gravel bed and current formed by an underwater spring. With only a few exceptions, however, trout living in lakes travel up the inlet streams to spawning grounds. They are inclined to gather off the mouth of the inlet for some time prior to running. A rise in the level of the stream, such as might be caused by a rain or the melting of snow, seems to prompt them to start the journey.

Not all trout make a spawning migration. Many are too immature to spawn, and some large trout do not spawn each year. About three-quarters of the trout population remain behind, and a few non-spawners make the trip futilely. These non-spawners may be prompted to run through instinct, or they may follow along to feed on the eggs of other trout. Some rainbow trout are known to run out of large western lakes in the fall along with the brown trout, although rainbows normally run and spawn in the spring.

Spawning maturity depends on growth and development, not age alone. Rapidly grown male trout in a hatchery are occasionally ready to spawn at the end of the first year, but under normal wild conditions a trout would not be ready to spawn until at least its third year. Steelhead trout follow a slightly different pattern from nonmigratory trout. The steelhead as a rule spends two years in its parent stream, then goes out to sea where it spends another two or three years before returning to spawn. A steelhead may return from the sea several times to spawn. Rainbows living in large lakes live a steelhead existence, their lake taking the place of the ocean.

This spawning migration is a mysterious and wonderful thing. Apparently trout are much like salmon in that they seem to return to the scene of their birth when it comes their turn to spawn. This is not invariably true, for occasionally even salmon are seen hammering away vainly at the base of a falls which drops directly into salt water, but for the most part these fish know instinctively where they are bound.

Probably the most remarkable of all spawning migrations is that of the sockeye or red salmon. This fish spawns only in the inlets or gravelly shores of certain suitable lakes located far up the headwaters of rivers. In some cases the salmon may have an upstream battle of more than two thousand miles to reach such a location, but if the journey is exceptionally long and difficult, he starts just that much sooner in order to arrive at the proper time. It is beyond man's power to understand what force directs him to enter the proper river, then guides him on his difficult journey up the many-branched river, until he arrives at his mountain lake. All such actions beyond our ken we attribute, conveniently, to "instinct."

A trout's journey, although occasionally it may be quite extensive, is not so complex as the salmon's. At the trip's end, the female selects a suitable gravelly spot in shallow running water and builds a crude nest. She churns up the bottom with her powerful tail so that the fine sand will be carried downstream, leaving a bed of coarser gravel, known as a redd. This gravel forms a lodging place for the eggs and protects them to a certain extent during the incubation period.

A pair of trout may spawn through a period of a week, the female scooting along on her side spawning the eggs over the gravel and the male following to fertilize the spawn. The pair retires to deeper water temporarily, then returns to spawn again. When all the eggs are deposited, the parent trout drop back downstream to their native haunts, leaving the eggs and their future offspring to the elements. Although the journey may have been one of several miles, the trout seem to return to the very pools from which they started.

The spawning process itself is so haphazard and the existence of the young trout after hatching so full of pitfalls that many thousands of eggs must be spawned to bring a few trout to maturity. A female trout spawns from eight hundred to one thousand eggs for each pound of her weight; that is, a four-pound trout may spawn four thousand eggs.

Brown, brook, and Dolly Varden trout spawn in the fall or early winter; rainbow, cutthroat, and golden trout spawn in the spring, those in

When a trout feeds, he sucks considerable water into his mouth cavity; then, if he has no cause for suspicion, he ejects this water through his gills, straining out the particle of food with his gill rakers (notice the flared gill covers and escaping bubbles of air taken from the surface). The food is then swallowed, or—if it happens to be a bit of debris mistaken for food—is ejected back out of the mouth.

A cautious approach and a deliberate first cast are the secrets to success on clear, confined waters, and the Gawk pictured above (author) is in the very act of setting the hook in a Greater Spotted Racer, one of many he failed to land in this particular Montana creek.

the lowlands as early as February and those in the high mountain lakes and streams as late as June.

Hatching and Survival

Thirty days after spawning, small black dots appear in the fertilized egg. It is in this "eyed" stage that trout eggs, kept dormant at a low temperature, can be shipped great distances for introduction into a new area. About eighty days after spawning, the tiny trout emerges and for the first two weeks subsists on the egg sac which remains attached to the body. The hatching of the egg, like much of a trout's existence, depends on the water temperature. An egg spawned in the late spring or under the influence of controlled temperatures at a hatchery may hatch in thirty days, while one spawned in the fall might not hatch for almost four months.

A young trout doesn't stand one chance in a hundred of growing up and being caught by a fisherman. Only the shallow water in which he is born protects him from the ravages of larger trout, and he is the constant prey of birds, small fish, mink, snakes, turtles, frogs, and the like. Surveys have indicated that 85 per cent of each brood fail to survive the first year and a half. Only 2 per cent of the trout in the wild can be expected to survive until the fifth year. At the most, fisherman catch about one-half of one per cent of the wild trout spawned.

Growth

Immediately after the trout hatches, he is known as an alevin. By the time the egg sac has completely disappeared two or three weeks later and he is foraging for himself, he is about three-quarters of an inch long, and during this next stage of his life the trout is known as a fry. The tiny rudiments of scales are first beginning to form on the body. Next, when he is from three to five inches long, with conspicuous dark blotches, or parr marks, along the sides, the trout is generally referred to as a fingerling. If he gets by his host of enemies through this stage, he can finally call himself a trout.

Under average conditions in a typical stream, a trout at the end of the first year will be from three to five inches long; at the end of the second year, from six to eight inches long; at the end of three years, about ten inches long; and at the end of five years, fourteen inches long. Under the systematic care and ideal conditions of modern hatcheries, however, trout can be grown at the rate of an inch a month for the first ten months or a year. A good hatchery can produce half-pound trout at the end of the first year, and legal-size fish can be turned out in six or eight months. Rainbows retained for breeders in a hatchery reach a weight of about ten pounds in four years. After that they become too big and strong to handle conveniently in the stripping operation.

Under similar circumstances browns and rainbows will grow faster than eastern brook trout. Some eastern fishermen who are partial to the brookie wonder why more of these trout are not stocked. This is part of the answer: it's more economical for the hatcheries to grow rainbow trout. Also rainbows and browns do better in the larger, warmer, and more heavily fished streams than does the native brook trout.

Growth in fish is a considerably different matter from human growth or that in the higher animals we see about us. Growth as we know it is a fairly constant thing up to a certain age when it tapers off and ceases entirely. A trout's growth, on the other hand, may be interrupted many times by periods of inactivity but is continuous throughout his life. He may stop growing time and again, as he often does during the winter, but when conditions again become suitable he resumes where he left off, no matter what his age. The greatest growth will be during the period of greatest vitality—that is, before the age of ten years, if he lives that long—but just as long as he does continue to live and eat he will continue to grow.

The amount that a trout can grow in later life seems to be determined to considerable extent by the amount he grows before reaching maturity. The pattern of growth is set early. Litter-brother trout separated as fry and placed in different environments could vary as much as five inches to five pounds at the end of three or four years' time. After a trout has reached maturity, however, it would be difficult to change his rate of growth for the better. If conditions are ideal from the start, a trout takes advantage of the situation and puts on weight at an amazing rate of speed; but when nature is not so bountiful, he will mature and carry on at a much smaller size.

The rate of growth depends directly on two factors: food and water temperature. The size of the body of water in which a fish is found would seem to play an important role, too, but this is due principally to the feeding opportunities afforded by larger water. Some trout, especially an eastern brook trout, can do surprisingly well in a very limited area if the food is there and the competition for the food not too severe.

The availability of food and the ease with which it is captured is the most important factor. A trout can grow only as he eats. The trout's food is equally important from the fisherman's viewpoint because it is the food of the moment which he must imitate if he is to be successful. The variety of trout's food will be treated more fully in a later chapter.

Food is generally more abundant and obtainable in lakes than in streams, and the largest trout are taken from still waters. Also, generally speaking, the least food is found in the high mountain lakes and creeks above timber line, more in the large rivers and lakes of the valleys, and the most in brackish or salt water.

Temperature controls a trout's life from birth to death. In relation to growth it is important in that it controls the activity of the trout. A trout does not actually hibernate, but in very cold water it becomes inactive and feeds but little. The chars—the eastern brook, Dolly Varden, and lake trout—are more inclined to feed in cold water than are other trout, but even these forage more at moderate temperatures. Not only is the fish itself inactive at low temperatures, but his food as well becomes dormant. Consequently, during the winter months trout do not grow appreciably, and those at very high altitudes, as I have mentioned, never attain very large size.

Hatcheries locate their rearing ponds where there is an abundant supply of spring water which remains constant and moderate in temperature the year around, thereby making it possible to obtain a steady growth throughout the year. A trout living in sixty-degree water will consume almost ten times as much food as one living in forty-degree water. A hatchery at Blaine Springs, in Montana, which has a constant temperature of fifty-four degrees in its rearing ponds grows a ten-inch trout in fourteen months, while the Mount Whitney Hatchery in California with spring water at the optimum temperature of fifty-nine degrees throughout the year rears trout to an average of a foot in fourteen months. The temperature makes that much difference regardless of the food and care. Of course, spring water would not contain much food, but the natural supply is of little concern to the hatchery since it provides its own.

Some of the most outstanding trout growth under natural conditions is witnessed in western reservoirs. These are often located in an arid region because it is there that the water to be provided by the reservoir is most needed. Any Westerner knows that much of this arid land is naturally rich and contains great potential. Once it is irrigated it blooms luxuriantly and provides ideal farmland and pasturage. Although not so

evident, the same thing occurs beneath the surface of the water when the land is flooded by a reservoir. Underwater vegetation flourishes, microscopic organisms and insects grow on the vegetation and on each other, minnows and small fish feed on these smaller forms of life, and the trout in turn are afforded a very abundant food supply.

Many of these reservoirs have large shallow areas in which the constant western sunshine can have the greatest effect in producing life. In the deeper areas of the lake the temperature remains low and thus if the shallows become too warm at any time for comfort, there is always a haven to which the trout may retreat.

In the arid Southwest where formerly no trout could possibly exist, such reservoirs have provided some remarkable fishing. The reservoir becomes a catch basin for muddy, silty rivers and its depth allows the water to cool. The river where it enters such a reservoir may be hot and muddy, but where it comes out beneath the dam it is clear and cool with a constant year-round temperature. The food is abundant. A large dam like the Hoover Dam on the Colorado River will assure excellent fishing in the Colorado for years to come, even though it is located in a desert.

Elephant Butte Reservoir on the Rio Grande in New Mexico with its unlimited supply of sunshine resulted in an almost unbelievable trout growth. However, the existence of trout under such desert conditions hangs by a narrow thread. When the level of the reservoir is pulled

A big one comes to the net.

too low, the temperature of the lake water creeps above the point necessary to sustain trout life, and it's all over, like a real estate boom and bust.

Some eastern lakes and reservoirs which were normally quite barren of trout food have produced unusual trout growth with the introduction of an ideal food supply. One of the best foods for very large trout is smelt, a distant relative of the trout which normally lives in salt water and enters fresh water only to spawn. Many of the large squaretails of Maine lakes and the rainbows of the Finger Lakes of New York, for example, and even the giant coasters, rainbows, and lake trout of the Great Lakes, owe their size to the existence of smelt.

I remember one reservoir that was sufficiently deep and cold to support trout, but it contained an insufficient food supply to produce much fishing. Then a small form of herring, known as a sawbelly, was introduced. These small fish live on plankton and other microscopic organisms too small for any but the tiniest trout. Thus the microscopic life of the reservoir was converted into swarms of mouth-sized sawbellies. Years ago, two- and three-pound trout from neighboring streams won the prizes in the local fishing contests, but after the sawbellies were introduced into the reservoir, contestants talked in terms of ten pounds instead of two.

Anywhere that unusually large trout are caught, either in fresh water or salt, it will generally be found that the food and temperature conditions are just about ideal; and, conversely, where trout don't grow large it will be because either the water temperature remains too low most of the year or because there just isn't enough food to go around.

Color of Flesh

There has been considerable conjecture on the coloration of the flesh of trout, why some are white meated and others are salmon pink. One thing is known: the salmon color is caused by a deposit, in the flesh, of a fatty matter called lipochrome which crustaceans happen to contain in large quantities. Salmon feed extensively on shrimps at sea, and there are also many varieties of fresh-water crustaceans on which trout feed. Such crustaceans are undoubtedly one source of

flesh coloration. However, there is much that is not known. It is not evident why some salmon in a school will have plain white flesh in contrast to their brothers, or why some trout in a pond will have deep-colored flesh and others alongside will be colorless. Apparently there is an inherent ability in some trout, lacking in others, to make use of this substance. Those not so constituted will have white flesh regardless of what they eat.

It also is not known what other natural foods in addition to crustaceans are a source of this fatty matter. The unnatural foods fed in hatcheries rarely contain it, and so the hatchery fish are generally white fleshed.

Most of us are inclined to feel that the fish with the colored flesh is the better eating, whether this is actually so or not. A white-meated salmon brings less money to the fisherman on the market because the customers think that a salmon should just naturally have salmon-colored flesh. Some years ago an enterprising salmon canner in Alaska bought up all the white salmon he could get his hands on at the reduced rate, then cagily put on the label: *Guaranteed not to turn red in the can.*

Age

Only a guess can be hazarded as to the maximum age to which a trout lives. Wild things constantly prey on one another, and the enemies of the trout are so many that it would be rare for one to have the opportunity to die of old age. A trout must be alert and lucky to survive at best, and one that falters is soon gone.

I know that trout in the wild reach an age of fifteen years on occasion. Through a microscopic examination of a trout's scale it is possible to determine his age, and I have seen an enlarged photograph of a scale from a 14½-year-old brown trout which was in good condition when caught.

Trout kept in captivity reach an age of twenty years. Some hatcheries have kept spawners up to fifteen years of age, but trout up to ten years produce more eggs for the food they consume; so the old ones are rarely kept. One hatchery I've visited has a pool of about a dozen old-timers which they have kept around for exhibition purposes. These huge rainbows are eighteen to twenty years old and look as though they're good for a long while yet.

Enough excitement for any fisherman. A steelhead jumps on an Alaskan river.

Trout in the wild may occasionally live to twenty years. I have heard stories of trout which have reportedly been kept in a spring hole for thirty years, but I have my doubts about their accuracy. Government biologists reading the scales of lake trout in the Great Lakes turned up one twenty-year-old laker to my knowledge. A more widespread practice of trout-scale reading will reveal much along these lines.

Trout-Scale Reading

The scales on some trout, especially the eastern brook trout, are so small that some fishermen do not realize they exist. Brook trout and Dolly Varden have the finest scales, golden next, then cutthroat, rainbow, and finally brown with the largest scales. The number of scales, counted in a lengthwise series, is an important factor in classifying various species and subspecies of trout. The scales of the brook trout are so small, for instance, that he has about twice as many (two hundred and thirty to two hundred and forty) in a lengthwise series as does the brown (one hundred ten to one hundred twenty-five).

A trout has the same number of scales when he is a fingerling as he does when he is adult. As the trout grows, the individual scales must grow. When a scale is removed from a trout or salmon and placed under a low-powered microscope, it is possible to see how this growth takes place. Each time the trout grows, a new layer is laid down on the outside rim of the scale, forming a new edge and leaving a conspicuous line where the old rim was. A trout may add ten or fifteen such concentric rings on a scale in a year's time. However, the rings added in the summer when the trout is growing rapidly are wide apart, and those in the winter when he is practically dormant are few and close together. Thus, by counting the number of alternate series of wide summer bands and narrow winter bands, a person can determine the age of the trout in question.

Perfection in the technique of scale-reading takes considerable experience; however, it is not so much the technique as the fact which is of interest to fishermen. An experienced man in this business can determine not only the age with considerable accuracy, but also the number of times a sea-run trout has been to salt water and, within limits, how often a trout has spawned. The more rapid and generally more constant growth afforded by salt water in contrast to fresh shows up on the scale and gives a clue to the trout's ocean existence. The rigors of the spawning period have a pronounced effect on a trout's physical condition, and this spawning operation may show up as an erosion along the edge of the scale rather than as normally added growth rings.

Chapter 4

HABITS

Trout stream success doesn't rest on whether you are right-handed or left-handed, have blue eyes or yellow, smoke filtered cigarettes, or vote a straight party ticket. There are things upon which it does depend, however. Foremost among these is your knowledge of the ways of a trout: his habits, his essential characteristics, and the influence of his peculiar environment. This sets him apart from all other game fish. Once this is understood, and put into practice, a man is well on his way toward becoming a trout fisherman—and a general knowledge of the habits of trout and the type water they prefer will help any fisherman anywhere. A man who is well informed on the ways of trout can visit a strange river and be assured of fair success. He can look at the surface of the stream and picture the character of the water below where the trout makes his home.

Reading a Stream

The moving water of a stream arranges fish in a definite pattern according to its flow. An experienced fisherman detects this pattern. He knows the combinations of currents and eddies which make the best feeding stations. This ability to "read" a stream is essential. Locating a trout comes first; catching him comes last.

It is the current of a stream which brings a trout his food. It does the work while he remains relatively stationary. Yet, though the current is the food-bearer, he doesn't buck it any more than necessary. A trout possesses the original streamlined form and he is essentially a fast-water fish; still, not even a trout has the endurance to hold out against a strong flow continuously. In other words, the current of a stream is his servant, but it would soon become his master if he tried to fight it.

The all-purpose rule to follow in locating trout in a stream is that a feeding fish will take a position where the current will bring him the most food with the least effort on his part, and the larger he is the better this rule applies. He may lie tight against the fast water where he can dash into the current for food, but he will be taking advantage of the slower water along its edges.

If a man learns to read a stream—learns which are the most likely spots in which to expect a trout—he can use his time efficiently. This method of concentrating on the hot spots is what I like to call controlled fishing as opposed to random fishing. This knowledge comes best with experience—if the fisherman remembers the type water in which he has strikes from good fish. Little trout don't count; they're likely to be almost anywhere. Often the large trout won't tolerate the little fellows in the choice holes. There are three trout in the shallow riffs to every one in slower water. However, the majority of trout under eight inches will be in the riffs, and the majority over eight will be in the deeper water.

Individual wild trout do not move much, at least after they are mature. From the time they are fry until they are fingerlings, they drop downstream rapidly from the shallows in which they were spawned to shallow riffs, or the shallows along the edges or tails of pools. From that point they move but little and only as they grow will they take over a deeper, choicer hole. The larger trout will claim the better spots around the pool, and unless forced to they will not leave that vicinity. Aside from the spawning migration, once a mature trout has chosen his home he moves about a limited area only, from feeding to resting station or to hiding place.

A trout always has an immediate hiding place

all picked out. This may be merely deep water close at hand, or it may be an opening under a rock, or an undercut bank, or a hole in the bank like a muskrat hole. If aware of danger, he'll calmly move out of sight into his hiding place and wait a few minutes until the danger is past. If badly startled or pursued, he may be forced to leave the pool entirely, pronto.

There are a lot of things around a trout stream besides man that enjoy trout dinner. So a trout is shy and the least annoyance will put him down. A wild trout mildly startled will be out feeding again in a matter of minutes. If he is frightened two or three times, he may stay down for hours. A "civilized" trout may act differently, however. Where there's a steady stream of people walking the bank, he can't afford to be scared all the time; he'd starve to death. He gets accustomed to them as does the mallard duck which drops into Central Park in New York City and soon thinks no more of people than he would normally of muskrats.

In a fast-moving stream one of the most obvious places to look for a trout is in the lee of an obstruction. Rocks in the current form perfect shelters for feeding trout. Behind each rock is a slick or eddy. In small pockets of this kind, the feeding fish will head upstream and lie against the main current between the main current and the backwater formed by the rock. In very fast water the trout may be forced to lie tight up against the downstream side of the rock for protection. In a smooth section of stream, where the water may be moving fast but not turbulently, there will often be a trout directly ahead of a rock taking advantage of the point where the current splits to go around the obstruction. In fast, slick water this is a favorite spot of a feeding rainbow. A brown will take such a station in somewhat slower moving water, but a brook trout will rarely lie ahead of a rock. He prefers the protection of the slower water behind.

When a rock is very large and has a sizable hole behind it, some trout may be found headed downstream into the backwater formed by the rock, and others will be found headed upstream just below the point where the backwater plays out and the current starts moderately downstream again. In both cases, of course, the trout are headed upcurrent. In streams which carry a lot of sand and silt in flood, the holes behind rocks fill up with refuse. If there isn't a deep spot in the lee of the rock, it won't hold a good trout.

Sometimes overlooked, small streams can provide a lot of action.

Anywhere in a stream that there is deep water right against the bank there will likely be a trout. The friction of the bank slows down the current, and even where there doesn't appear to be a slow spot or an eddy, there may be a trout lying close up against shore.

Just as the bank slows down the water immediately against it so does the bottom of the stream. Although the current may appear steady and too fast for trout on the surface, there may be many trout lying close to the uneven bottom. Such trout are difficult to locate and catch, however. For one thing, it is impossible to judge exactly where they are and, for another, it is difficult to get a lure down to them. A heavy hatch may bring them to the top, the abundance of insects making it worth their while to battle the current, and then there's good fishing; but they're either up or they're down in such water. When they're down, a dry fly is of no use. A deep run with submerged boulders or an uneven bedrock bottom will certainly contain fish and the only thing to do is to go down to them with a spinner, spoon, or deep-running spinning lure.

Any projection from the bank, such as a rocky ledge, will form a sheltered spot for trout. If this sheltered spot is of any size and consists of a backwater, most of the trout will be headed downstream into the current. When you are fishing such holes along a bank, this is a good thing to remember if you are to keep out of sight. A hot spot in a backwater is at the upstream end just where the backwater current rejoins the main current.

Then there are the pools—stream-wide holes with fast water at the head, a deep placid middle section and the gradually shallowing tail. Pools are the most logical and productive places of all for good trout. They afford everything: a heavy current for feeding on waterborne food, deep water for rest and protection, and a large, shallow, smooth-surfaced area near the tail for foraging and feeding on surface insects.

Pools are generally found below cascades or falls, at sharp bends in the river, often below bridges and, of course, below dams. Some streams, like the Beaverkill and neighboring Catskill streams, consist of a continuous series of pools and short rapids, one after another for miles. This makes ideal fishing water. The riffs provide feeding areas for small trout, the pools for large. Other streams, like the Owens of California or stretches of the Gunnison of Colorado, for instance, are practically devoid of pools, and they are difficult to fish. Most of the famous trout waters of the Rocky Mountains have a good share of big pools, and in any such river which is not fished too hard it would pay the fisherman the biggest dividends to concentrate on these pools alone. However, in a heavily fished stream with few pools, these will take the worst beating and it will be worthwhile to look elsewhere for results.

For all-round, day-in and day-out fishing, the heavy current at the head of a pool is the most productive spot. There will be fish feeding there most of the time, and fast water eliminates the necessity for very fine terminal tackle. The deep, quiet water of the pool will harbor some big fish and some resting fish, but they are difficult to get at in the deep water and hard to deceive where the water is so calm. But never overlook any deep run, even though it doesn't empty into a pool. The moderately moving water along its edges will harbor feeding fish.

The shallow tail of the pool is not the place to fish, generally. Most of the time this is the kindergarten, and the little fellows should be left alone. But there are exceptions. Sometimes in the early morning or evening a big trout will be seen foraging through these shallows, generally intent on making a meal of one of the youngsters. Again, when there's a heavy evening hatch on, good trout often drop back into this shallower, faster water at the tail to feed on floating insects. Finally—a special case—sea-run trout often display a salmon's preference for the tail of a pool. If they are in, they generally can be seen.

Big rivers, such as the great brook-trout rivers of northern Canada, some Alaskan rivers, and many South American rivers, present their own peculiarities. The pools are huge. Good fishing spots are located alongside the fingers of current at the head of pools and especially wherever two such currents converge in a V. There the trout will lie at the very base of the V. Otherwise, as where water gradually accelerates at the natural outlet of a lake, the increasingly rapid and shallow water at the tail of the pool is the ideal feeding spot.

There are many different types of trout streams, each one with its own peculiarities. The rocky, uneven stream with many obstructions is the easiest to figure out. Such a stream has fast

The meandering meadow stream provides the best locale for fine-tackle fishing.

and slow water, deep and shallow, and a variety of protective holes behind the rocks and ledges and in the pools. Trout may seem to be everywhere in such a stream and may hit a lure in the fastest water, but such fish generally have dashed out from behind an obstruction to get the lure.

A stream which runs through miles of gravel, such as the Gallatin of Montana, is more difficult to figure out and fish effectively. The gravel and sand bottom conforms to the flow of the water and eliminates obvious holes.

A steadily roaring river, such as the Yellowstone below the falls, can be difficult too. Where there is a backwater, it will have lots of trout, but otherwise the fish must take advantage of the bottom, where they are difficult to reach, or they must lie against the bank in pockets too small to notice. The main river is too heavy to buck.

Some slick-surfaced, steady-flowing streams are just slow enough for a trout to breast the current anywhere while feeding. Such are Silver Creek and the flat water of the Yellowstone River above the falls. When a hatch is on, hundreds of rises can be seen made by trout which lie everywhere just beneath the smooth surface. The faster current along the outside of a bend in such a river may concentrate the food and fish along that shore.

Meandering meadow streams also have their peculiarities. In this slower water a trout might be anywhere, but the best ones will be near the deep water or along a protective cut bank. Also, they often lie below a weed bed, since much of their insect food comes from the weeds. This is especially so when the nymphs are rising from the weeds preparatory to hatching. These meandering little streams of the meadows afford as delightful fly fishing as a man could want. It hurts to see so many of them in the West disappear under reservoirs.

Trout have pretty much the same characteristics and habits wherever they live. In one stream a fisherman might find a good trout in what seems a peculiar place, and if he remembers it he will find trout in similar spots in other streams.

Night Activity

Trout are active during the night hours, especially in the warmer periods. Where the water is low and clear and the fish are unusually shy as a result, they may do most of their feeding from dusk to dawn when they can move about with more safety. Also, if, as in some streams, the water becomes too warm for comfort in the summer, the trout will be active only in the cool of night.

The fact that trout can maneuver well during the dark hours has been well established. Fish culturists who set traps for migrating trout to strip them of spawn have noted that the intensity of the migration is as great at night as it is during the daylight hours.

There is some indication that bright moonlight has a depressing effect on the night activity of trout. This is not due to the presence of the moon, but merely to its light. When the moon is obscured by a dark cloud, the activity resumes.

When Trout Feed

When does a trout feed? That's almost like asking when does a bird fly. He feeds when he gets ready. Fortunately for the fisherman, he's ready most of the time. Trout feed when there is a concentration of food available and as long as it is available. Their search for food is constant. They take advantage of good times when food is plentiful and this tides them over the lean periods. If the water conditions are right and he is undisturbed, a trout's appetite is practically insatiable. A trout rarely gets so full when there's an abundance of food on hand, whether it's a fly hatch or a school of small minnows, that he won't try to take just one more bite. During a heavy hatch I've taken trout whose bellies were so distended that it must certainly have been painful. Yet they took one more fatal bite.

Aside from the seasonal reproductive instinct, a fish is concerned primarily with two things: food and survival. He is intent on either making

Where a tributary joins a river or lake is a good spot to try your luck.

a meal of some other hapless creature or avoiding being eaten himself.

This constant appetite can be dampened by two things: his wariness and the water condition. No matter how hungry he is or how much food is present, his appetite is overshadowed by his caution. A trout stops eating when the water is too bright and clear, when he is frightened or suspicious, when the water temperature drops too low, as in winter, or when the water becomes too warm for comfort as at midday in the summer in some streams. But when conditions are right a trout can be caught at any time with the right lure presented in the right way, because he is always hungry.

Of course much of the fascination of a trout is that he is not always predictable. The man or beast whose next move can be called ahead of time is a dull character. Certainly this is not true of a trout. Many a fine rule on trout behavior must be discarded with experience. A great deal is "known" about trout that isn't true. However, it is safe to set down a few generalities which have been found to hold true.

For instance, under normal conditions the greatest concentration of feeding trout will be found in the early mornings and evenings, especially as spring and summer progress. The evening is the best. The reason is that this is the time of the greatest activity among aquatic insects and when the biggest hatches come on. The minnows and small fish come out to feed on the insects; the trout feed on the minnows, small fish, and insects; and a merry time is had by all, except the insects. A smarter person than I am would fish mornings and evenings and rest during the day.

Special conditions can alter this period of greatest activity or bring on another of equal intensity regardless of the time of day. For instance, a power dam increases its load at a certain hour each day and the water above contains numerous minnows which come through the turbines at this time injured or dead. The trout below the plant naturally go on a feeding rampage when this happens. Or a summer storm breaks loose, clouds a stream and brings with it many earthworms and insects. The trout of course start feeding.

Everything hinges on whether or not water conditions are suitable, but if they are a trout will feed whenever and as long as there is good food at hand. At a time when there is insufficient food to warrant the energy spent in searching for it, he will rest and wait for a more productive period. He gorges himself when the opportunity permits and waits it out when the pickings are lean, just as any wild creature or even primitive peoples do.

An intense feeding condition appears to arise in the autumn. A trout then seems to go on a wild feeding spree apparently in a last attempt to fatten up, like a bear, for the coming winter. In states where autumn trout fishing is permitted, the fishermen can often make a killing late in the year.

But although a trout's appetite is practically ever present, the overpowering instinct of self-preservation cannot be too strongly emphasized. The chances are that a wild trout doesn't know a man from a moose, but he cautiously assumes that anything bigger than himself is an enemy until proved otherwise, especially if it is headed his way. A large trout can be alarmed even by a tiny spinner if it is pulled directly toward him. Anything coming at him with determination is to be avoided. Only cautious trout live to produce their cautious offspring.

The bank walker is inadvertently the trout's best friend. He keeps the trout in a constant state of jitters and on guard. The trout may return to his feeding station soon after the bank walker passes, but he'll be nervous and hard to fool for some time. A trout that has had no cause for alarm is far easier to take than one which has been recently disturbed, although both appear to be feeding.

How long does a trout stay scared? This depends on the water conditions and how hungry he is. In shallow, clear water he may stay down for a long while, possibly until evening, whereas in deep or cloudy water he feels more secure. In rising water he won't stay down so long because rising water brings a lot of food; but when the rain is over and the water begins to drop, the chances are his belly is full and he can afford to be more cautious. When a heavy hatch is on, he won't stay down for more than a couple of minutes. During the evening rise I have seen a trout merely change his feeding station twenty or thirty feet across a pool when disturbed by a careless cast, then go on feeding. If the hatch is a dense one, almost nothing can put a trout down, he is so eager to get his fill, but at the end of the hatch when he's pleasantly

A long way down and farther back up, but the Yellowstone River is worth the effort for any fisherman.

plump, one bad cast might send him to deep water for a couple of hours.

Temperature

The activities of a trout, since he is a cold-blooded creature, are enormously affected by the temperature of the water in which he lives. His life, and sometimes his death, can be attributed directly to changes in water temperature. His appetite and, in turn, his growth are directly influenced.

From the very start of things, the parent trout are prompted to make their trip to the spawning grounds by a change in the water temperature. Under artificial conditions trout have been made to change their time of year of spawning by altering the water temperature, but in the wild they revert to normal. As I have mentioned, the spawned egg may hatch in thirty days or not for ninety days in the wild depending upon temperature. And again in captivity fertile eggs can be kept dormant for long periods of time and shipped anywhere on the earth by holding them at a low temperature.

Of principal concern to the fisherman is how water temperature affects the appetite of the trout. A fish must eat in order to be caught. In general, a trout eats little during the cold winter months. His appetite picks up as the water warms, and this trend continues unless the water becomes too hot during summer middays; then his appetite falls off.

Specifically, we can get some idea of the optimum feeding temperatures by observation as we fish. Many of us have done this for years by noting the times at which trout feed well and observing the stream temperature at the moment, but at best this is a haphazard procedure. As the scientist takes his subject into a laboratory and analyzes it, so can the fisherman. His laboratory is the hatchery. When he takes into consideration certain obvious factors which make a hatchery different from a stream, he can learn all he needs to know.

A constant temperature of around fifty-eight to sixty degrees Fahrenheit seems to be about ideal for rearing trout. Below that temperature they do not feed and grow so well, and above it their vitality is weakened by the lack of oxygen, and disease sets in. This is the point at which we must consider the difference between the hatchery and the wild stream. The water in a rearing station is crowded to the limit with trout, and disease has a much better chance under such conditions than in a sparsely settled stream. In the wild the best temperature for trout, resulting in both increased feeding activity and vigor on a line, is between sixty and sixty-five degrees. Above seventy degrees, however, they will go off their feed.

An example of the difference water temperature can make in a trout's appetite was described to me by the manager of the Mount Whitney Hatchery in California. A trough of trout fry, given as much food as they wanted, consumed less than one-quarter pound at a temperature of forty degrees. At a temperature of sixty degrees the same trout consumed two pounds of food, a ratio of almost ten to one between sixty and forty degrees temperature.

Temperature controls a trout's eating habits in that it also has some control over the activities of the trout's food in the stream. However, insect hatches are not controlled by water temperature alone. They are equally influenced by the condition of the stream aside from its temperature, and of course are greatly influenced by the time of day.

Stream condition therefore is a big factor in fly fishing. A water temperature below forty-five degrees is generally considered best for bait and spinners. From forty-five degrees up, wet flies may be in order, and from fifty-five degrees up, it's dry-fly time. These rules can be set down only generally, however. A clear, constantly flowing spring might come out of the ground at fifty degrees and afford excellent dry-fly fishing, and a high, roily river at sixty degrees would be good only for worms.

When the water temperature becomes too high, it takes the starch out of trout. A trout breathes oxygen and he requires a high content of it in water. As water becomes warmer, the oxygen escapes into the atmosphere. When the oxygen content becomes low, the trout loses his energy. If it becomes too low, he dies. In two streams of equal temperature, the water in the bubbling, splashing stream will contain more oxygen than that in the slow-moving stream. Therefore, trout can remain alive and active among the fast waters of rapids at a much higher temperature than they can in still water.

The brown trout can stand a higher water temperature than can either the rainbow or brook. The rainbow is almost as hardy as the brown while the brook trout requires the coldest water. In pure still water, the lethal temperature for brook trout is between seventy-five and seventy-nine degrees. Browns might stand water up to eighty-five degrees if it were well aerated. A trout exposed to temperatures over seventy-five degrees for any length of time would be weakened and fall to disease even if the lack of oxygen didn't kill him.

Every summer for years we camped on the East Branch of the Ausable River in upper New York, as beautiful a trout stream as was ever conceived. In late June one season a drought began to take effect on the stream. The water was very low; and, when hot weather set in, the trout began to die by the hundreds. Wherever a cool brook or spring emptied into the main river the trout gathered at its mouth, forming a black mass in the design of the merging current. The trout were so near dead that they could be lifted from the water without a struggle. A bucketful of water lifted and poured back into the river gathered the suffocating trout in an eager circle. Just in time it began to rain and a large percentage of the trout survived. But a fisherman is a strange creature. We lost interest in fishing the Ausable. There were more than enough trout there. We knew because we had looked them over one by one. There was an eastern brook trout in the pool directly behind camp far bigger than we had ever dared imagine, but we didn't try to catch him. We didn't fish any more because the mystery was gone. We had seen every trout in the river. With no mystery, there's no fishing.

Fresh sea-run brown trout, Río Grande, Argentina.

Chapter 5

SENSES

The reason for going trout fishing is to catch trout. There are other reasons—other rewards, let's say—and anyone who hasn't experienced a day on a trout stream which has been both full and fruitless is not very aware. In fact, he's barely alive. Nevertheless, we go fishing to catch fish, and a major share of a day's success is measured in these concrete terms. Therefore, where a trout is concerned, it is essential to learn all we possibly can about him. When we do get a picture of how he reacts and why he reacts, either favorably or unfavorably for us, then there is no reason why we can't have our pleasure on a stream and our trout too.

Vision

Too many fishermen ignore the cardinal rule in trout fishing, and that is to keep out of sight. Trout everywhere are shy and have good eyesight. He will generally see the fisherman before the fisherman sees him, and when he does, it's all over for the time being.

A trout's vision is acute and he relies on it almost entirely for both food and protection. If you examine a trout you will notice that his eyes are on the side of his head so that he can see both to the right and the left at the same time. They also protrude somewhat from the streamlined surface of his body and are movable in the sockets, which all in all gives him a wide range of vision. He can see objects to the sides independently with one eye or the other, or he can concentrate both eyes on the same object when it is in front of him or above him. An analogy might be that a person feels an object to his right with his right hand and to his left with his left hand, but ahead of him he might feel it with

both hands. The eyes of a trout operate in a similar manner: independently to the sides and in unison ahead.

A trout's blind spot, as a mink or otter knows, is behind and below. A Conservation Commissioner for Alaska once told me of watching an otter enter a pool from downstream and take the hindmost of a school of salmon without disturbing the others. The dry-fly fisherman, since he fishes upstream and thus approaches the trout from behind has a great advantage over other trout fishermen. He can use a short line with little danger of being seen.

Above-Surface Vision

Have you ever swum under water on a very calm day and looked up at the surface? If you have, then perhaps you have noticed the fish's "window" through which he can look out of his watery home and see the tops of trees, the clouds, and the sky above. Around this rather confining window, the under surface is a mirror shining like slightly uneven, burnished steel. Everything below the surface is reflected, somewhat contorted of course, in this mirror. The body of anyone standing to his neck in shallow water to one side is reflected above so that it appears like a two-ended, headless creature joined grotesquely at the neck.

In perfectly calm water this window and the manner in which the trout sees through it can be reduced to mathematics, but we all know how rarely a trout stream is dead calm; so in practice we must treat the subject with the necessary flexibility. It is a disastrous approach to apply set formulas to any living, breathing creature.

In the theoretically perfect calm, a trout can

see out of the water through a round hole [see out of the water through a round hole] er. Light rays passing perpen-
surface, the center of which is directly ab   een the two are unaffected, but
eye and the limits of which are about fo   at an angle are bent. The greater
degrees on all sides from the perpendicul   e more they are bent until they
can be pictured as a cone of vision w   nt where they are reflected off the
point of the cone at the trout's eye and th   a ricocheting bullet, causing the
open end at the surface. The round por   ight rays near the limits of the win-
the open end of the cone has about twice   t so sharply that objects around the
ameter of the trout's distance beneath   greatly compressed to the trout,
face. In other words, the deeper he g   mirror at the carnival which makes
wider becomes his above-surface vision;   n appear short and dumpy. For in-
nearer he approaches the surface, th   -foot man standing thirty feet from
confining becomes his window. If a tro   position would appear in his normal
three feet deep, his window would be   less than a foot high.
across; but if he were only six inches   u place a stick or your rod tip in the
the surface, as if often the case when he   notice how the part under the water
ing on floating insects, his window w   be bent up sharply at the point where
only a foot wide. Beyond this window is   he surface. Also, if you have ever shot
ror.   object beneath the surface, you have

This all has to do with the physical   that you must aim considerably be-
light passing between air and the de   arget for a hit. The light rays passing

The trout's "window," showing how a fisherma

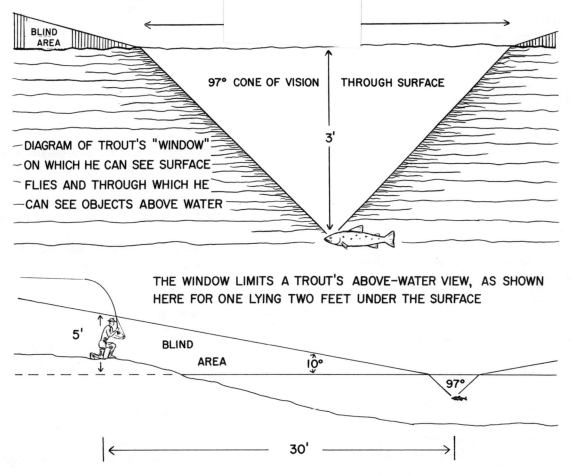

BLIND AREA

97° CONE OF VISION │ THROUGH SURFACE

3'

—DIAGRAM OF TROUT'S "WINDOW"
—ON WHICH HE CAN SEE SURFACE
— FLIES AND THROUGH WHICH HE
—CAN SEE OBJECTS ABOVE WATER

THE WINDOW LIMITS A TROUT'S ABOVE-WATER VIEW, AS SHOWN
HERE FOR ONE LYING TWO FEET UNDER THE SURFACE

5'

BLIND AREA

10°

97°

30'

at an angle through the water's surface are bent to the extent that the object appears above its actual position.

This window means a great deal to the fisherman. It restricts the trout's above-water vision sufficiently to give the fisherman a natural blind. A man kneeling by an open meadow stream, although he would seem to be in direct line of vision of a trout, can actually be completely out of sight behind the mirrored surface. The fisherman who keeps his head and rod tip down has a ready-made blind as effective as a boulder or clump of willows.

Of course, a fisherman is hampered in his attempt to see into the water by this same property of light, just as the trout is prevented from seeing out. Modern science, however, has given the fisherman a great advantage—polarized lenses which eliminate much of the reflection from the water's surface thereby helping the fisherman see the fish for which he is working.

It is possible to work within range of a trout's window without disturbing him if sufficient caution or patience is exercised. A feeding trout is principally concerned with things near at hand, but of course is disturbed by anything unusual which takes place above or around him. A fisherman who works very slowly and cautiously can get surprisingly close to a trout. It is the quick move that startles him.

Occasionally a bait fisherman takes a trout at his very feet within plain view. This man has casually walked up to the stream and dumped himself down on a rock overlooking the pool. He's as conspicuous as a fly on your nose, and the trout warily seeks the refuge of a rock or overhung bank. But a trout's memory is short and his desire for food ever-present. In five or ten minutes he reappears and if the fisherman makes no move—or is asleep by then—the trout takes no notice and a tempting worm may be his undoing.

A large trout probably became large through an extra share of caution and he won't feed for some time after being startled. Young ones are often caught in plain view, but old ones—unless the bait fisherman remains quiet for a long time, or is a sound sleeper—are seldom fooled by anyone in sight.

An old fishing adage says never have the sun or moon at your back. Most old rules are reliable because they have been well tested, but in this case I have my doubts. I believe it to the extent that it's dangerous to cast your shadow across a fish. That will put him down for sure. But that's as far as I'll go.

Where possible, of course, it's best to stay out of sight completely, but where that's impracticable I feel that a trout is less likely to see the fisherman when the sun is at the man's back than when it is behind the trout. In the bright morning sun, for instance, I will choose the east bank, and when the sun is in the west, I prefer that bank. A trout can see separate images out of each of his two eyes. If one eye has the bright light of the sun shining directly into it, he won't see well on that side, any more than you or I can look directly into a bright light without being dazzled by it. This is especially true since a fish has neither eyelid nor contracting iris with which to reduce the intensity of the sun's light. Also, when the sun is behind the fisherman, it penetrates the water and makes the trout quite evident. On the other hand, when the sun is behind the trout, a fisherman walking along the sunlit bank is about as inconspicuous as if he had a spotlight on him.

Maybe I'm wrong, but it seems to work for me —as long as I don't cast a shadow on the fish or make a startling move.

On-Surface Vision

The trout's window and the mirrored surface around it go far to explain the deadly effectiveness of a dry fly, which more often than not has surprisingly little resemblance to the natural insect. I have often seen feeding grayling lying so close to the surface that their large dorsal fins actually protruded into the air above. They are a dead cinch for a dry fly. Such a grayling's eye is little more than an inch from the surface; therefore, his window is only a couple of inches across. He makes up his mind to take a fly while it's still well outside this range of clear vision.

Prior to the brief moment in which the fly floats down through the window, however, he sees the impression it makes on the mirrored surface upstream from the window. The stiff hackles of a high-floating dry fly will make pinpoint pricks in the mirror much like the spread legs of a floating insect. The shallow-lying fish is attracted to the fly at this time; and, in water

An Eastern brook trout about to be released to the waters of Gods River, Manitoba.

cipal thing to remember in attempting to imitate a natural floating insect. Consider how it is going to look to the trout, not how it looks to you when it is held in your hand with the sun at your back.

Underwater Vision

A trout's underwater vision is less complex from the fisherman's point of view than is his ability to see on and above the surface. Naturally a fish is as much at home in his medium of water as we are in ours of air. Except for the turbulence of the water and the limited range of view afforded by some streams, the situation is not much different from that to which we are accustomed.

It may be that a trout is shortsighted. Many factors would seem to indicate this, and possibly distant objects are noticed only in their movement. A trout will rarely appear to notice a free-floating fly at a distance of more than three or four feet. On the other hand I have seen a hungry trout in clear water come a distance of several yards to hit a spinner. I am inclined to believe that the apparent shortsightedness of a trout is merely a matter of concentration on objects close at hand when feeding out of the current, but when cruising for food, or when nervous and on the lookout for danger, he is capable of seeing for a considerable distance.

A trout in quiet, clear water will see anything which splashes and shatters the mirrored surface even at a distance of thirty feet. He could be shortsighted and still notice such a disturbance because the breaking of the mirror on a bright day is very noticeable from below, almost like a shower of sparks. A large trout on the prod for food may be attracted, somewhat suspiciously, to such a distant splash, and his desire for food may overcome his caution if the lure is handled cagily from that moment on. A conspicuous splash too near a shy trout, however, will certainly startle him and put him down.

The mirrored undersurface of the water around the trout's window plays another role when the fisherman is using sinking lures. Since this surface reflects everything beneath it, the trout often "sees double." He sees not only the lure itself but its reflected image above.

In short, an underwater fly or other lure used

moving at a fairly good clip, he has little opportunity to change his mind while it is within his range of clear vision. If the fly has bulk and size reasonably close to the natural, it will be taken. These pin-pricks caused by the stiff hackles of a good dry fly explain why a high-floating fly is so successful, regardless of pattern, while a soggy, half-submerged fly rarely is.

Deep-lying trout in a lake or in a very still pool have a larger window and time for a leisurely scrutiny of the fly. Many is the time under such conditions that I have presented a sufficiently close imitation to arouse a trout's interest, only to have him come to within an inch or two of the fly, give it the once-over and turn aside at the crucial moment. It's disheartening, but a challenge to perfect the imitation.

A trout sees a floating fly or insect from only one angle, of course, and that is from below. There is no source of light in the water, and little reflected light from the bottom. The light comes from the sun and the sky above; that is, the brightest light is always behind the floating fly from the trout. Therefore, he sees an insect in silhouette or in whatever shades or colors would be given it by transmitted light. This is the prin-

in still, clear waters must be the most exact imitation of the trout's natural food for consistent success. In his own medium he can see the lure clearly and in detail without the handicap of refracted light and backlighting which are so prominent with floating flies.

Color Vision

Some folks say that a trout can't see color, that he's completely color blind and sees everything in black-and-white. In fact, fishermen seem to be born with this idea. Well, don't you believe it. He can see color as well as you or I, and maybe better.

A fisherman's experience should tell him this. He knows that sometimes a fly with a touch of red will knock 'em dead, while an identical pattern of yellow will be ignored. And the success of fluorescent yarns in steelhead flies is another indication. But an idea once imbedded can be difficult to uproot.

For fishermen who have not proved this to their own satisfaction, the scientists have taken a hand and proved it without room for doubt. Many experiments have been carried out, but the most conclusive are those which indicate the trout's reaction to color in connection with food. It is demonstrated that the trout in the experimental aquarium respond to the color which means food is on the table, and ignore others. When the food color is changed from red to blue, for instance, the trout soon associate blue with food and ignore red and other colors. Such experiments have been carried right through the spectrum and indicate that fish in general can not only distinguish pure colors from one another, but also are adept at spotting the various shades. Moreover, their eyes are apparently more susceptible to colors at the ends of the spectrum—the ultraviolets and infrareds—than are human eyes. Experiments have also indicated that color sensitivity tends to diminish with fading light, which is hardly surprising as our eyes register the same diminution.

A good backcast is the secret to fly casting.

So don't ignore color in trout fishing. Maybe it is not so important as size, shape, and action of a lure, but it can be a decisive factor in stream success.

Night Vision

During World War II American scientists devised a gadget known as a snooperscope which gave the sniper eyes in the night. It consisted of a projected infrared ray, which is invisible to the human eye unaided, plus a scope on the rifle which picked up these rays. In other words, it permitted the rifleman to light up and spot his target unbeknownst to the enemy.

The night vision of trout is uncanny by our own standards, and an analogy might be drawn between a trout's eyes and a snooperscope. If a trout's vision extends beyond ours into the ends of the spectrum, this may account for his ability to see at night. It is a known fact that certain objects—the wings of moths, the fur of some animals, various insects—fluoresce when exposed to ultraviolet light. Possibly a trout can see things which we can't. I don't know.

Of course, many nocturnal birds, animals, and insects can see well at night, but in all cases that I know about this is because of a reflector in the back of the eye which passes the available light through the eye twice and thereby doubles its power. When you shine a flashlight in a cat's eyes, or those of an owl, these reflectors shine back brightly. Or step out on the lawn on a dark summer evening and shine the flashlight in the grass. The many double pin points of fiery red are spiders' eyes. It's the same thing.

A trout, too, has such reflectors, but he has more than that, i.e., the need to eat. Trout often feed at night, especially in the summer in some streams where the midday heat is too much for the sensitive trout; then in the cool of the evening and in the dark shadows of the night they come out and slosh around like dogs playing in the water. Since the size of the trout, the slickness of the rocks underfoot, and the annoyance of branches overhead are all exaggerated when unseen, fishing in the black of night is hard on the nerves and the temper, but it's an adventure.

Smell and Taste

At the time of the Alaskan trout bounty one man told me he had recently accounted for fifty thousand trout tails. His method was to carry a sack of salmon eggs up a coastal stream, tramp on it in a riff above a large pool, wait a couple of hours, and dynamite the pool. This hardly creates a pretty picture, but nothing could prove as conclusively that a trout can detect either an odor or taste in the water and respond to it. This is the one big advantage the bait fisherman has over anyone using artificials. The odor or taste of his bait, especially fresh bait, permeates the water for a considerable distance and attracts the fish.

One day three of us were fishing a high-altitude trout lake, and we weren't doing too well. The water was extremely clear, and it was so calm that the smoke from a cigarette went straight up your nose. We worked hard on these shy, suspicious fish and we caught a few, but only on the most exact of nymph imitations on a fine leader. Then along came a fellow with a can of worms.

There were no worms naturally at this little rock-bound lake. The trout couldn't have known what a worm was—but a worm must smell like food to any fish. That fellow caught trout until it was a pity. He didn't use a fine leader and he didn't have any finesse, except that he knew enough to leave his bait alone once he had cast it out and to sit as still as though he were frozen. He also put his worm where the little inlet stream would wash over it out into the lake. It was twenty or thirty minutes between bites, but they couldn't stay away. We worked like mad to try to keep this worm fisherman from outclassing us, but it was a tough battle.

It's a definite fact that trout can smell or taste an odor in the water, and they will often travel long distances to run it down if it appeals to them.

Taste may also play some part in the refusal of certain foods. It's a common thing to see pennybugs and water spiders skating around a trout pool undisturbed. I suppose trout eat them if they get hungry enough, but I imagine they like the taste of them the way I like carrots.

Hearing

A trout has earlike structures in his head which apparently give him the ability to hear, but just what influence this has, I can't say. I do know that I have tried to disturb trout by making a variety of noises, but have never succeeded in bothering any by noise alone. I have lain unobserved beside a pool and watched trout for any reactions while I talked, whistled, shouted, and caused various other commotions. None of these disturbances affected them in the least.

Possibly because trout have lived for untold generations in roaring trout streams, their sense of hearing has deteriorated. Perhaps some trout living in quiet ponds are more sensitive, but I doubt it. It appears that only the balancing function of the ear, not the auditory, is active. My conclusion is that a trout fisherman can shout and carry on all he pleases, but he won't disturb his quarry by noise alone.

Median Line

Fish have another sensory organ closely connected with the ear which higher animals do not have. This is known as the median line; or lateral line. This sensory organ can be seen as a thin, almost hairlike line running down the fish's side, starting near the upper edge of the gill cover and continuing to the tail. All fish have a median line. In some species of fish such as a codfish or snook it is quite evident, while in others it might easily go unnoticed.

Anatomically, the median line consists of a large nerve which runs down the fish's side just under the skin with numerous small branches which protrude through the skin and scales to the surface. Each scale along this line has a tiny hole through which these branch nerves extend. A trout's scale is so minute that such a nerve hole can be seen only with a microscope, but on a large-scaled fish, such as a tarpon, this nerve hole in each median-line scale is as large as a pinhole.

All the functions of this sensory organ are not obvious. However, it is known that through the minute nerve ends of the median line, the fish gets the "feel" of the water. It enables a fish to keep his balance, to travel in a straight line, and, in the case of a trout, to keep his head directed into the current. If the median-line nerves of a trout were severed, he would be washed tumbling downstream to the sea.

Blind fishes, like those in Mammoth Cave, must have highly developed median lines to make it possible for them to operate entirely in the dark. Apparently through this organ they receive echoing waves from rocks and other objects around which they must navigate. A trout's ability to swim and feed at night may be analogous to these blind fishes' ability to exist in total darkness. That is, it may be a function of the median line in trout rather than an ability to see in the dark.

Although not everything is known about this organ, it is evident that it is very sensitive to vibrations in the water, and if a fisherman frightens a trout by walking too heavily along a quaking bank, it is likely that the fish receives the warning through the median line rather than through his ears. The median line probably plays as important a role as a trout's eyes in warning him of danger. In quiet water a fisherman can't wade too carefully.

Chapter 6

TROUT FOOD

It would be more astounding than helpful to present a complete menu of trout food. A camper might dump some spaghetti into a stream and afford a mouthful for a surprised trout, and hatcheries raise fat ones on pellets made up of about everything except what a trout would normally find in a stream. The rare items of diet—the caviar and *pâté de foie gras*—will not be covered in this chapter. The staples will be. Most of the basic items of a trout's diet will be mentioned, some briefly where they are of little value to the fisherman, others of prime importance in more detail. These are things every serious trout fisherman should know. He catches trout by presenting to the fish his natural food or a facsimile of it in the proper manner.

Plankton

First, in order to get a good picture of the stream of life which eventually produces a trout, we must start briefly at the bottom of the scale. In every uncontaminated body of water there is a free-floating mass of tiny organisms so small that they are either invisible or unnoticed by the human eye. A glassful of lake water will contain thousands of such organisms. Billions float and drift near the surface of the lake. By late summer they often become so numerous that in mass they are quite conspicuous; the water becomes tinged or cloudy with them, and the lake is said to be "blooming" or "working."

This society is composed of, first, algae, very minute forms of plant life which convert the energy of the sun into food; and, second, small animals which feed on the plants. Typical of these plants is the diatom. This is the plant which, upon dying, leaves minute silicified skeletons that make up diatomaceous earth, much used in industry as an abrasive and insulator. Typical of the preying animals are small crustaceans, like cyclops and daphnia, or water fleas. Water fleas are well-developed organisms complete with eyes and legs, large enough to be evident except that they are almost completely transparent. In a concentration in a lake there may be over a million water fleas in a cubic yard of water.

This enormous free-floating mass of life is given the general name of plankton. Small trout feed extensively on certain of the plankton animals. Some fish, such as golden shiners, sawbellies, ciscoes, little redfish, alewives, lake herring, and lake whitefish subsist almost exclusively on plankton, thereby converting this abundant but minute form of life into mouthsized trout food. Plankton is so plentiful in the ocean that the largest creatures the world has ever known, the baleen whales, live primarily on it by filtering the minute organisms out of the sea water with the baleen or brushlike arrangement in their mouths. The largest of the sharks, the giant basking sharks, also subsist on these tiniest of living things. Plankton exists wherever there is uncontaminated water: in the sea, in lakes, in streams.

This plankton, together with water weeds and the algae, or green slime, which grow on the weeds and the bottom, form the basis of food, the pasturage, for underwater life. The crustaceans and insects feed on the algae and on each other, and fish feed on the crustaceans and insects and other fish. The more fertile a stream or lake is, the more plankton, algae, and larger forms of life there will be and, of course, the more trout.

Since trout can be caught legally only as they eat, the fisherman would do well to know just what a trout does eat. In the first place, a trout is strictly carnivorous; that is, he feeds exclusively on other animal life, not on plants as do some fish. The food of trout falls into four classifications: crustaceans, insects, other fish, and miscellaneous foods.

Crustaceans

Crustaceans can form an important item of diet for young trout, and sometimes for the older ones. The crustaceans found in various trout waters include the tiny water fleas, the scuds, the fresh-water shrimps, and the crayfish. The importance of these as food is illustrated by the fact that one female daphnia, or water flea, might give birth to thirteen billion offspring in a period of sixty days, which is a family to be proud of. The water fleas are too small and transparent to be imitated by artificial flies.

The scuds and shrimps are larger, one-half inch or more in length. These are thin-bodied, semitransparent creatures which are very active: swimming, cimbing, jumping, and diving with speed and ease. Some species prefer quiet ponds, but others, such as the Caledonia shrimp, are equally at home in trout streams. The scuds are not so prolific as the water fleas; yet a single pair may produce a family of twenty-five thousand a year. They constitute ideal fish food since they live on herbage and decaying matter and do not compete with trout for insect food. No commercial patterns of flies are tied specifically to imitate these crustaceans; but, wherever scuds make up an important item of trout food, any one of many sparsely tied wet flies fished by the action method makes an effective imitation.

Crayfish, or crawdads as they are commonly called, are the largest of the fresh-water crustaceans. They are well known to every fisherman east of the Rockies. This is the favorite food of the small-mouth bass, but is a minor item in the trout's diet. Certainly young crayfish must be eaten quite often by trout, although I have never discovered one in a trout's stomach. Crayfish are themselves carnivorous and are known to eat their share of trout eggs and fry.

Insects

Insects form the bulk of the trout's diet. All young trout feed primarily on insects. Under certain circumstances, older trout will turn to a fish diet, but a trout never gets so large or exclusive that he will not eat insects. A trout is continually foraging for food and eating insects no matter how large he is. When he catches a minnow, he's lucky: he might have to swallow a hundred insects for an equal amount of food. Yet when there is a concentrated hatch of insects on, no delicacy can tempt a trout away from the food at hand. Large trout, small trout, and minnows feed on the hatch side by side, apparently oblivious of each other.

Aquatic Insects

Insects are divided into two groups: aquatic and land. Land insects form merely an incidental part of the trout's food. Aquatic insects belong to nine distinct orders: stone flies, May flies, dragonflies and damsel flies, water bugs, net-winged insects, caddis flies, moths, beetles, true flies. These all have immature, underwater forms, known as larvae or nymphs, and mature, winged forms above water. Some, like the caddis, pupate in between these distinct stages of life, as does the caterpillar in his cocoon before he becomes a butterfly. Others, like the May fly, emerge as winged insects directly from the nymph. Fully 90 per cent of the insects eaten by trout are in the underwater larval or nymph stage.

Stone Flies: Stone flies are thoroughly distributed through the trout streams of North America. Like trout, the nymphs prefer cold, running water. They are most at home in rapids; and are also found along wave-washed shores of lakes. If placed in stagnate or warm water, they die. They are seclusive in their habits and live under rocks and in crevices. They will be found clinging to the bottom of flat rocks which have been picked up from stream beds and overturned quickly. As soon as a rock is turned over, the nymphs scurry off to the sides and drop back in the water. Small May-fly nymphs and caddis-fly larvae may be found under the same rocks.

Adapted to his life under rocks, the stone-fly nymph is flat-bodied with legs which protrude horizontally out to the sides. He looks like a bug that has already been stepped on. The various species run in size from a half-inch to two inches. Some are black in color; others, like the most common species, are mottled with a brownish-green and yellow design. All have two conspicuous tails and two long feelers.

Stone flies are nowhere as numerous as May flies or caddis flies are inclined to be, but they are widespread and trout know about them. Because they live such seclusive lives under the rocks, they don't become a major item of trout food, but the trout eat them whenever they have the opportunity. These nymphs are large enough to be fished as natural bait on a No. 12 hook, and there are few if any baits more appealing to a trout.

The stone-fly nymph is a weak swimmer. He depends on the two stout claws on each foot to hold onto the rocks in fast water, and when he happens to be washed off he is at the mercy of the current. Therefore, in fishing a stone-fly nymph, natural or imitation, you should allow it to float freely with the current and not give it any action with the rod and line.

Stone flies are a good early season lure. Some of the nymphs hatch into adults as early as Feb-

ruary, and other species continue to hatch through spring and early summer. At high altitudes, the hatching season is retarded.

The adult stone fly is also flat-bodied and secretive. He has long wings which are folded flat along the back, and he has the same two tails and long feelers characteristic of the nymph. All species are dull colored: brown, black, or gray. Their adult life is short and for the most part uneventful. They rest quietly and unnoticed under the leaves of trees and bushes along the stream bank until they mate, return to the water to lay their eggs, and die. If you want them for bait, they can be shaken from the branches and picked up without a struggle. They are weak fliers. When one finally gets going, he's just as likely to fly right into you as not. One on the wing is easily knocked down or caught in the hand. Trout manage to get a good share when they're hatching and when they are spawning their eggs. However, they seldom hatch in the swarms characteristic of May flies and caddis flies.

Some of the trout's preferred natural food.

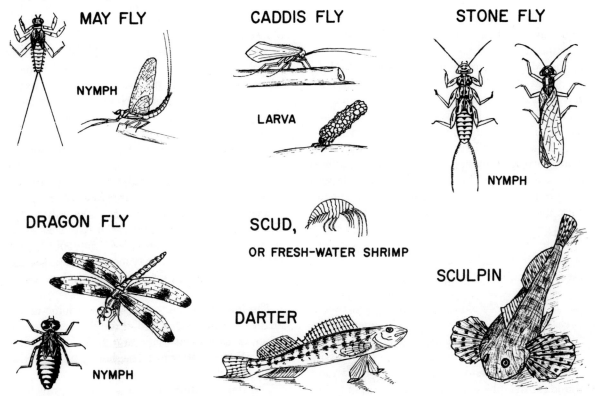

May Flies: The dainty and graceful adult May fly is well known to every man who ever cast a fly to a rising trout. The vast majority of dry-fly patterns were conceived to imitate various of the many species of this insect. These are the Duns and the Drakes, the Spinners, and the Spent Wings. May flies come in an almost unlimited variety of sizes, colors, and patterns. If pale olive May flies are hatching, the trout won't look at an iron-blue fly. And if size 14 flies are hatching, they won't consider a size 12 imitation. Trout know their May flies.

May flies are widespread and vastly numerous. They compose the major part of trout insect food everywhere. Not only are more May-fly nymphs eaten than any other kind of nymph, but due to their manner of hatching, far more May flies are taken off the surface than any other insect.

May-fly nymphs have adapted themselves to many ways of life and different conditions. The only limit to their distribution is the pureness of the water. They are found both in still and fast water. Some burrow in the mud on the bottom, other flat-bodied specimens live under and around the rocks, like stone flies, and probably the majority live among the underwater vegetation. They live on algae which they scrape from the weeds and rocks, seine out of the moving water and root out of the mud. They also eat certain water weeds.

The May-fly nymph is easily recognized by the series of feathery projections along the back and sides of his abdomen. These are his gills. He usually has three tails, sometimes just two, and his feelers are short. May-fly nymphs vary in size from little fellows barely a half-inch long to the giant burrowing nymph of lakes which is almost two inches long. The life cycle of this largest nymph is two years, but some of the smaller ones live only six weeks and may go through four generations in one summer.

These May-fly nymphs are the constant prey of trout from early spring through fall. Some species are quite active and can jump and dart among the weeds with considerable agility. Most can scurry rapidly along the bottom, and two or three species are fair swimmers in open water. One of the swimmers, a dark-colored nymph a half to three-quarters of an inch in length with unusually long, slender tails, is one of the most abundant nymphs early in the season. He swims about the vegetation and also can navigate in still open water, although slowly. He is an ideal nymph to imitate with an artificial because the fly can be fished under motion. Another nymph, slightly smaller and paler and with shorter tails, is an even more active swimmer and occurs the year round near underwater vegetation. He also is a highly favored food with trout and can be imitated with a moving fly. Most May-fly nymphs, however, are pretty much at the mercy of the current unless they have their hooked feet attached to a rock or weed. Therefore, their imitations should be fished naturally or very slowly.

When the May-fly nymph matures, he swims to the surface of the water and floats there, just beneath the surface, while the nymph case splits down the back and the winged May fly emerges. The winged fly, in turn, floats for a few moments until strong enough to fly to shore. During this hatching period the May flies are oblivious to danger and practically helpless. This is when the trout have a picnic.

A heavy May-fly hatch is one of the most amazing sights in the outdoors. Early and late season flies hatch rather sparsely at different times during the day, but the evening hatches of late spring and early summer sometimes fill the air with swirling clouds of insects. Traffic along a lakeside or riverside road is occasionally blocked by the masses of May flies when they become plastered on the windshields. Empty nymph cases may pile up in windrows along a lake shore. The vast numbers of flies rise like a mist, and the fish from below and birds from above literally gorge themselves. Occasionally the swifts and swallows commence dipping over the stream before any May flies appear, almost as though they sensed a hatch was coming. It's a good sign for the dry-fly fisherman.

No matter whether the life cycle of a certain species is six weeks or two years, the individuals of that species mature and hatch like clockwork, at the same season and same time of day. A hatch of one species may continue for several days, occurring always at the same hour each day.

The life of the adult is very short. Some of the smaller species hatch, go through their mating dance, spawn their eggs, and fall to the water spent all in a matter of a few hours. At the most, adult May flies live but two days.

The dainty adult May fly, with his gracefully

curved body, outstretched forelegs, long tails, and upright wings, is familiar to almost everyone who has spent much time around a trout stream. However, there are stages of the adult life that are not so familiar and which are important to the fly fisherman.

When the May fly first emerges from the nymph case, he is known as a dun. He is invariably drab in color. The many dry flies known as Duns were designed to imitate May flies in this stage. The duns rise from the water and fly ashore where they rest quietly, the resting period varying from a few minutes in some species to as much as two days in others. Then the fly molts once again and emerges bright and shiny.

After this second molt, the May fly is known as a spinner, and he is ready for his mating dance. This mating dance will occur in the evenings, sometimes the same evening of hatching from the nymph, sometimes twenty-four hours later and sometimes forty-eight hours later. Each species has its characteristic dance. The males gather in a swarm and the females fly out to join them. The females are evident by the large egg sac they carry, and dry flies like the Female Beaverkill were designed to imitate May flies in this stage. Some May flies bounce along the surface spawning their eggs. Others alight on a rock and actually crawl underwater to deposit the eggs. Many such are washed away by the current in the process.

Soon after spawning the flies drop to the surface spent, with wings outspread horizontally. Trout consume many such spent flies, and the numerous patterns of spent-wing dry flies are designed for use at this time. During the season of heavy hatches on a stream, the trout so gorge themselves on May flies that it is difficult to tempt them with other lures at any other time of day.

Not all May flies hatch in May, of course. The March Brown dry fly, for instance, was designed to imitate a fly which appears during the heat of day in the early season, and many of the largest hatches occur on June and July evenings. The largest of the May flies, the big burrowing form of lakes and mud shallows of streams, rarely hatches before late June.

No set rules can be laid down as to just when specific hatches, for which certain dry flies were

Fly fishermen in action at dusk. These silhouetted gentlemen are Corey Ford (with pipe) and Alastair MacBain.

designed, will occur. There is so much of a variation in seasons and altitudes across the country that there is no uniformity in hatching. In any on locality, however, a fisherman can soon learn what May flies hatch when, and experience on the stream will soon prove what patterns of flies serve as the best imitations. The same hatches will occur with regularity each year, and the same pattern of dry flies will continue to be effective.

Dragonflies and Damsel Flies: The big eyed dragonflies, sometimes called darning needles, with their four large, outspread wings, are a common sight around lakes and streams in the summer. The closely related damsel fly is of more delicate construction and holds its wings erect over its back when at rest. These two are the hawks of the insect world, hovering and darting about in pursuit of all manner of insects. I've always thought I would like to have a pair of trained dragonflies, one to sit on each shoulder when the mosquitoes are thick.

The adult dragonflies and damsel flies are rarely of food value to trout, but the nymphs are very important to the fisherman. They are important because they are large and because they are the strongest swimmers among the underwater insects. The dragonfly nymph can be fished rapidly, in spurts, and therefore can be used to cover a lot of ground. The dragonfly nymph is literally jet propelled and swims powerfully by ejecting water through a rear orifice. Both dragonfly and damsel-fly nymphs are strictly carnivorous and are constantly in pursuit of other insects which they grasp by a quick movement of a long pincer arrangement located under the lower jaw. They even capture and eat minnows and small fish on occasion. Although nowhere as plentiful as May flies and caddis flies, they are well distributed throughout trout waters and a favorite trout food. The live nymphs make good natural bait.

Water Bugs: Water bugs include such familiar creatures of still pools as water striders, water boatmen, water scorpions, water measurers, and the like. They are incidental trout food and of little interest to the trout fisherman. No artificials are designed to imitate them.

Net-Winged Insects: This group includes the familiar hellgrammites and related insects. The adults are dobson flies, alder flies, and fish flies. These adults carry their wings folded flat along the back, in the manner of the stone fly, but are easily distinguished from the stone fly by the absence of the two long tails. Like stone flies they are weak fliers and are more inclined to run than fly when pursued. These flies vary in size from less than an inch to as much as three inches.

The larvae are carnivorous and very secretive, living under rocks and vegetation where they are not easily available to trout as food. These larvae pupate and emerge some time later as winged insects. The hellgrammites and other larvae make excellent bait fished naturally. The adult insects are short-lived and active in the daytime. The dry fly known as the Alder is an English pattern and, as is unfortunately the case with many such flies, was designed to represent an insect quite different from the American alder fly. The English alder belongs to the same order of insects as our alder, but is much different in appearance, having its wings folded in a peak in the fashion of the caddis fly.

Caddis Flies: Caddis flies rival May flies in abundance and are possibly even more numerous. Because of their manner of life they do not make up so great a percentage of trout food as do May flies, but they are second only to May flies in importance.

The larvae of caddis flies can be found in their protective cases clinging to rocks, gravel, and wood in fast water and roaming freely about in slower water. They populate all trout waters. Like May flies, they have adapted themselves to a great variety of water and conditions. Adult caddis flies are familiar as the insect with wings folded peak fashion over the back, like the ridge of a tent or house, and with two long feelers pointed forward. They have a mothlike flight, and in summer evenings are often seen swarming along the stream's edge or dancing over the water surface. Thousands may be found crawling over every object, including a fisherman, near the stream.

The larvae of all species of caddis flies live in a protective tubular case. Depending upon the particular species, these cases are cemented together employing a great variety of material and in characteristic designs. Some cases are made of sand, some of gravel, some of tiny sticks, and some of the shells of small snails. The larva itself

Larger trout are generally produced by the greater feeding potential of big water, as evidenced by these lake rainbows, rather than by a stream habitat.

is a grublike creature. The legs are grouped forward where they can be protruded from the case; and the body, where it is protected by the case, is soft and white. Two hooks at the rear end of the body serve to hold him in, and he can pull back completely out of sight if danger approaches. Many species roam clumsily about the bottom and the weeds in search of algae. One species, with an intricate spiral-designed case, is a free-swimmer. Still other species are cemented firmly on or between rocks, and the opening of their tubular home faces upcurrent. Some of these construct tiny webs to catch the plankton floating downstream.

This forbidding case protects the larvae from many would-be enemies and undoubtedly discourages trout on occasion. If a trout gets hungry enough, however, he eats the caddis, case and all. A trout's stomach will sometimes be crammed with the rock and stick cases of the caddis larva, especially early in the season before many other insects are stirring around.

This underwater form of the caddis is called a larva because it goes through a pupation period before it emerges as a winged insect. A nymph, in contrast, transforms magically directly to a winged insect merely by discarding its nymphal case.

When the caddis larva has matured, it cements its case to the bottom, seals the front door, and pupates like the caterpillar in his cocoon. At the end of this period, the pupa emerges and swims to the water's surface. Some species emerge from the pupa directly on the water, others walk ashore on the surface and crawl up on the grasses and bushes before emerging in the winged state. Trout make the most of this hatching period. Some species have concentrated hatches, like May flies, and others seem to hatch in smaller numbers throughout the year. The adults are inactive by day, and swarm, fly, and mate over the water in the evenings and nights. Trout and dry-fly fishermen are both active at this time.

Caddis flies are more difficult to imitate successfully than the May flies. Few dry flies have the characteristic triangle shape of the caddis as it sits on the water. However, many dry flies, including the various Sedges, are tied as caddis-fly imitations. Caddis flies in some quantities are found along trout streams almost any evening throughout spring and summer, and attempting to match the particular insects on hand can be both fascinating and aggravating.

Moths: The larvae of a very few species of moths actually live underwater in trout streams, forage on algae, spin their cocoons, and hatch into pretty little moths. They are too few in number to be of concern to the trout fisherman.

Beetles: A half-dozen or so beetles are acquatic. Some, like the water pennies and whirligigs, are a common sight on ponds and quiet pools of trout streams, but make up too small a portion of a trout's food to be of any concern to fishermen.

Flies: The final group of aquatic insects includes the true flies whose larvae live underwater: the mosquitoes, midges, black flies, deer flies, and horseflies, bless them. The more of these that trout eat, the better we all like it. The larvae of most of these unpleasant characters prefer stagnant water, but many are found in company with trout. We can all remember times when the hatches were so good that we've given up trout fishing as a bad job. In addition to these unpopular insects, this group also includes the nonbiting midges and crane flies.

Mosquitoes, black flies, and punkies, or "no-see-ums," are almost too small, both as adults and larvae for successful imitation. Black-fly larvae live in rapid water and can be found in such quantities in streams of the Northeast that they appear almost like moss clinging to the rocks in the current during the spring and early summer. Fortunately, trout and other small fish feed heavily on them and also on the adults as they are hatching from their pupa cases. The adult is the pleasant little white-stockinged fellow that crawls persistently over the face and arms and down under the shirt looking for a choice spot from which to remove a hunk of flesh while the fisherman is trying to concentrate on tying on a new fly. Like deer flies and horseflies, the black fly is active only in the daytime, leaving the evening and night to the mosquitoes and punkies. The larvae of deer flies and horseflies live in the mud in shallow water and are seldom available to trout.

The nonbiting midges are the delicate little black-and-gray flies which are forever getting slapped down just for looking like a mosquito. These are perhaps the most numerous of all aquatic insects available as food to trout, minnows, and carnivorous insects. One investigation of brook trout showed that they averaged one hundred of these larvae each in their stomachs, and I have caught trout whose bellies were bulging with at least a thousand of these tiny things. The wormlike larvae swarm over the bottom, decaying vegetation and plant stems, usually living in a frail mud tube with which they surround themselves. Many are bright red, and thus are called bloodworms. They are important principally as a means of converting plankton and algae into trout food in vast quantities, but the larvae can hardly be imitated successfully by the fishermen. The merest body tied on a No. 14 or 16 hook is the closest imitation. Trout also feed heavily on the hatching flies, and this is the most difficult of all hatches to imitate with a dry fly. About the only thing which will work is a tiny Black Gnat midge in a size 18 or 20.

The adult crane fly has the long legs and body shape typical of the mosquito, but his wings are outspread, he is much larger, and is usually brown in color. Crane flies, sometimes called gallinippers, are a common sight along a trout stream, sometimes swarming, sometimes dipping along the surface as they deposit their eggs, and sometimes sitting on streamside vegetation bobbing up and down in the manner of a sandpiper. The larvae are wormlike in shape and either white or brown. Some live in riffles and in very fast water. Trout feed heavily on both the larvae and the adult flies. A Brown Spider or a Brown Variant makes a fair imitation of the adult crane fly.

Land Insects

Insects fallen or blown into the stream from shore constitute a minor item in a trout's diet. Trout feeding at random in the summer supplement their regular diet of aquatic insects with occasional beetles, bees, millers, caterpillars, ants, flying ants, grasshoppers, crickets, and the like. At such times a dry fly which isn't designed to imitate any particular insect but is just naturally "buggy looking," like a Spent Woodruff, will take a lot of trout.

On rare occasions certain land insects may form a major portion of a trout's food, and a good trout fisherman will be alert to such situations. A breeze off an alfalfa field might deposit many bees on the water, or a summer meadow stream might catch so many grasshoppers that it would constitute a "hatch." One May while I was fishing in Vermont the large, brown beetles, commonly known as June bugs, were flying in such quantities in the evenings that the trout fed on hardly anything else. Their sides were distended and bumpy from having swallowed so many of these large insects. When any such condition arises, the fisherman will take advantage of it immediately.

Other Fish

Minnows and other small fish make up a large portion, by volume, of the food of big trout. Under normal stream conditions, any trout, no matter how big, will take many, many insects for every one minnow, but one minnow has a lot of bulk in comparison with insects. Trout know this, and large ones will take a pass at a minnow every opportunity they get. That's why the many minnow-imitating flies and lures are so effective on the larger trout.

Under certain conditions, especially in lakes, a trout may turn almost entirely to a fish diet. The huge Kamloops variety of rainbow trout, the largest American trout not including the laker, has for untold generations built its way of living directly around the pursuit and capture of little

Fast water and hungry brook trout await the angler at the headwaters of the Peribonca River, northern Quebec.

redfish, the land-locked Pacific blueback salmon, or on the young of the migratory salmon. Almost all of our largest trout, no matter what species or where found, have attained their size because of the presence of similar school fish which they can pursue and on which they can gorge themselves regularly. A large Kamloops rainbow may have four or five ten- and twelve-inch little redfish in his stomach at one time.

The best school fish are those which feed primarily on plankton. These convert the microscopic life into trout food and do not compete with trout for other food. Certain of the freshwater herrings and whitefish, such as the alewife, cisco, and sawbelly, are ideal because they are both plankton eaters and school fish. Smelt and little redfish are school fish as well and fine for trout large enough and fast enough to prey on them, but they compete with small strains of trout.

Such school fish are a regular source of food for a few large, lake-dwelling trout only, and present a special situation calling for special fishing tactics. All stream trout and a majority of those living in lakes have a varied diet, not only of insects but of fish as well.

Stream trout feed on so many varieties of minnows, probably fifty or more, as well as the young of chubs, suckers, whitefish, and squawfish, that it would be useless to try to name them all. Because of their abundance, the four which probably make up the majority of trout food are the black-striped dace or horned dace, the red-finned shiner, the darter, and the sculpin. The shiner makes a particularly attractive natural bait because of its bright sides.

The darters and the sculpins are favorites with trout because they live in the same habitat and because they are relatively easy to capture. The darters are confined primarily to the trout streams of the East and Midwest; the sculpins are found in trout streams everywhere in America. The darter lives in fast water and rests motionless, poised on his ventral fins like stubby arms. He moves about after food in short, rapid spurts and remains otherwise motionless on the bottom.

The sculpin is a broad-headed, bottom-living little fish with distinctive, fanlike pectoral fins spread to each side like wings. He is found in trout streams everywhere and is particularly abundant in the West. In the East he is known

variously as miller's thumb, blob, mufflejaws, and stargazer; in the West he is known almost universally as bullhead. He rests on the bottom and moves in short spurts like the darter. He is often nocturnal, resting under rocks in the daytime. This little fellow is undoubtedly one of the very best of all natural baits for trout.

No trout has any scruples against turning cannibal and eating his own kind. However, the young trout are generally too quick for the old boys, and unless hard pressed for food the big ones don't bother with smaller trout. It's easier to catch minnows.

Miscellaneous

Miscellaneous trout foods would include an astonishing and not too appetizing list of creatures, such as snails, spiders, mites, mice, leeches, and even small turtles, snakes, lampreys, and eels. In some small, mud-bottomed ponds, snails form a major diet of brook trout. Sometimes snails cling upside down to the calm underside of the water surface and eat algae; at such times trout may actually rise to them. Generally speaking, though, only two miscellaneous foods are of interest to fishermen. These are worms and eggs.

Worms are the most universally used of trout baits, although trout eat a limited amount of them in the natural state. Earthworms are most abundant in a meadow stream with cutting banks, or after a heavy rain when they have been drowned out of their burrows and washed into the water. These are popular as a bait because they are easy to gather, because they remain alive and wriggly for a long time, and because they apparently smell as well as look like food to trout.

During the spawning season trout eat a lot of their own eggs and the eggs of other trout. It is doubtful that they do their race any harm by this practice because, as I have mentioned, the free-floating eggs which they get are rarely fertilized. Trout are not grovelers and don't pick up the fertilized eggs down in the gravel. It takes the sculpins and crayfish to get these. Although the spring and fall spawning seasons are the only times that trout would eat eggs naturally, salmon eggs remain a popular bait the year round, especially in the West.

Chapter 7

BAIT FISHING

Bait fishing is the introductory chapter to the world of fishing. My first experience with a trout came in a little, splashing stream rather fittingly named Mountain Brook, and that first gentle tug on the line—so small yet so impertinent in its abruptness and command—awakened in me a curiosity which could never be fully satisfied.

If most of us tend not to pursue bait fishing, it is not due to any ethical compunction but rather to the challenges and rewards of other forms of trout fishing, especially fly-rod fishing. For my own part, a great deal of my fishing pleasure derives solely from the act of casting. In addition, I know that I can take more trout on artificials than on bait. However, there are a few individuals who have continued with bait as their primary method, and more power to them. If you can be more successful and get more enjoyment out of the sport by using bait, or spinning lures, or a casting spoon, or whatever else you may desire, then go right ahead and stick to that method.

When I see a good bait fisherman in action, I am frankly awed by his ability. I admire mastery in any field and am probably overly impressed by something well done which I cannot do myself. Although I also enjoy watching a good fly fisherman, there's no mystery in his wizardry. I know how he does it. But when I witness a man who can cast a worm upstream and roll it along the bottom with the current, then I am impressed. I take a back seat and watch him perform. I feel an equal respect for the man who can fish a minnow with a master's touch.

The artificial-lure fisherman has many advantages over the bait fisherman. He has a great variety of offerings which can be resorted to at a moment's notice to fit any particular situation or condition. He can also cover much more ground and a greater variety of water. The bait fisher-man in turn has some distinct advantages. The principal one, of course, is that he is fishing with something that the trout knows without question is food. He knows by its odor, he knows by its sight, he knows by its feel when he takes it in his mouth. Perfect imitation and deception are the keys to fishing with artificials, but these problems are of little concern to the bait-fishing man. Proper presentation is the key to his success. The bait fisherman, once he has located a good fish, should be able to take him in short order, whereas the fly fisherman may work for weeks on a big trout with a limited chance of hooking or landing him.

Worms

For best success any fisherman should have some idea of the natural feed of the trout in his fishing waters, but this is not so essential for the bait fisherman as for the man using artificials. A worm, for instance, just naturally looks and smells like food to any trout whether he has ever seen one before or not. I have watched worm fishermen take trout from rocky, high-mountain lakes, from desert waters, and even from northern tundra streams, none of which harbor worms naturally. Such fishermen pay a good price for imported worms, and their money isn't wasted. Obviously to a fish—any fish—worm is a four-letter word spelling food.

All species of angleworms make good trout bait. The liveliest, and probably the best, is the firm, red worm commonly found in the vicinity of the manure pile. At least it is one of the best for clear-water conditions where a small worm is the proper choice. The common worm of the garden patch is next in preference, and the nightwalker, or night crawler, is the least appealing because of his large size. The best way to gather worms is with a spade, of course, but the fisherman can often replenish his supply along the stream by overturning rocks and pulling sod. Nightwalkers, when desired, are procured at night with the aid of a flashlight. A moistened blue-grass plot is the best place to find nightwalkers on the surface after dark. Many a fisherman will recall that in his early days the capture of these giant worms was almost as exciting as fishing itself.

Worms once gathered can be kept in captivity until the time comes to use them. The worm box should be kept in a cool, shaded spot, of course. It will have a layer of rich earth covered with leaf mold, sod, or moss. If the box is waterproof, care must be taken not to allow too much water in it, as worms are easily drowned. It should be kept covered against the danger of rain, and moistened occasionally. An open-topped box should have holes drilled in the bottom and covered with copper screening for drains. The

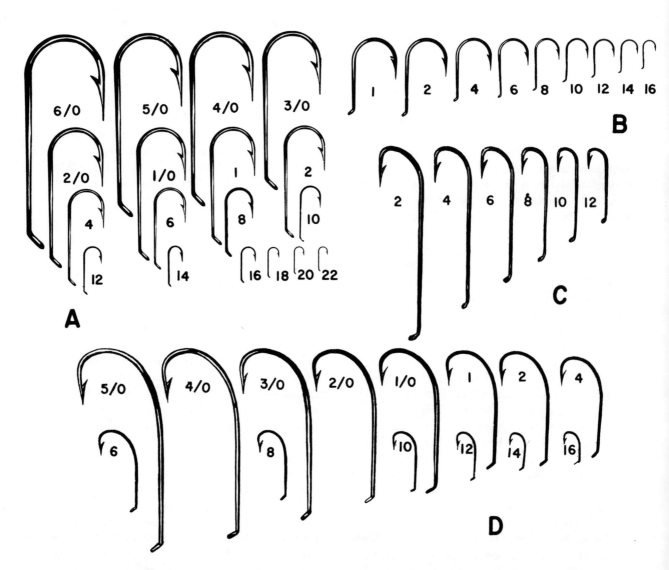

Hooks. (A) Gaelic Supreme hand made hooks with turned down eye, used for wet and dry flies; (B) Gaelic Supreme hooks with turned up eye, used for spider and variant flies and as short shank bait hooks; (C) Irish Limerick hooks, long shanked; (D) Improved Sproat hooks for fly tying and bait. All hooks shown actual size. ILLUSTRATION COURTESY OF HERTER'S, INC., WASECA, MINNESOTA.

worms should be fed occasionally by scattering corn meal, coffee grounds, bread crumbs, suet, or even sugar lightly on the surface.

In some areas where angleworms are scarce or nonexistent, the fisherman may want to raise his own. This can be done in the cellar in a galvanized tub about two feet in diameter and ten inches deep, or its equivalent in any watertight metal drum. The inside should be tarred or painted to prevent rust. The most satisfactory worms to raise are the red earthworms, or brandlings, found around manure piles or leaf mold. According to a Department of the Interior Sport Fisheries leaflet, up to six thousand worms can be raised in such a tub in one year, and following are their instructions:

Fill the tub with fertile soil to a depth of about eight inches. Add sufficient water to make the soil moist throughout. Take 1 pound of corn meal and ½ pound of vegetable shortening or lard and mix with the top 2 or 3 inches of soil. Put in 100 or more red worms, and cover the soil with a burlap bag or strips of wood to delay evaporation of the moisture. Each tub of worms will require about 1 pound of vegetable shortening and 2 pounds of corn meal for food each month. If larger containers are used, more food will be required. The food should be placed on the surface of the soil every 2 weeks. After the tubs have been started, the addition of water at the time the food is added should be sufficient. The soil should be kept moist but not wet.

Many fishermen like to scour and harden worms before fishing with them. A worm can be scoured by leaving him for a day or two in clean, moist moss, such as sphagnum moss commonly used by florists. The drier the moss is wrung out, the more it will tend to harden the worm, simply because it dehydrates him somewhat. Some fishermen add a few drops of cream to the surface of the moss during this scouring operation. Whether this actually enhances the worm's appearance in the eyes of the trout or whether it is merely a ritual in the form of a last supper, I do not know.

The container in which the angleworms are carried while fishing must have holes punched in it to prevent the suffocation of the worms, and it should contain moist grass or moss, not earth.

Worms are good trout bait any time, but are most effective during the high water of spring or after any summer storm which discolors the water. Since a worm must breathe air, he is often drowned out of his burrow by a heavy rain and forced to come to the surface. Those which are washed into a stream become trout food. The best time to fish is while the water is rising. The trout are looking for them then, and no particular finesse or fine tackle is required if the water is cloudy, as is generally the case at such a time.

Under such conditions a feeding fish is generally deep, picking up his food as it washes along the bottom. An excellent worm rig for such a time has a heavy sinker, say a quarter-ounce dipsey, tied to the terminal end of the leader. A foot up the leader is tied a loop onto which is slipped the snelled hook for the worm. The sinker thus goes to the bottom and the worm is held just off the bottom where it will do the most good.

Worm fishing in the low clear water of summer is a highly developed art. The best worm fishermen under such conditions work upcurrent. A spinning outfit is ideal for worming. With fly-casting tackle a long rod is an advantage, and it should have a soft action so that there will be no harsh movement to snap the worm from the hook. The cast is a gentle, sweeping movement with extended arm. An amount of line and leader about equal to the length of the rod should extend beyond the rod tip and an equal amount will be held loosely in the left hand. The worm is swung gently behind and in a continuous movement tossed ahead with just enough force to carry out the slack held in the left hand. The cast is generally made quartering upstream and the line kept barely taut by raising the rod tip as the worm floats downstream. For best effects the worm will move downstream in tune with the speed and direction of the current. The leader should be six or eight feet long and fairly fine, and the hook should be small. The amount of weight used depends on the strength of the current. The best fishermen don't use any added weight where the current is sufficiently slow to permit the worm to sink of its own weight, but in a heavy current or deep water it is certainly advisable to use the number of split shot necessary to take the worm near the bottom.

Eggs

The worm is the most universally popular of all baits for trout, but it is run a close second by the salmon egg because of the extreme popularity of this bait in the West, except where outlawed. Eggs are readily available preserved and packed. They can be obtained in different shades of yellow, orange, and red, according to the fisherman's choice, and also come packed singly or in clusters.

All trout will eat eggs, and are especially prone to do so during the spawning season. They eat the eggs for food and because they are excited by them. Where fishing is permitted during a spawning run, such as during a spring run of rainbows, the catching of one female trout is the only prerequisite to taking a tubful of fish. The roe of the first trout is removed and this becomes the ideal bait for others. Although not a very high-minded method of taking trout, it is nevertheless effective. Natural roe such as this can be formed into a cluster by tying it in a small square of sheer nylon stocking material. The nylon sack so formed is invisible in water.

Eggs are fished much as are worms. They are more effective if floating free in the water than if resting on the bottom. A trout doesn't grovel for food. He likes his victuals served up naturally by the current.

Stump-Knocking

Down in the lowlands of North Carolina there is a unique method of fishing known by the equally unique name of stump-knocking for mud chubs. The mud chub is the little warmouth bass, close kin to the rock bass. The outfit is a short rod with a line no more than a foot long and the fishermen—the stump-knockers—poke this short line with bait into the holes among the cypress knees, roots, and fallen limbs where the mud chubs live. Practically this same technique is used effectively by trout bait-fishermen working small brushy streams. By stripping the line very short, they can poke their bait into secluded corners where the fly fisherman could not possibly fish. If they do this with enough caution and manage to keep out of sight of the trout while making their approach, they can take a likely mess of fish. The important thing, and the thing that many beginners overlook, is that the trout must see the bait before he sees or suspects the fisherman. Some fishermen like a telescope rod for this brushy-brook fishing as it can be made a convenient length for each condition as it arises. A single egg or a small worm can be used equally effectively for this type of fishing.

Minnow

The minnow is not used so commonly as the worm or salmon egg simply because of the inconvenience of its capture and transportation. Properly fished, however, the live minnow is without question the best of all baits and lures for large trout. There are a hundred, more or less, varieties of minnows, shiners, dace, darters, etc., in America. The fisherman should use a species native to the waters in which he is fishing not only because the trout, being accustomed to it, will strike more readily, but also because of the danger of introducing a harmful alien species to the water. It is illegal to use goldfish for bait in many localities, for instance, because a goldfish is nothing but a small species of carp, and carp have done more harm to game-fish waters than any other causes except pollution and erosion. Carp act like pigs: they root in the mud and roil up the water to the point where it is uninhabitable by game fish.

A live or freshly caught minnow makes a better bait than a preserved one. For one thing its appearance is better, and any odor it might give off, such as from bleeding, smells like food on the table to a trout. The smell of Formalin or other preservative would not be so appetizing. This question of smell is principally important in still-fishing and makes little difference when the minnow is being used as a moving lure.

The most common method of catching minnows is by means of a minnow trap baited with bread crumbs and the like. A makeshift homemade trap can be fashioned by knocking out the center of the inverted dent in the bottom of a wine bottle and tying a piece of muslin across the mouth of the bottle. For best results with a trap, choose a quiet, weedy cove in the stream, stir up the mud to attract the curious minnows, and then set the baited minnow trap.

Some fishermen resort to catching minnows with a small hook, such as a No. 16, baited with a tiny piece of worm. This seems to entail as much trouble as catching the trout themselves. For those who wish to raise their own bait fish, the Bureau of Sport Fisheries, Department of the Interior, Washington, D.C., issues detailed pamphlets on the subject.

Minnows to be kept alive can be left in the stream in a well-perforated container. If they are to be transported, they must be kept cool and the water changed often. The best type minnow bucket has an air container in the bottom which releases a steady stream of bubbles into the container to keep the water aerated. Minnows that are killed will keep better in moist moss than in water. Also, minnows that are killed to be used the next day can be toughened by immersing them in a strong solution of salt and water.

Shiners and other brightly colored minnows are best for spinning, and the minnow need not be alive. Other than for spinning, the best of all minnows for trout, especially big ones, is undoubtedly the homely little fellow known as sculpin, stargazer, miller's thumb, and many other names. He is found in trout streams all over the country but is most numerous in the Rocky Mountain area where he is known almost universally by the name of bullhead. He is easily recognized by both his appearance and habits. There is none other like him. The bullhead is brown or mottled brown and he has a broad, flat head with the eyes set on top. He gives the impression of being about one-third head and of being roughly tadpole shaped. His pectoral fins are broad and protrude to the side like spread fans. He is a bottom-living minnow and swims in short spurts, then rests motionless with his belly flat on the bottom. He is primarily nocturnal in habits and generally hides under rocks during the day.

Bullheads

There are two good ways to catch bullheads for bait. The most common method of the western fisherman is to gather them at night in a riff with the aid of a flashlight. Like most wild things, he is blinded and almost mesmerized by a strong light. If he is to be taken alive, he can be scooped up with a small net or vegetable strainer with a little practice; otherwise he can be speared with a sharp fork. In the daytime he is caught by means of a small seine made of wire screening turned up six inches on three sides and left flat on the fourth. This trap is placed in a shallow, fast riffle with the open edge upstream; then the fisherman enters the water fifteen or twenty feet above and walks rapidly down, making as much of a fuss as possible and turning over all rocks as he goes. The bullheads turn and scurry with the current when so disturbed. They are more inclined to stay in the screen trap if it contains a few handfuls of moss under which they can hide.

Whether they are to be fished as live or dead bait, it is best to keep them in a minnow bucket until ready to be used since they turn white and unattractive after they have been dead a few hours.

There are several ways of fishing a bullhead. He can be cast quartering upstream and rolled under the current in the manner of worm fishing, he can be still-fished, or he can be fished by the method described in the chapter on "Taking Big Trout." The latter is undoubtedly the best because the minnow is fished on a long deceptive line, and a lot of ground can be covered. For those who prefer still-fishing, he is a pretty sure killer in a hole where there is known to be a large trout. He has an advantage in his hardiness and liveliness on the hook, but is at a disadvantage in that he will immediately seek cover under a rock. The bullhead is a particularly effective bait because he is a staple food of a large trout. This is part of an eternal battle in a trout stream: the bullhead himself is one of the most efficient of trout spawn eaters and, in turn, one of the most favored of trout foods.

A live minnow to be still-fished can be hooked lightly through the back just ahead of the dorsal fin. This gives him the freedom to swim about. A very light float, such as a quill float, can be used to advantage to hold the minnow just off the bottom where he will do the most good and also to prevent his taking refuge under something. This is especially important with bullheads. A minnow to be cast can be hooked through the lips so that he can be retrieved in a natural, head-foremost manner; or he can be rigged as described for bullheads in the chapter on big trout. It is possible to strip-cast a minnow on a long, soft-action rod if a light enough line is used, but a more effective job can be accomplished with a spinning outfit, which will be discussed in the chapter on "Spinning."

The Snake River in Wyoming has some of the best fishing in the country.

Grasshoppers

A trout feels about a grasshopper the way I feel about apple pie: it should be eaten promptly. Even I might pass up an apple pie if it were set in a bear trap, and a trout feels the same way about a crudely fished hopper, but when it comes naturally his one inclination is to eat it. The grasshopper is a good midsummer bait. The trouble is that it generally doesn't occur to the fisherman to try a grasshopper until a trout reminds him by rising to one; then he dashes around madly slapping his hat on the ground, falling on his face, grabbing thin air and generally making himself look ridiculous. The time to catch grasshoppers is at night or early in the morning before the sun has warmed them up. In the evening or at night with a flashlight grasshoppers can be picked off the tops of tall stems of grass just like picking berries.

A grasshopper is most effective when alive and fished naturally on the surface with light tackle. He still makes good bait, though, when fished underwater like a worm or salmon egg. If hooked carefully through the collar on the back of the neck, he will remain lively and attractive for some time.

Miscellaneous Baits

The term miscellaneous baits reminds me of a man with whom I used to fish for golden trout. He was a good fly fisherman and had an ample supply of dry and wet flies. When we arrived at the lake he would remark that goldens were finicky and a fellow could never be certain what they might want, then he would start producing various and sundry cans, bottles, and boxes. He had a different kind of bait in each pocket, including worms, eggs, grubs, beetles, grasshoppers, stone-fly nymphs, hellgrammites, and even May-fly nymphs. Needless to say, he caught trout.

There is a multitude of insect forms which live among the weeds, mud, and rocks of every trout stream, as indicated in the chapter on "Trout Food," and these constitute the major part of a trout's diet unless he turns to a meat diet. Of these many forms of aquatic insect life, the only ones large enough to be used satisfactorily for live bait are the stone-fly nymph, the caddis-fly larva, the dragonfly nymph and the hellgrammite, or dobson-fly larva. Most fishermen find the May-fly nymph too small to handle, but it is worth a try. Trout normally eat more May-fly nymphs than any other food.

As we have seen, the stone-fly nymph is a flat, mottled green or brown nymph an inch or more long found scurrying along the underside of an overturned rock. The caddis-fly larva is a grub-like creature which lives encased in a tubular structure made of sand, twigs, pieces of leaves, or one of several other available materials. The larva moves about and feeds by protruding its head and feet out of the open end of the case. Hungry trout will eat caddis-fly larvae, case and all, but most fishermen who use them for bait reason that they are more appetizing when evicted from their stronghold. These caddis worms must be fished on a small hook, a No. 12 or smaller, and a fine leader.

The dragonfly nymph is more practicable as a live bait because he is larger. This is a predatory nymph which unlike most others can swim at a pretty fair clip. This is important because it means that he can be fished on a taut line and still appear natural to the trout. He should be moved along in short jerks as this is his method of swimming.

The hellgrammite is well known to most fishermen. Some call him dobson and some clipper. This is the largest of the aquatic insects and is the larval form of the dobson fly. The hellgrammite has a bait-collar similar to a grasshopper and is hooked in the same manner for best results. All these numphs are ideal food as far as the trout are concerned, but the hellgrammite has advantages from the fisherman's point of view because of his size and ease of handling.

These various aquatic insect nymphs and larvae can be gathered for bait along any stream. Stone-fly and small, flat May-fly nymphs will be found clinging to the underside of flat rocks in the riffles. Hellgrammites will also be found under rocks, but generally in slower water. Caddis-fly larvae may be found on stones, wood, weeds, or crawling about the mud bottom. Dragonfly nymphs will be found in quiet water, either on the bottom or swimming free. A variety of nymphs live around the water weeds.

A wire vegetable strainer is a help in catching nymphs, and to be kept alive they should be placed immediately in an aerated minnow bucket. Two people working together can catch nymphs quickly with the aid of a window screen. One person stirs up the rocks, weeds, or mud; the other stands in the current below and strains the insects out of the water. Many May-fly nymphs will be caught by this method, but most of them will be too small to attempt to use for bait. If May-fly nymphs are to be tried, the burrowing form is the largest. Their tracks and holes can be seen in the soft mud and they can be sifted out by picking up scoopfuls of mud in the vegetable strainer. Never take more nymphs from a stream than are immediately needed. The future of the trout depends on this food supply.

There are still other baits used occasionally by some fishermen, such as ant larvae, bee larvae, and beetle larvae, or grubs. Most of these are difficult to fish with as well as difficult to gather. Any of the natural foods mentioned in Chapter 6 make satisfactory baits. Like all trout fishermen, the man who uses bait must be alert to notice whatever trout are feeding on at any particular time and place and take advantage of the situation immediately.

Chapter 8

FLIES AND FLY TYING

The fly fisherman should know the various aquatic insects on which trout feed, and be able to spot and identify the fly being taken during a rise. He won't be able to name the insect specifically, other than that it is a May fly, caddis fly, stone fly, and so on, but he will certainly be able to see its size and color. Then he can select something similar from his fly box and go to work. Nine-tenths of the time, presentation is more important than pattern.

Dry Flies

In a generalized sense, dry flies are used in three different situations. First, the dry fly can be fished at random, regardless of whether or not a trout has been seen to rise. This random fishing is for the man who really loves to float a fly. He works upstream dropping his fly in the pockets, runs, and points of rocks, wherever he judges a trout might have a feeding station. In very deep or in cloudy water, this might be a waste of time, but generally through the late spring and summer months it is a delightful and productive way to fish. The trout are feeding on a great variety of food, almost anything that comes their way. Ninety per cent of their food is being taken underwater, but with a feeding station near enough to the surface, the trout will willingly rise to anything tempting. Any one of a hundred different dry-fly patterns can be used successfully for such random fishing. The fisherman selects a pattern, with reasonable size limits, that will float high and that is easy to watch and keep track of. A few patterns popular for such fishing are: Brown Hackle Bivisible, Brown Variant, Royal Coachman, Wickham's Fancy, Black Gnat, Brown Spider, Greenwell's Glory, Light and Dark Cahills, Hare's Ear, Gray Hackle, Woodruff, Tup's Indispensable, Skue's Hackle, Pink Lady, and so forth. The list is endless.

The second dry-fly condition is similar, but in this case a specific fish has been seen to rise. If a man is already fishing a dry fly at random, he's ready to give the fish a try; and the wet-fly fisherman will often shift to a dry fly at such a time because he realizes that a rising fish is easier to take on a floating fly than otherwise. Many a dry-fly fisherman sticks to one pattern of fly for random fishing, and such a man will merely float this favorite fly over the trout he has seen rise. He knows it is just naturally buggy looking and the rising fish will take to it as well as anything. Another dry-fly fisherman may be a bit more critical, and if the rising fish is a good one, he may study the situation for a few minutes to see if he can determine just what natural has brought the trout to the surface. The chances are again, however, that any such sporadically rising trout, when there's no heavy and obvious hatch on hand, will take any one of a hundred different dry-fly patterns so long as it is presented well.

The third dry-fly condition is that rare and wonderful moment when a heavy hatch has brought all the fish in the stream to the surface. This requires specific imitation, which is the most fascinating form of dry-fly fishing. The heavy hatch brings out even the old lunkers, and all the trout are concentrating on the abundance of this one insect and disregarding all other forms of food. The fisherman will naturally go after the largest of the rising fish, and he will be the most difficult to please.

Fortunately for the dry-fly fisherman, the distortion resulting from the dented water surface caused by the hackles of the high-floating fly or the legs of the natural insect prevents the trout from getting too clear a view. All that is necessary, then, is that the natural fly be imitated in general, not precisely. The English Ginger Quill is not an exact replica of the pale watery dun, which it is designed to imitate; yet it has the same general color and bulk, and on the correct size hook it is a deadly imitation. When floating high, the natural and the artificial appear sufficiently similar to the trout.

In attempting to match any particular hatch, the name of the pattern of fly selected has little to do with the situation. Except in very unusual cases, the individual species of May flies and caddis flies in America do not even have names, so there can be no specific patterns of artificials to imitate them. The fisherman who carries a variety of dry flies, in different sizes and shades, regardless of their specific names, can match the hatching insects no matter where he is. If he

Some of the more popular flies.

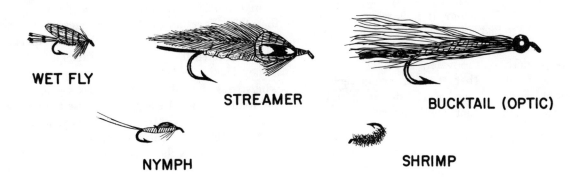

VARIETIES OF UNDERWATER (WET) FLIES

WET FLY

STREAMER

BUCKTAIL (OPTIC)

NYMPH

SHRIMP

VARIETIES OF DRY FLIES

HACKLE

PALMER HACKLE

SPIDER

SPLIT WING

REVERSE WING

HAIR WING

SPENT WING (VIEWED FROM ABOVE)

FANWING

VARIANT

doesn't have anything that will pass muster, but he knows a little something about fly tying, he can put together a fly which will do the trick. I have tied a good many such nameless flies, many of them with such a minimum of fly-tying skill that I would not have been proud to show them to anyone but a fish, but they served their purpose.

Dry-Fly Requirements: The first thing to look for in selecting a dry fly, more than just pattern, is the hackles. These must be stiff and should have a sheen to them. Soft hackles which will become soggy make poor dry flies. A dry fly to be successful must not merely float; it must float high—up on the hackle points. The hackle should be evenly applied so that the fly has a uniform appearance. The wings, if it is winged, should be well matched and balanced so that the fly won't spin when being cast and so that it will cock properly on the water. The hook should be of fine wire so that it adds no unnecessary weight, and the eye of the hook should be tightly closed, so that it will not cut the leader.

Types of Dry Flies: Dry flies fall into two general categories: simple hackle flies and winged flies.

In turn, there are three general types of hackle flies. One of these is palmer-tied; that is, the hackle extends from the eye of the hook back to the bend. Such a fly generally has no body, only the hook, hackles, and thread go to make up the entire fly. The Brown Hackle Bivisible is a good example. This type is fine for random fishing, especially where the current is a bit rough, because it will float long and high, even after a good ducking.

Another has the hackle concentrated forward and often has a body of quill, peacock herl, fur, or the like. It is similar to the winged fly, minus the wings. It can be used for all types of fishing, the principal disadvantage being that it is often not so easy to see on the water as a winged fly.

The third type of wingless fly is the spider. This is tied with long hackles on a short-shank hook, usually without any body and with no tail.

Winged flies have upright or spent wings. Spent wings are designed to imitate the May fly in the last stage of life, when it is known as a spinner. It has spawned its eggs and fallen to the water exhausted with wings outspread or spent.

Such spent wings are most commonly imitated with small hackle feathers.

Upright winged flies fall into several categories. Wings made from the primary feathers of starlings, ducks, and other birds, as described later in this chapter, are the most universal of the upright wings. These can be single, double, or reversed. A specialized type of upright wing is the fanwing. Fanwings are relatively difficult to tie, and the wings are not too stable, but they are a great advantage to the fisherman in watching a fly on broken water. The Fanwing Royal Coachman, which looks like no insect ever seen by man or trout, must appear particularly buggy from underneath. It's effective in bringing up lunker trout in random fishing. Variants differ from ordinary dry flies with upright wings in that they have unusually long hackles, in the manner of a spider, and no tail. Other specialized flies have upright wings of hackle or hair. Some dry-fly patterns have attempted to lay wings back over the hook in a peak shape, like the folded wings of caddis, but these are not too successful. A heavy, translucent body, as of fur (a Hare's Ear or a Tup's fly are good examples), seems to imitate the caddis shape better than such wings.

Wet Flies

Wet flies represent any one of many foods to the trout: the numerous nymph and larval stages of aquatic insects, drowned land insects, crustaceans, or minnows. Therefore, wet flies are open to limitless variations. Nymphs, streamers, bucktails, spinner flies, and the like are merely specialized forms of wet flies.

Regardless of these specialized forms, there are two general types of wet flies: the specific insect imitation and the attractor type of flies. The latter are by far the more numerous. They don't copy any particular trout food but have design or color to attract the eye of the feeding fish.

The presence of a fly floating on the surface, although its form is not evident, is far more obvious to a trout than is one underwater on his own level. In clear, still water drop a small stick on the surface and notice the shadow that the disturbed water surface casts on the bottom. This surface distortion, plus the fact that a dry fly breaks the mirrored undersurface of the

Just below a falls or rapids the big ones lurk waiting for their food to be brought down to them. This is Gods River, Manitoba.

water, makes a dry fly in still water immediately obvious to a fish. A dry fly is seen against the light of the sky background, but a wet fly may be camouflaged against the dark colors of the bottom, and might pass within a couple of feet of a feeding trout unnoticed.

There are two things which help to catch the eye of such a fish: motion and color. This is why wet flies are generally fished in motion and are designed in bright patterns. This is the reason for the attractor-type wet fly.

Small and natural-colored flies can be used to best advantage in small or clear streams where the chances of their being seen are good. Also, if the specific location of a good trout is known,

whether in a small stream or large, then it pays to work on him with natural-colored flies fished with the current. The chances of catching an old and wise trout are better on a natural appearing wet fly than on one of the attractor types.

In cloudy water, or in large streams where a lot of ground must be covered and the fish attracted from considerable distance, it is best to use bright patterns. For instance, on some of the larger Rocky Mountain rivers I have found steelhead or salmon patterns much better fish getters than the conventional Brown or Gray Hackles.

The same general approach holds true of lakes. There is no way of knowing the exact location of a feeding trout in a lake, and the

In the Bridger Wilderness Area, Wyoming, fishermen pack in their gear on horseback.

chances of laying a fly right on his nose are slight. It is hoped that trout may be attracted from considerable distance; therefore, a bright pattern is normally used. In a small, clear pond where the trout can be seen, a small natural fly scurried near the bottom in front of his nose will be more deadly.

Wet-Fly Requirements: Since the wet fly is conventionally fished against the current, the first requirement is that it be streamlined. The wings and the hackle should point back toward the bend of the hook so that the fly will move through the water smoothly. The hackles, in contrast to those on the dry fly, should be soft so that they will conform to the current. The hackle

may have sheen to it, however, without harm. And, finally, the wet fly should be sparsely dressed. In my opinion, the majority of inexpensive commercial wet flies are too thickly tied. A guide in New Brunswick once remarked to me: "Some of the flies dudes bring up here sure are pretty, but I never heard of a trout killing a chicken."

Fly Tying

Some folks feel that they haven't arrived as trout fishermen until they have created a new pattern of fly and named it after themselves.

Creating a new pattern is no trick. The trick is to try to keep from creating a new pattern. Nine out of ten flies we amateurs turn out are new designs. I start out to tie a Royal Coachman and finish with a Flunky Footman. But that doesn't bother me, and it doesn't seem to bother the trout. Lots of dumb trout don't know the names of all the patterns in a tackle catalog. Some trout don't even know a Dotterel Dun or a Waterhen Bloa when they see one, to say nothing of a Coch-y-Bonddu.

Most of us tie flies to meet certain conditions, or to fall within the limitations of our skill and the material at hand. The object is to tie flies that will take fish, and the wide range of successful standard patterns proves that this includes a multitude of sins. I've never felt sorry for any trout I've taken on one of my homemade jobs; he should have known better.

Except for a natural outlet, the location of feeding trout in a lake is seldom as predictable as in a stream or river, but with a long line and a little luck, a fellow may tie into a keeper occasionally.

When I want a really fine fly I turn to a professional flytier. There are a few of these scattered around the country whose ability is the ultimate in craftsmanship. No one, whether he has ever wet a line or not, can help but admire their creations, and this is especially true of us fishermen who have attempted to tie flies half as well. Craftsmanship in general is rapidly disappearing. No longer are fine, hand-tooled guns and reels available in this country, and even some of the excellent rod companies have been forced to cheaper and faster machine methods. But we fishermen can be thankful that the individual flytier is still with us and going strong.

Most of us amateurs can't hope to match the precision and perfection of this handful of artisans, but we can tie simple flies that are capable of catching trout under all but unusual circumstances. Tying such flies is no trick. There is really very little mystery in it. Anyone with no more than two thumbs to a hand should be able to tie a passable dry fly with very little practice. Maybe he will never become an artist at the game, but he will catch trout on his home-tied flies, and there's satisfaction in that.

The following intends to give merely the fundamentals in fly tying from a strictly amateur viewpoint. There are many schools of fly tying and I don't profess to be an expert at any of them, but the methods suggested here will be sufficient to give anyone a start. Those who want to continue into the unlimited field afforded by the multitude of fly patterns should turn to one of the several fine books devoted solely to this subject.

Tools

The tools necessary to start the job are a vise to hold the hook, a couple of pairs of hackle pliers, a small pair of sharp-pointed scissors, a pair of dime-store tweezers, a dubbing needle, and a bottle of either rod varnish or lacquer. It goes without saying that the vise and pliers should have a firm, uniform grip and the scissors should be sharp. Dubbing needles are inexpensive, or one can be made by mounting a large sewing needle in a piece of wood or cork for a handle. Rod varnish is good for touching up the thread of the finished fly because it dries hard and permanently, but it also dries slowly. Lacquer may not take so firm a grip, but it dries almost immediately.

Basic Dry Fly

Stiff, glossy, good quality hackles, with little or no webbing to soak water, are the most important part of a dry fly. All else is incidental. Deception is easiest if the fly sits completely on top of the water film. A live insect doesn't have to tread water to stay up; he stands high and dry, making about the same relative impression on the elastic water surface as would a mouse standing on a stretched piece of cellophane. Stiff, dry hackles merely dent the water in this fashion.

A perfectly good and effective dry fly can be made with nothing but a couple of good hackles, a hook, and winding silk. Wings, which cause most of the trouble in fly tying, are put on more for the fisherman than for the fish. Upright wings are a definite help to the fisherman in keeping an eye on his floating fly, and under very precise, flat-water conditions may be a help in producing strikes. Most often a trout will take a plain hackle fly as readily as a winged one.

Don C. Harger, fisherman-flytier in Oregon, tied up a series of wingless, quill-bodied hackle flies for me in an almost complete range of May-fly sizes and shades. They are beautifully though sparsely tied with stiff, shiny hackles and have the characteristic May-fly tails. I have yet to find a May-fly hatch which I have been unable to match with one of the various shades and sizes of these simple, wingless flies.

Hackle feathers come from roosters. Hen hackles are no good for dry flies, and not all rooster hackles will do. A rooster has usable hackles on various parts of his body, but those most commonly employed are on the neck. A complete rooster neck, with small hackles at the top and larger at the bottom, can be purchased from any fly-material dealer. A complete neck is the most economical way to buy hackles if the fisherman plans to do a lot of fly tying. If not, assorted hackles may be purchased in order to have a few hackles of various shades, rather than complete necks bought for each shade. Natural-colored hackles are preferred to dyed ones.

The Model Perfect hook is as good a selection as any for the dry fly. There are numerous other models and bends from which to choose if the fisherman desires, but it is important to select a light-wire hook for dry flies. Inspect each hook before using it to make certain that the eye is well closed. A partially closed eye will cut a leader like a knife.

Spools of thread put up especially for fly tying can be purchased, although sewing silk in the proper size will do well. For medium-sized flies, use a size coo thread; for small flies, on a No. 16 hook or smaller, use size oooo thread; and for bucktails and large flies, on a No. 8 or larger, use size oo thread. Note that the size of the hook decreases as the number increases. Professional flytiers wax thread thoroughly before using it, but the amateur can get by with untreated thread. The cementing varnish or lacquer will soak through and hold unwaxed thread fast.

The fly-tying operation on a plain hackle fly is surprisingly simple. Mount a No. 10 or 12 hook in the vise with the eye facing right, if you are right-handed, and the point of the hook and barb covered by the jaws of the vise. Take the tip of the thread in the left hand and hold it alongside the shank of the hook between the thumb and forefinger; then, with the right hand, wind over and around the hook close to the thumb until the thread is caught under itself. This sounds easier than it is the first time it's tried, but with five minutes' practice it becomes as automatic as winding line on a reel. This is all that is necessary to get the operation started. Whenever it is necessary to have both hands free for other things, throw a half-hitch around the hook shank or hang one of the pairs of hackle pliers on the thread to keep it taut.

Next, select a stiff hackle feather with hackles about as long as the shank of the hook, strip off the fuzzy part and most of the webbing near the base of the feather, and whip it on the hook with the point forward and clip off the base of the quill. Now clamp the tip of the hackle in the jaws of the hackle pliers and wrap the hackle over and around the shank of the hook. Most hackles have a light and dark side. I like to wrap the light side forward; it's a help in seeing the fly on the water. When the hackle feather is wrapped on all but the last half inch, whip over the hackle tip with the winding thread, binding it along the shank of the hook almost to the bend. If judged properly, this will leave the stiff tip of the hackle protruding as a tail to float the after end of the fly.

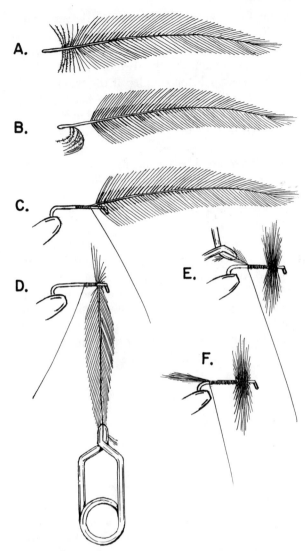

Steps in tying a basic dry fly. (A) Select stiff hackle. (B) Strip fuzz from base of hackle. (C) Tie in hackle to hook in vise. (D) Wind hackle. (E) Wind in end of hackle to bend of hook. (F) Tie off thread leaving hackle tip protruding as tail, clip thread, and varnish body.

The fly is finished now except for tying off the end of the thread and touching up with varnish or lacquer. The thread can be tied off immediately with a series of half-hitches (as I normally do), although this system is frowned upon as not being very secure. It is better to use a whip finish. Professional flytiers always whip-finish at the head, not behind the hackle. The thread can be wound forward through the hackle without disturbing it, but any fibers which should be-

come bent down in the process can be teased out with the dubbing needle.

When the whip finish is secure and the thread clipped off close, the head is touched with lacquer or varnish and the fly is completed. This is a sparse fly, ideal for smooth water. For a more heavily hackled fly, tie in two hackle feathers instead of one at the same spot and carry through the operation the same as before. Some flytiers wind two such hackles at the same time, but most of us must wind them one at a time in order to get them taut.

This is an exceedingly simple dry fly, and just as effective as it is simple. There is nothing about it to soak water; so, even if submerged for a few moments, it can be flicked out with a false cast and floated again immediately. I have taken hundreds of trout on various sizes and shades of this design, and the largest rainbow I ever took on a dry, a discerning old lunker better than four pounds, mistook such a fly tied on a No. 12 hook with a single badger hackle for a slate-gray May fly. With the materials at hand, a simple dry fly like this takes but a couple of minutes to make.

Whip Finish: The whip finish is difficult to master at first. Before attempting to learn any such knot it is essential first to understand what is to be done. The whip finish on the head of a fly is exactly the same knot as on a rod winding, but of course it would be impracticable to use a waxed loop of thread on anything as small as a fly. Another method must be used to finish the winding with the end of the thread bound under the last few loops.

By following the sketches on p. 72 it will be seen how this is accomplished on a fly. The end of the thread is held in the left hand and the first two fingers of the right hand form a loop, as shown in Fig. A. The right hand is then swung around toward the body and up to the position shown in Fig. B. Next the fingers are pointed away from the body and spread apart, as shown in Fig. C. The wide loop thus formed by the spread fingers is slipped over the head of the hook (Fig. D). Finally, the right hand is brought down to the original position, as shown in Fig. E. This forms the first of several loops to be wound over the end of the thread, which remains parallel to the hook during the entire operation. Now swing the fingers up, as in Fig.

B, point away and spread apart, as in Fig. C, slip the loop over the head of the fly, as in Fig. D, and return the hand to the original position again, as in Fig. E, and the second loop is completed. This motion is continuous in actual operation, but is outlined in steps here for clarity. Continue this operation until four or five loops have been formed; then, as in Fig. F, pull the end of the thread with the left hand and release the final loop with the right hand. In order to bring the knot up securely, press down on top of the last loop with the index finger of the right hand to prevent its slipping, as in Fig. G. Practice this on a bare hook until familiar with it before attempting it on the head of a fly.

Another method of making a whip finish, recommended by some flytiers, is illustrated on p. 73. It is accomplished, as can be seen, with a dubbing needle. The end of the line is allowed to drop in a loop through which is placed the dubbing needle. The needle is then rotated

about the head of the hook several times; and, finally, it serves to hold the loop taut while the thread is pulled from under the last few windings thus formed. On the surface this would appear to be much the simpler of the two methods of putting the whip finish on the head of a fly. Once the first method is mastered, however, it is the more satisfactory of the two to use.

Body Materials: The hackle fly described above is a basic dry fly. If a body is desired, there is a wide choice of materials. A quill body imitates the appearance of a May fly's body. Quill is usually obtained by stripping a piece of peacock herl clean with the thumbnail and forefinger. The fibers come off easily if the herl has been soaked for a while in warm water, and the warm water also tends to soften the quill so that it will wrap willingly about the hook shank. Some fly patterns call for fur dubbing, which gives a translucent effect. The fur of all manner of ani-

Whip finish at head of fly.

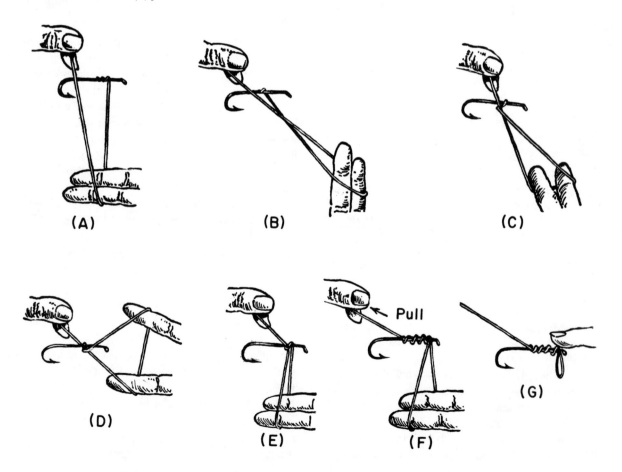

(A)   (B)   (C)

(D)   ← Pull   (G)

(E)   (F)

mals from a water vole on up to a polar bear have been used for dubbing. The Hare's Ear gets its name from the source of the dubbing, the Ramsbottom and Tup's Indispensable have equally revealing names, tup being another name for ram. Other body materials include horsehair, raffia, silk floss, wool, tinsel, gold-wire ribbing, peacock herl, gut, plastic, and almost anything else that can be thought of. Flytiers haven't missed anything. Review a fly-material catalog and you will find that they have gathered their supplies from every corner of the earth, from certain feathers on rare birds of the Brazilian jungles to the red hairs on an orangutan's ear.

Whatever body material is chosen don't overdo it. Many cheap commercial flies are useless because they are tied coarsely. As a result, they are weighty, they appear too bulky, and they soak up water readily. Take a good look at a natural May fly, midge or crane fly, especially as he would appear to a trout from beneath. There's not much to him. A caddis fly gives the most appearance of bulk owing to the way he folds his wings over his back like a tent, but there isn't much to him either. His wings don't stop much light.

The daintier a dry fly can be kept and still float high, the better it will serve. A material like cork could be used for a body, and hackles wouldn't even be necessary. Such an imitation insect would always float. However, a cork body would float with its belly in the water, like a floating twig, but stiff hackle points merely dent the water like the feet of a live insect.

Making whip finish with dubbing needle.

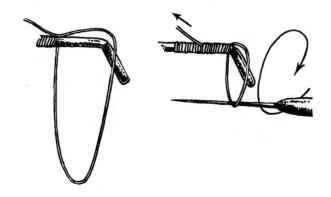

Body materials are wrapped on the hook in the fashion of the quill. Whatever the material, it is generally tied in after the hackle feather and the wisps for tails have been tied in, then it is wrapped on the shank of the hook before the hackle is wound.

Other Hackle Dry Flies

Spiders and palmer-tied flies are wingless, bodiless hackle flies. The Brown Spider Bivisible is a wicked fly on wise old browns. It's as dainty a fly as there is, and that's often what's necessary to fool the smart ones. It has such a small hook, however, that strikes are often missed, but that's a risk to be taken. A spider is usually tied on a No. 16 short-shank hook and the hackles are stiff and long. A spider sits up on the surface like a daddy longlegs.

A palmer-tied fly has hackles tied continuously from the eye to the bend of the hook. It requires several hackle feathers, and these are tied in intervals along the shank of the hook. They can all have fibers of the same length, although the fly is generally more effective if the fibers are progressively shorter toward the bend of the hook. Such a fly has a smooth taper from head to tail.

The bivisible effect on hackle flies is obtained by two or three turns of white hackle at the very head of the fly. The fibers on this white hackle will be the same length as those immediately behind it. The bivisible is a distinct advantage to the fisherman in watching a fly. The darker hackles of the fly show up against light water, and the white hackles show up against dark water.

Bucktail dry flies can be made from deer hair as described in the section "Streamers and Bucktails" at the end of this chapter.

Wings

Wings, when used, are generally tied in after the butt of the hackle, the tail wisps, and the body are on the hook, but before the hackle is wound in place.

A simple pair of spent wings can be made of a pair of small hackle feathers. These are tied in at the butt parallel to the shank of the hook, then forced into the outspread position by taking the winding thread around the feather butts in a figure-of-eight fashion. These small hackle-feather wings can also be tied in an upright position, like ears, as on a Skue's Hackle. Another method of making hackle wings is to wind on a hackle feather, as in the basic fly described, then to divide the hackles top and bottom and force each half out to the sides in spent-wing tufts with a figure-of-eight winding of the silk.

Fan wings are difficult to handle. The little curved feathers from the breast of a duck make the best fan wings. The all-white feathers, as for the Fanwing Royal Coachman, come from the white domestic duck. A pair of these is matched, tied in by the feather butts, and held in position

by the winding of the thread. This is not so easy as it sounds.

The wings on most patterns of flies come from the primary feathers of the wings of starlings and from the primary and secondary feathers of the wings of ducks. The starling feathers are supposed to have just the proper translucency, but are even more difficult to handle than duck feathers because the fibers are short. I gave the starlings a bad time trying to learn to tie winged flies.

The webbing for the two fly wings is selected from the same spot on the equivalent feather from a right and left bird's wing, as shown in Fig. D below. A narrow piece of webbing is torn out for single wings. For double wings, a piece

Tying a typical winged dry fly.

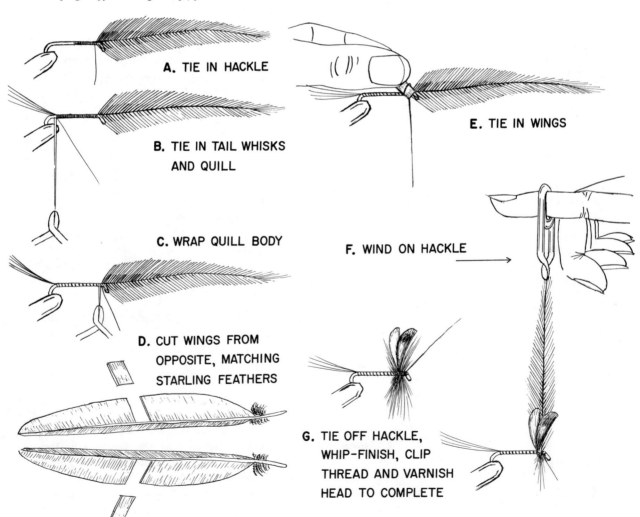

A. TIE IN HACKLE

B. TIE IN TAIL WHISKS AND QUILL

C. WRAP QUILL BODY

D. CUT WINGS FROM OPPOSITE, MATCHING STARLING FEATHERS

E. TIE IN WINGS

F. WIND ON HACKLE

G. TIE OFF HACKLE, WHIP-FINISH, CLIP THREAD AND VARNISH HEAD TO COMPLETE

twice as wide as each intended wing is removed and folded over on itself. The tendency is to make wings too wide, so keep the pieces of webbing narrow.

Tying these in smoothly is a job for only the most skillful of amateurs. The two pieces of webbing to become wings are matched and held together between the thumb and forefinger of the left hand. These are to be the right and left wings, but are tied on as though one. They are held in position by the left hand, with the butt of the webbing facing right, toward the eye of the hook. The longer the fibers chosen and the more of the butt that can be left protruding beyond the winding thread, the less the chance of the wings' splitting. When the fibers are in position and held tightly, the winding thread is brought up and over the protruding butts of the webbing and down on the other side; then the thread is carefully pulled taut, pressing the layers of fibers together as if you were squeezing an accordion. Two or three additional winds of thread are taken to the right, not the left, of this original turn to whip the feathers on securely, and the remaining butts are clipped off.

The hackle is then wound in tightly behind the wing feathers to force them up and forward. The wings are lifted up during this process to allow the hackle to get in securely behind. The last couple of turns of hackle are taken ahead of the wings, the tip of the hackle whipped in with the thread and clipped off, and the whip finish put on the head of the fly. Finally, the right and left wings are separated from one another and forced out about thirty degrees from one another for the completed fly. Some flytiers separate the wings prior to winding on the hackle and force them apart with a figure-of-eight winding between them.

The wings can be put on in a reverse fashion; that is, with the butts pointing to the rear rather than forward. Some patterns call for one style and some for the other.

Wet Fly

Anyone who can tie a winged dry fly can handle a wet fly as well. The procedure is essentially the same. The basic difference is that the hackles on a dry fly must be stiff and protrude at right angles to the hook or, if anything, a little forward of right angles. The wings also are erect. In a wet fly the hackles may be soft, and the hackles and wings should lie back in a streamlined fashion. Another difference is in the hook. A heavier hook is generally in order for wet-fly fishing. A good model is the short-shanked Limerick.

A good wet fly should be neat and trim. Once a trout's attention is focused on it, he can get a better look at an object underwater than at one floating on top; so a wet fly must be presentable. The saving grace for the wet fly is that it is often being pulled past the fish hastily, or it is being used in fast water where the trout must strike quickly. Strangely, seldom does the care go into a professionally tied wet fly that goes into a dry. Many cheap ones are sold that are just plain coarse and too bulky for much good. Others are tied like a woman's Easter hat.

Hen hackles are commonly used on wet flies because they are soft, but cock hackles can be used. In tying flies from a complete rooster neck, there will be many hackles too soft for the best dry flies. In fact the most important step in tying a dry fly is the ability to discard all but the choicest hackles. The others are suitable for wet flies.

A typically tied wet fly is the Butcher, and it is a good one, too. The materials necessary for tying a Butcher are a few scarlet hackle fibers, or other whisks of scarlet feather, for the tail; flat silver tinsel for the body; a Black Minorca hackle; and, for the wings, secondary mallard wing feathers from the iridescent, blue-black patch on the drake's wings.

The thread is started as with the dry fly and the butt of the hackle feather tied on in the same manner. The thread is then carried back near the bend of the hook where the scarlet whisks of red feather are tied in for the tail and the end of the silver tinsel is whipped on. The thread is carried forward, followed by the tinsel which is wrapped on like an old-fashioned puttee. The tinsel is finished off with three or four turns of the thread, the excess clipped off, and the wings are tied in. The butts of the wing feathers are clipped off and the hackle wound in front of the wings. The hackle fibers should be short and fairly sparse. The tip of the hackle is tied in at the head of the fly and the excess

Ted Trueblood, who taught me how to take trout in lakes. This is Wyoming's Bridger Wilderness Area.

clipped off. If the hackles protrude too much at right angles, they can be laid back with a turn or two of thread at the head of the fly, then the thread is tied in with a whip finish, the head is touched with lacquer or varnish, and the fly is finished.

As with the winged dry fly, tying in the wing feathers is the most difficult part of the battle. Single wings are used on the Butcher. When you match the webbing for these wings, the iridescent parts of the mallard feathers are chosen, with the iridescent sides facing out, of course. The wings lie back along the hook, turned down, and are not separated. They should not be too large. Large wings, especially if not tied just exactly right, will make a fly spin. The big job is to prevent their splitting when tying them in. They should be held as firmly as possible between the thumb and forefinger of the left hand and a considerable amount of butt should be allowed to protrude beyond the point where the thread

grips the feather. Then if the thread pulls the fibers together, like a bellows, and doesn't twist them, the wings should not split. Some flytiers put a drop of lacquer on the tips of the webbing before tying them in to prevent their splitting, but the trouble comes not from the tips but from the point where the thread is wrapped.

Nymphs

There are few if any good nymphs sold commercially. A nymph is fished naturally with the current or moved very slowly, and in low, clear water where the nymph is most effective the trout can get as good a look at it as a shopper can at the banana he is buying. The nymph fisherman doesn't have the benefit of surface distortion or a rapidly moving lure. There's nothing to interfere with the trout's looking it over. A shopper doesn't buy an apple for an orange, and a trout doesn't bite a doodle bug for a nymph.

A fairly passable May-fly nymph can be tied with three long whisks of hackle for tails, a quill body, and a small hackle at the head. The hackle is divided with a few strands left underneath for legs and the remainder tied down in a hump on the back for a wing case. The excess remaining from forming the wing case is clipped off. A dark hackle is a good idea if the nymph is to be used in May, June, or July. The wing case of a May fly turns dark just before it hatches, and an excellent time to fish a nymph is just prior to a hatch or during the first stages of a hatch. The trout are then feeding heavily on the nymphs rising to the surface in preparation for the hatch.

This is as good a simple nymph as can be tied, but nothing to rave about. Among other things, most such nymphs tied of feathers or fur simply don't sink readily enough, especially in the small sizes. The only really good nymphs I have ever seen are the amateur creations described in the chapter on nymph fishing.

Streamers and Bucktails

Streamers and bucktails are designed to imitate minnows and should be so shaped. Streamers are generally brightly colored to attract the attention of the trout, and bucktails and squirrel tails are in natural colors. If a fisherman discovers a particularly successful streamer, he should not have much trouble copying it. Streamers and bucktails are on the whole very simple to tie. Exceptions would be flies like the Gray Ghost, which has everything from white belly and dark back to eyes, gill covers, and a stripe down the side.

A simple streamer can be made with a silk floss body, a bright tab for a tail, and two hackle feathers slightly longer than the hook tied in at the head so that they lie parallel to either side of the hook.

A very deadly streamer is the White Maribou made from the fluffy feathers of the maribou stork. The body of this streamer is generally of silver tinsel. A maribou feather is tied in at the head by the feather butt. Outside this on either side is a strip of peacock herl and, finally, at the head on either side is a jungle-cock feather for an eye.

Bucktails are tied from natural deer hair. Ac-

A fat brown trout from a Montana mountain creek.

tually hair from the tail of a doe or fawn, if available, is better than from that of a buck as it is not quite so coarse. It is tied on the hook with the dark hair on top and the light on the bottom, just the way it comes off the tail. The hair should not be put on too thick, and the hindmost wrappings of thread should not be too tight or the hair will flare out like a shaving brush. Hair dry flies are made of bucktail wound so tightly that the hair protrudes at right angles.

The body of a bucktail is commonly made of silver tinsel. The head can consist merely of the lacquered whip finish, or it can be improved by giving it an optic effect. One method of accomplishing this is to wrap a heavy head with thread, lacquer it shiny black, and finally paint eyes on either side. Another method is to split a buckshot halfway, clamp it over the head, lacquer it and paint eyes on it. Still another method is to wind two little glass beads on either side for eyes. The hook for streamers and bucktails should be long shanked. A good model hook is the Sproat.

Chapter 9

FLY TACKLE

The graphite rod, a product of space technology, is the latest of many recent innovations in tackle. As in other aspects of our lives, improvements in the fishing-tackle field have come more rapidly in the last fifty years than during the previous five hundred. Significant changes have been made within the memory of many of us. For example, we have witnessed the uniform tempering of bamboo, the impregnation of bamboo, glass as a rod material, and now graphite. The leader, that essential deceptive separation between the harsh line and the delicate fly, has been constantly improved ever since the first synthetic monofilament, nylon, replaced silkworm gut. Finally, there have been many improvements in line materials, tapers, and densities.

In selecting a fly-fishing outfit, we start at the end and work back. The line is the crux. It is chosen for the work it must do: float a dry fly, cast a streamer, sink a nymph, or carry a fly an exceptional distance. The type of work to be done determines the particular type and weight of the line, and the weight of the line, in turn, determines the proper rod for the job.

The Line

The line is to a fine fly rod what the conductor is to an orchestra. The rod may have the ability to perform superbly, but it is up to the line to transform this potentiality into reality. A line that is too heavy will bog down the rod, one too light will fail to bring out its hidden strength. In the first case the rod works too hard, in the second case the fisherman works too hard, and in neither case can a cast be made with perfection or ease.

The first thing to be understood by a beginner in fly fishing is that it is the line which is cast. The line is cast by the rod, and the leader and fly are carried to their destination by the momentum imparted to the line. This is in direct contrast to bait casting and spinning in which the weight of the lure and the force with which it is propelled pull the line with it. In fly fishing it is the weight of the line in the air during the false casts that cocks the rod and brings out its power to shoot the line forward.

Consequently, the selection of the proper weight and taper of line to match the rod is vitally important, as important as the bow to the violin or the lens to the camera.

Unfortunately, there is no rule by which the correct weight line can be determined by the weight and dimensions of a rod. Too much depends on the design of the particular rod, the material of which it is made, and its individual characteristics. No two rods are likely to be identical even if machine-made and turned out one after the other. However, the reputable rod maker will specify exactly which weight line is best for each of his rods. In a less expensive rod, without such a maker's recommendation, an experienced rod dealer can set up a rod, feel its action, and select a line which will fit. This is about all a beginner has to go by. An experienced fisherman can make a couple of casts and know. If the rod isn't working, the line is too light and he can feel it. The same is true if the rod is overworked.

Lines are designated by numbers to indicate their weight. These numbers generally run from 2 through 11, No. 2 being the lightest and 11 the heaviest. These numbers are accompanied by letters to designate the particular line. The letters preceding the number indicate the design:

for example, L signifies level; DT, double taper; WF, weight forward; and ST, shooting head. The letters F or S following the weight number stand for floating or sinking. There are some lines which are designed to float but which have a sinking tip. These are designated F/S. For instance, a DT6F line is a 6-weight, double-tapered floating line; a WF10S is a 10-weight, weight-forward (or distance) sinking line.

The numbered weight of a fly line is not the total weight of the line but the weight of the first 30 feet, which is the amount of line normally carried in a cast to work the rod. The following gives the weight in grains for the various numbers:

Weight:	80	100	120	140	160	185
Number:	2	3	4	5	6	7
	210	240	280	330		
	8	9	10	11		

The first two weights are so light that they are used only rarely, for extremely specialized fishing. No. 4 is about the lightest common size, so we will start there. (NOTE: Rod weights are given for bamboo. A similar rod in glass is somewhat lighter for the same purpose and in graphite much lighter.)

The very light No. 4 line is designed for the most delicate approach on small streams, for leaders tapered down to two-pound test. It is used on fly rods from 6 feet to 7½ feet in length and weighing from 2 to 3 ounces. These rods must be fairly slow in their action.

The No. 5 is a more practical weight for small streams and a delicate approach. This would most often be used on 7-to-7½-foot rods weighing from 2¾ to 3¼ ounces in a medium to medium-fast action. It should also be used on even longer rods if the rods are soft; that is, if they have slow action.

The No. 6 line is the most widely used weight for normal trout fishing. It can handle dry flies, wet flies, and small streamers well. The rods it takes are of such a weight that they can be cast all day without fatigue and yet are powerful enough to cast 60 feet easily. Rods for No. 4 lines are good for only about 40 feet and those for No. 5 for about 50 feet. Unless a person is going in for big-stream fishing, steelhead fishing, or certain lake conditions which demand a long cast, the No. 6 weight line is the best all-round choice. For the most part it would be used on rods from 7½ to 8½ feet in length weighing 3½ to 4½ ounces. The lines, floating or sinking, would normally be double-tapered.

The No. 7 line is used for the same type fishing as the No. 6 but it takes a somewhat longer or heavier rod and reaches out a bit farther. It therefore demands more of the fisherman, generally too much for all-day dry-fly fishing, which involves hundreds of false casts.

Nos. 8, 9, 10, 11 are designed primarily for conditions which require a long cast and where delicacy of presentation is not of prime importance. Most of them are designed as weight-forward lines for distance and they are most often sinking lines. Others are shooting heads. With a 9- or 9½-foot rod, in weights of 5¼ to 6¼ ounces, casts of 100 feet are possible with the heavier of these weights.

For fishing under all conditions on all manner of trout water, I personally do everything with two outfits, an 8-foot rod with a DT6 line and a 9-foot rod with a WF9. If I were to use a shooting head on the latter, I would choose one weight heavier; that is, an ST10.

Keeping these designations in mind, we can now examine line design and what exactly is meant by double taper, shooting head, and the like.

There are four basic fly line designs: level, double taper, weight forward, and shooting head. The level line requires no explanation. As the name implies, this line is the same diameter throughout (as shown by A in the diagram on p. 80). It is a passable all-purpose line.

The tapered lines, however, are what interest us most. First and foremost among them is the double taper (B). The middle section, or belly, of the double-tapered line is level. However, at either end the line gradually tapers down to points a size or two smaller and lighter in weight. The graduated distribution of weight from the belly to the point is the important thing in the taper, and the leader should continue this taper from the line to the fly.

The double taper has the widest use of all the tapers. It can be employed to advantage in all types of fly fishing, but it is most effective when used with light lures, such as dry flies, small wet flies, and nymphs. The heavy middle section—the belly of the line—gives the weight necessary in the cast and delivers the impetus to the lighter tapered section, the leader and the fly. The taper, with its gradually lessening weight toward the tip, makes the line roll out smoothly and easily in the cast. In a well-delivered cast, the belly of the line should fall to the water first, while the lighter sections of the line, then the leader, unfold and descend gradually. The fly floats gently to the water last of all.

The reason for the double taper—that is, the taper at each end—is simply one of economy. Only one of the two tapers is used at a time, and when one end of the line becomes worn and useless the line can be reversed and a practically new line put into play.

The third type (C) operates on the principle that, since it is the weight of the line that makes casting possible, it should be concentrated forward where it will do the most good. This WF taper utilizes both the principle of the gradual taper from the belly of the line to the leader, as in the double-tapered line, and the front-taper feature which concentrates the casting weight of the line forward where it will have the most effect.

This line has a gradual taper from the belly forward to the leader. The heavy belly extends for a short distance and then tapers back sharply to a level line almost as light as the forward point. This level section, which is continuous to the end of the line, is known as the shooting line. When it is used properly and the line is the right size for the rod, all of the taper—that is, all of the heavy belly forward of the shooting line—should be beyond the rod tip during the false casts. When released on the final forward thrust, the shooting line is pulled forward by the mo-mentum given to the belly of the line by the rod.

The fourth and final type of line is the ST, or shooting head. It operates on the same principle as the WF line, the only difference being that the shooting line is replaced by monofilament. Monofilament—which, of course, is single-strand, synthetic line, such as nylon, stren, and the like—not only shoots better but is a guide to the fisherman to indicate when all the belly is out of the rod as it should be in false casts. With such a line in moderate dimensions, a competent fly fisherman should be able to hold 30 feet of line in the air on false casts and shoot another 40 without difficulty.

Unless a fisherman has the rod, the ability, and the necessity to handle a WF, or distance, taper, he will do better to stick to the double taper. The distance taper is seldom recommended for dry-fly fishing, or any fishing in which more finesse than power is required. It is designed to be used for just what its name implies: distance casting.

Using the proper type and weight line for the rod and the fishing conditions at hand heightens the pleasure of fly fishing more than any other single factor. It is worth selecting the right one; and once the right one has been found, it's worth taking care of. The quickest way to ruin a line is to step on it and grind the finish on the gravel. This sounds like an extreme measure, but I've done it. That's when I learned to hold the slack line in coils in my left hand when I retrieved it rather than allow it to fall aimlessly at my feet. This is no mere trick; the line can be shot farther and controlled much better from coils in the hand than from the ground or water.

The only other consideration in selecting a fly

Diagrams of fly lines with different tapers.

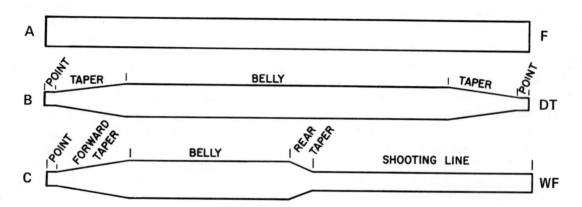

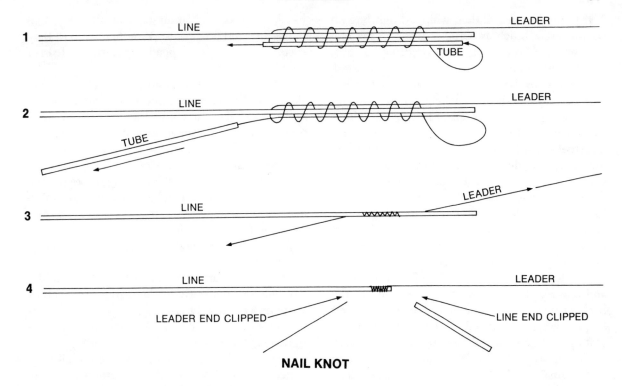

NAIL KNOT

*Step 1. Arrange fly-line end, leader material, and hol-
        low tube parallel to each other; wrap leader
        back around all three for six or eight turns;
        push leader end through hollow tube.*
Step 2. Remove tube.

*Step 3. Tighten knot by alternately pulling leader ma-
        terial from both ends.*
*Step 4. Clip excess line tip and excess leader material
        close to knot.*

line beyond its weight and taper is the matter of
whether to choose a floating or sinking line. In
almost all small-to-moderate trout streams a
floating line is used, and all beginners should
start with a floating model. A floating line picks
up easily without putting excessive strain on a
light rod, and it also responds more rapidly to a
strike than a deep line at the mercy of the current. However, in much lake fishing and in big-
water fishing, such as for sea-run trout, a sinking
line is in order. Sinking lines come in various
densities, and where it is necessary to get a fly
down to a steelhead through a heavy current, a
high-density sinking line may be required.

Modern fly lines rarely need much attention.
They are built to float—or sink, as the case may
be—without additional dressing and their finish
is smooth, pliable, and durable. If a floating line
does commence to sink, it probably means that
it is dirty. A light washing in mild soap and
water should rejuvenate it.

A few fishermen resort to dressings for added

distance. One method of dressing a floating line
is to run it through a piece of paraffin to clean it
and give it a slick shooting surface. The other
dressing is made of powdered graphite. This
makes a line so slick you can hardly hold it. It
will shoot a mile. It is wonderful—except for
one slight disadvantage. Everyone is acquainted
with graphite in its use as pencil lead. It is black
and easily transferable, so that within an hour
on a hot day a fisherman can wind up looking
like a grease monkey. Otherwise, graphite is perfect.

A break or crack in the finish can be sealed
satisfactorily with a touch of rod varnish. Apply
it very sparingly, for if it is put on too thick, the
line will become stiff and crack.

A bad spot in a line should be broken and
spliced. A line can be spliced so smoothly that it
will not be noticed in the casting. Fray both
ends to be spliced with a needle or pin for a distance of a quarter inch, then intermesh the two
ends as we do our fingers in folding our hands.

The whole business is then whipped tightly with winding silk, much as a rod is wound (see section on *Rod Varnishing and Refitting*, p. 86). Finally the splice is varnished or, if preferred, polished with beeswax. The completed splice will be only one-half inch long. For a stronger splice, scrape and fray ends of line, overlap for a quarter inch, and whip.

A reel should always be filled out with backing, either braided casting line or monofilament, behind the fly line and attached to the drum of the reel. When you are after large fish, it is wise to splice this backing directly to the casting line because a knot at this point might provide just enough of an obstruction in passing through the guides to give the trout his freedom.

If a fisherman has several different fly lines and one reel he can join the casting line to the backing merely by a junction of two permanent loops, a large one spliced on the after end of the casting line and a small one on the forward end of the backing. The backing except for the loop itself remains on the spool of the reel. The method of joining the two is as follows: the large casting-line loop is first threaded through the backing loop then passed completely over and around the reel. When pulled taut the two loops are locked together. Thus various fly lines are immediately interchangeable on the same reels.

A slick little gadget, actually a small eyelet with a barbed needle point, can be inserted in the end of a fly line for securing the leader. It won't pull out until this tip of the line becomes weak from wear. Otherwise, without using such an eyelet, I prefer to join the leader to the line by a pair of loops, the leader loop and a similar small one spliced in the end of the fly line. The line loop is passed through the leader loop, then over the end of the leader. The leader is then drawn through until the two loops join. This is as quick as tying a knot and forms a much smoother junction. If a knot is preferred, the nail knot, illustrated on p. 81, is by far the best hitch.

The Rod

Today we are blessed with three good to excellent fiber materials from which to select a fly rod (and Du Pont is presently developing another, presently labeled PRD-49). The three are bamboo, glass, and graphite, and all are potentially fine rod materials. Whether or not they succeed in being so depends upon the craftsman who fashions them.

A craftsman is a dedicated soul. He is highly skilled and takes such pride in his work that he will not sacrifice that skill for the sake of time, money, or the convenience of inferior materials. His reward comes from the satisfaction of a job well done, not from the glory, power, or riches which drive many individuals. Therefore, in the heat of the modern machine world, the craftsman is an endangered species. There are not many left, but we fishermen are particularly lucky. Some of the best of those remaining today are building fly rods.

Because of this, it is safe to say that all the bamboo rods currently made in America, such as those by Winston, Orvis, and Leonard, are excellent products. A few glass rods are also well designed and carefully made. And most graphite rods are reliable, although a few are not all they appear to be. Each of these materials has its own properties, so each should be discussed briefly.

A bamboo rod has personality. Since it is produced from a natural product, Tonkin cane, no two rods could ever be identical. Each is an individual, and after long acquaintance it seems to live and respond almost as an extension of the fisherman's arm, taking on a mellow character as no synthetic material ever could.

Bamboo is the oldest of our current rod materials, and for about one hundred years it was almost the only material used for making the finest rods. There are more than two hundred varieties of bamboo around the world, but rod makers are so particular that they will use only one relatively rare species, Tonkin cane, which is found exclusively in mainland China. Only the hard outermost layer with the finest cell structure is used, and only the best of that ever goes into a rod. About 95 per cent of the cane which passes through the rod maker's hands is rejected. The 5 per cent selected is as uniform as possible, and it is ideally resilient and durable, but the design of the rod is even more important than the material which goes into it. America has led the world in the field of fly-rod design for many years, ever since Leonard started selling split-bamboo rods in 1870. He established a tradition carried on by the artisans of today.

Bamboo is the heaviest of the materials used for rod-making and it lies between glass and graphite in both elasticity and strength, glass being the weakest in both categories, graphite the strongest. Few of us can cast a rod long enough to break down its molecular structure to any significant degree, but in this respect as well bamboo lies between glass and graphite; glass breaks down the most readily, graphite the least. Bamboo has the edge over both in durability, since the six wedge-shaped sections which go into a split-bamboo rod form a solid object whereas both glass and graphite rods are of hollow construction with relatively thin, vulnerable walls.

Anyone fortunate enough to possess a good bamboo rod of today or yesterday—such as those made by Thomas, Payne, Phillipson, Powell, Edwards, Orvis, Winston, or others of less renown—should treasure it. These rods are not only capable of a lifetime's service but are examples of craftsmanship at its best.

Glass rods made with similar care are also fine products. They must be properly designed to begin with, then carefully laid up and bonded correctly. Glass in a sense is like a synthetic bamboo. It is constructed in much the same fashion with the resilient fibers running lengthwise much as do the fine cells in cane; so the potential is there. It has the advantage that it is less expensive than either bamboo or graphite, but in this advantage lies its greatest disadvantage. There are thousands of glass rods which emphasize only this one aspect of the material, the cost, and they sacrifice design, proper bonding resins, and care in construction. At its very best, glass cannot compare with a fine bamboo or graphite rod, so poor ones are not even in the same league. Such rods are likely to work only in the tip, or only in the butt, and all are inclined to be too soft.

Graphite, on the other hand, seems to be precisely the material that rod makers and fishermen have been searching for forever. Years ago when bamboo was the only rod material and some rods were turned out as hastily and carelessly as are some glass ones today, the fisherman shopping for a good one would test it by whipping it down sharply and watching how rapidly the tip stopped vibrating. A weak or soft rod would continue to oscillate at the tip while a crisp one would almost immediately return to

the true and remain there. Not only would such a rod with a high "damping ratio," as it is called, have more punch, but in damping rapidly it would permit the line to shoot through the guides with less interference. A rod with a low damping ratio encumbers the line with each oscillation and sends it out in waves. Through habit I test every fly rod I pick up in this manner, and I couldn't believe it when I put my first graphite rod, which happens to be a Fenwick, to the test. It has virtually no vibration, or oscillation, at the tip. It comes to the true immediately at the end of the cast.

Due to this and its greater elasticity compared to other materials, most fishermen can lay out about 10 per cent more line (of the same weight) with a graphite rod as they can with rods of bamboo or glass. This may not happen immediately. Graphite responds so rapidly that it may take a while to get accustomed to it.

Of course, graphite is not really graphite. This would be too simple. It is a unique carbon fiber developed for space use to provide a lightweight material with high structural strength. It starts out as polyester, which is complex enough, and at the end of a series of operations becomes an extremely fine carbon filament after being heated to more than 3000° in an oxygen-free oven. These fibers are arranged side by side and bonded into a sheet. In building a rod, as with similar glass sheets, the sheets are wrapped around a steel core, or mandrel, and bonded together to form the tubular rod sections.

Graphite is so stiff and light (has such a high modulus of elasticity, technically speaking) that rods produced from it are much smaller in diameter and much lighter than either glass or bamboo for the same weight line.

With such superb characteristics, graphite is just about an ideal rod material, but there is a word of caution. For proper results in rod construction, a small amount of glass is necessary. Both Orvis and Winston, to my knowledge, use 94 per cent graphite in their rods. However, as they point out, glass costs about $.87 a pound at this time while graphite costs $100 a pound, so there is the temptation on the part of some manufacturers with less pride in their products to use more glass and less graphite.

However, it is safe and advisable to order directly from any reputable maker. Such companies have had years of experience behind them and the men who have devoted their lives to the business know far more about rods than any of us who are acquainted with only those few that we have used. Therefore, in ordering a rod from one of these leading companies, if you tell them the size you have in mind and the action desired, you can be pretty certain of getting what you are looking for. And the maker's recommendation for the proper size line to match the rod will help you get the most out of it.

The rod is the most expensive and important item in the trout fisherman's equipment. If you intend to get the most out of fly fishing, it is worth your money and time to get a good rod. This goes for a beginner as well as an experienced fisherman. Good tools are good teachers. With the right rod you will learn good casting habits from the start, whereas a poor rod will teach bad habits which will be difficult to overcome. And with reasonable care a good rod will last a lifetime.

Rod Care

A rod requires little more than common-sense care. There is just one important rule: when the fishing is finished, even if just for the time being, dismantle the rod, wipe off any excess moisture, then place the sections in their cloth bag and the bag in a rigid container. As long as a rod is in its aluminum or hard-fiber case, no harm can come to it. More rods are broken or harmed by careless handling in automobiles and away from the stream in general than during actual fishing.

For instance, it is easy to harm a rod during the simple process of dismantling it. The sections of bamboo should be dismantled by a direct pull, never a twist. A rod is built to stand a lot of bending, but a twist could easily separate the glued-together strips. An obstinate joint which insists on sticking can best be taken apart by two people who alternate their hands, as shown in the accompanying illustration. This insures a direct pull, and it is surprising how easily a tough one will come apart under such treatment. If you are alone, such a joint will sometimes respond to the following treatment. Grip the rod firmly with both hands on either side of the obstinate joint, place the ends of the thumbs firmly together and push apart with the thumbs.

Of course the wise thing is to avoid a sticky joint in the first place. This is easily accomplished by applying a bit of paraffin or graphite to the male ferrule. The handiest and best lubricant is applied by rubbing the male ferrule alongside the nose or in the hair before setting the rod up. Never use oil. Oil will form a suction which will only make matters worse.

Sticky glass ferrules can be lubricated with beeswax, graphite with paraffin. Glass and graphite rods, in contrast to bamboo rods, may be twisted apart.

In addition to following these precautions, the things to watch for in a well-used rod are chipped varnish, worn windings, worn snake guides, and loose ferrules.

A broken or worn winding which holds a guide in place will eventually have to be replaced, but as a streamside expediency a touch of varnish, or, quicker, any collodion such as nail polish will hold the thread in place temporarily. If the guide has actually been knocked loose, whip it on again with a bit of nylon leader. Such wrappings go well with a glass rod throughout, by the way, and are less trouble than the thread windings discussed later.

Nothing will shorten the life of a good fly line

Taking apart a joint.

as quickly as a worn snake guide. The knifelike edge of a badly worn guide will literally peel the finish right off a line. The first guide on the butt section and the tip-top guide receive the most wear and should be made of agate or a very hard steel alloy. These will not have to be replaced unless the agate becomes cracked, then they can play havoc with a line. Replace worn or broken guides before they can do their damaging work.

The slight give of a loose ferrule is an annoying thing when casting, and it is hard on the rod. Sometimes the mere heating of the ferrule with a match is sufficient to soften the ferrule cement inside and give it the opportunity to reset as it hardens. However, every fisherman should carry a bit of ferrule cement in his tackle box. Then a very loose ferrule can be removed, a bit of cement melted on the butt of the rod section and the ferrule replaced.

Broken Rod: Ferrule cement and matches can effect numerous streamside repairs. For instance, when a rod breaks, it does so most often where it is seated into the ferrule. Unless the rod was originally fastened into the ferule by means of a small metal pin, the broken stub is removed simply by heating the ferrule to soften the cement. A pair of pliers will overcome any stubbornness. Cut off the frayed and split end of the rod and fit it into the ferrule. If the break has occurred below the joint, at the female ferrule, it may be necessary to shape the rod slightly to refit it into the ferrule. If so, shave away the least possible amount, for to cut sharply or excessively into the rod is to invite another break at the same point. If the break is above the joint at the male ferrule, the rod may fit too loosely. In this case, a single layer of thread whipped around the butt of the section will make a snug fit.

When a good fit between rod and ferrule has been achieved, heat the tip of the cement with a match until it melts sufficiently to put a dab on the end of the rod, then heat the ferrule and slip it into place. After the ferrule is in place heat it moderately again to make sure the cement is well distributed, then hold it firmly in place for the moment required for the cement to harden. Any excess cement at the end of the ferrule can be wiped clean while it is still warm or chipped off when set.

A break in the middle of a joint is usually disastrous. The rod will likely be shattered for some distance and there won't be much left to salvage. With a clean break in a bamboo rod, however, a passable repair can sometimes be made. Make a diagonal cut at least 1½ inches long at the end of each broken section. These cuts must be made even and opposite one another so that they will fit together snugly. Glue this splice with cabinetmaker's glue and wrap as tightly as possible with nylon. Then order a new rod, or at least a new section.

Removing a Set: Occasionally, generally through misuse, a rod develops a "set," which is a warp or permanent bend. A slight set may not be serious. It often can be remedied immediately by reshaping the affected part with the fingers. A bad set is something else. It is generally caused by one of two things: the fibers may be broken or badly strained; or the strips in a bamboo rod may have slipped in relation to one another. Such a rod may have a lot of service in it yet,

Perfection in the art of rod building has reached the ultimate in the Orvis impregnated split-bamboo rod ("99" fly rod illustrated) and in the Winston split bamboo. The building of these rods requires the greatest care in the selection of materials, in skill, in craftsmanship, in inspection, and in pride in the completed product.

but a set usually indicates a weak spot which may give way eventually. Also, a set doesn't add to the appearance of a rod, and most of us take pride in our tackle.

The only remedy in the first case above, where the bamboo or glass has actually been fractured, is to whip the weak area tightly with nylon to strengthen it and hope for the best. In the second case, where the sections have slipped, scrape the varnish from the area around the set and expose this part of the rod to live steam from a kettle. It is sometimes possible to soften the glue in the rod in this manner and bend it back true. The section should then be bound tightly and allowed to dry thoroughly before revarnishing.

Rod Varnishing and Refitting: Graphite, glass, and impregnated bamboo are not varnished except on guide windings; otherwise, if you are fortunate enough to possess a good split-bamboo rod, take care of it. Varnish is the means of protecting the bamboo and glue of the rod from the moisture with which it is always in contact. To carry out this primary purpose this protective coat must be kept intact. A well-used rod should be varnished occasionally before the start of the season. This is a simple process.

The best grade of spar varnish should be used, and it should be applied thinly. Put the bottle of varnish in steaming water for several minutes before starting the varnishing job, and in order that the varnish be as thin as possible keep it in the pan of hot water throughout the varnishing process. Do not stir or agitate the varnish as the bubbles caused will prove a nuisance. Do the varnishing in a warm, dust-free room and varnish from the top of each section down. Concentrate on keeping the coat of varnish thin and watch for drops which will accumulate at the guides or at the bottom of the sections.

The rod should be kept in a dust-free, draftless location for a few hours, at least until the surface is no longer tacky. Then, if it is necessary to hurry up the drying process, the rod can be transferred out into the air and sunshine. A single, thin coat should dry sufficiently in a couple of days for the rod to be used.

A rod too often varnished or one on which the varnish has been badly chipped or cracked should be completely scraped and revarnished.

This is quite a job, but for those who like to tinker with tackle it is an interesting one.

First, the old windings and guides are removed by cutting through the thread with a sharp knife or razor blade and peeling them off. Next, the old varnish is removed by scraping it with the edge of a piece of broken glass held perpendicularly to the surface of the bamboo. Fine sandpaper stretched tightly across the flat surface of a piece of wood will take care of obstinate varnish. Finally, go over the rod with steel wool, brush off all dust, and the rod is ready for wrapping. A heavy thread, such as buttonhole twist, is best for rod winding.

Scars on the sticks will show the original locations of the guides and any other windings, and these will indicate where the new ones are to be replaced.

The manner of whipping on the thread may seem a little difficult the first few times, but after several attempts it becomes quite simple. Moisten the end of the thread so that it is easier to hold in place; then, in winding from right to left, place the tip of the thread under the left thumb parallel to the rod and carry the thread around the rod with the right hand to overlap the piece held under the left thumb. Continue this process for five or six laps, giving way slightly with the left thumb to make room for each succeeding wind. A half-dozen such loops of the thread wound over itself are sufficient to anchor the end of the thread. The left thumb can now be relaxed and the winding continued as far as desired.

To finish a winding, have handy a tight loop of well-waxed thread. A half-dozen turns from the end of the winding, lay this loop parallel to the rod with the loop end in the direction in which you are winding, hold it in place with the left thumb, and carry the last six winds over it. Finally, run the end of the winding thread through the loop and pull the loop out from under the windings, carrying the end of the winding thread with it. This end can now be cut off close to the winding with a sharp blade and the job is finished.

In whipping on a guide, I have found it handy to anchor it in place temporarily by tying it down with thread or even with a bit of Scotch tape. Such temporary lashings are removed, of course, as the winding thread takes over.

The varnishing is done as described above

with a couple of preliminary steps thrown in. Varnish or shellac applied directly to silk, and to a somewhat lesser extent to nylon thread, turns the winding a much darker color. If the finish is to be applied directly, this fact should be kept in mind in selecting the color silk for the winding job. Direct application has the advantage of cementing the winding thread securely to the rod.

However, if the natural color of the thread is desired, this can be accomplished by one of two means. The most often suggested method is to apply beeswax to the winding, rubbing it in thoroughly and finally boning it until it is hard and shiny. I have never had much success with this method. Somehow some varnish leaks through the wax and discolors a part of the winding. The other method is to coat the windings with a solution of equal parts collodion and banana oil. The banana oil is used merely to dilute the collodion.

I prefer merely to apply a coat of shellac to each winding, let it dry and then varnish, even though this does turn the winding thread darker. Thread has numerous tiny hairs which will protrude through the shellac and varnish and mar the appearance of the rod. These can be singed off with a clear flame before shellacking or varnishing if great care is taken not to scorch or smudge the thread. Another method is to tamp down the tiny hairs after applying the shellac and while it is still tacky.

In varnishing, work lengthwise from top to bottom after going around each winding to make certain it is thoroughly covered. Allow a week between each coat to give the spar varnish the opportunity to dry thoroughly, and apply three coats.

The Reel

The reel is a relatively minor piece of equipment in the fly-fishing outfit. Under most circumstances it is no more than a storage bin, merely a reservoir for the line not in use. The fly reel is not employed in making a cast and rarely in retrieving one. A trout fisherman might well cover a mile of stream without once touching the reel.

Nevertheless, there are a few considerations in the selection of a fly reel. These are, in order of importance: line capacity, weight, click or other

drag mechanism, take-down and, for the fisherman who takes pride in such things, appearance.

The capacity of a reel depends on the type of fishing you have in mind. For everyday trout fishing a reel with a drum just large enough to hold thirty-five yards of fly line is sufficient and advisable. Trout under three pounds don't make single sustained runs longer than the length of the standard fly line. When up against sea trout, steelhead, salmon, and large trout in lakes, it's a different story. For steelhead and salmon it is wise to have a reel capable of holding one hundred yards of 15-pound monofilament backing in addition to the casting line.

But a reel too large for the fishing at hand should not be used. Select a lightweight model in the capacity considered necessary. It is foolish to attempt to keep the weight of the rod down and then add a useless extra half pound of weight in the reel.

A reel should be filled near to capacity. A fly reel is single action—that is, has no multiplying gears for a rapid retrieve of the line—and therefore it has a narrow drum which, when full, will take up considerable line with each turn of the handle. If the fly line by itself does not fill the drum, it is well to fill out the drum with backing, or a cork arbor, whether any large fish are expected or not. This will save excess winding, and the fly line will be less cramped.

The click or other form of drag on a fly reel should have just enough resistance to prevent overrunning of the reel when stripping out line. Many reels have adjustable clicks and some large ones have drags and clicks, both adjustable. The click should be smooth, not too ratchety, and should afford more resistance when the reel is turned backward than when reeled forward.

A large fish on a fly rod should be played against the reel. When the trout is running, the tip of the rod should be held high and no pressure should be applied to the line other than the mechanical friction of the reel. There is little chance of a fouled line when it is playing out directly from the reel, and the click or drag provides a constant and relentless resistance which affords nothing solid against which the fish can effect a tackle-breaking surge. The drag should be adjusted sufficiently light to allow the reel to turn without danger of parting the leader no matter how much line is run out.

Of course, with equal drag or click tension, a reel with a full spool will give line under less pressure than will a reel with a nearly empty spool. This is a simple matter of leverage. Therefore, the farther a fish runs, the greater becomes the reel resistance automatically. Toward the end of a run when the fish is naturally tiring, the reel resistance increases and stops him.

The best way to land a large fish where conditions permit is to give him his head and let him run himself out and, after he has expended the first burst of energy, even to encourage him to run again and again. A migrating fish like a steelhead or salmon may take it into his mind to turn tail when he feels the barb and head for his home in the sea; then it behooves the fisherman to take out after him pronto. A local stream trout, however, will seldom leave the pool which had always been his home and haven unless he is harried into doing so by an excitable fisherman.

Some modern fly reels have no audible click whatsoever, but employ only a silent drag. Such a drag is every bit as effective and efficient as a click. But I am old-fashioned in this respect. I like to hear the angry screech of a reel when a good fisherman is working out line for a long cast, and to me a fine reel singing to the tune of the run of a big trout is as much a part of trout fishing as the sound of the murmuring water or the song of the phoebe overhead.

A simple means of taking the reel apart is important to remove grit which is certain to get in it occasionally (at least that's true if other fishermen spend as much time as I do sitting down or rolling around in a stream).

As we in America have long led the world in rod-building, the English have excelled in lightweight, handsome reels. These are exemplified by the beautiful Hardy reels. I have a Hardy Perfect which I was fortunate to obtain when quite young, and such a reel not only performs excellently but also will outlast the busiest fisherman. This is a fact which I will prove someday, but I should testify to it while I can.

The Leader

Everyone knows that there is a large variation in the diameter of various monofilaments in relation to the claimed pound test. Some of this variation is real, as indicated for Stren in the chart below, and some of it is imagined. Therefore, in discussing leaders we will use the old X system since this refers to a definite diameter. Actually, as in lines, it is weight that we are most interested in, but there is no available information on this to cover the large family of monofilaments.

A leader should continue the taper of the line on down to the fly. Since various size monofilaments are available in convenient ten-yard packages, every serious fly fisherman should learn to tie his own. Such home-made leaders are not only much less expensive but they are far better than any made-up leaders which can be purchased. Not only can the correct leader for the particular occasion be whipped together on the spot, but no commercial leader I have ever seen has the proper taper. They are not heavy enough at the butt; therefore, they do not deliver the proper impetus from the line down the leader to the fly.

AVERAGE STRENGTH OF NYLON AND STREN IN VARIOUS DIAMETERS

Size	Dia. in Inches	Pound Test	
		Nylon	Stren
6X	.005		2
5X	.006		3
4X	.007		4
3X	.008	3.7	5
2X	.009	4.5	6
1X	.010	5.5	7
0X	.011	6.2	8.5
9/5	.012	7.4	
8/5	.013	8.7	11
7/5	.014	9.7	
6/5	.015	11.5	14
4/5	.017	14.5	
2/5	.019	18.0	

For the man who wants to tie his own, the reasoning behind this business of taper should be understood. The principle of the leader taper is the same as that of the taper on the end of a fly line. The energy of a moving body is known as its momentum, and its momentum is a product of its mass and speed. With equal momentum, if a body's mass is greater, its speed is less; if its mass is less then its speed is greater. That is, if two bodies of the same size, say a baseball and an iron ball, have the same energy imparted to them, the one with the less mass, the baseball, will travel faster.

With a little imagination it is not difficult to see how this applies to the taper in line and leader. The momentum of the moving line is transferred to the taper; and, as the mass of the line and leader become less, the energy is transformed into speed, giving it the ability to pull the wind-resistant fly with it. This is the principle of a popping whip. The whip is tapered from the handle down to the finer tip, and when the whip is popped the energy imparted by the hand is transformed into speed until the tip is traveling at such incredible speed that it forms a vacuum in the air and causes the popping sound.

But back to leaders and fishing. The taper in the leader also has the very decided advantage of putting the finest and least conspicuous part of the leader near the fly and the fish. This inconspicuousness is the primary purpose of the leader, although its ability to extend the fly and drop it to the water gently and naturally is also important.

Dry-fly leaders and leaders used for single nymphs or single wet flies should be tapered directly and uniformly from line to leader. Leaders for very large flies and spinners which have sufficient weight to carry themselves out need not necessarily be tapered. Small dry flies and nymphs handle well on a long, gradually tapering leader. A bulky or wind-resistant lure will cast better with a short leader having a pronounced taper. In lake fishing from a boat where the wind can be kept at the caster's back, a tapered leader is not necessary; the wind will carry the fly out. Conversely, for casting into a wind the leader should be kept short, start heavy, and taper sharply. These are general rules.

Next, how long should a leader be and how fine should it taper? A leader finer than necessary for the conditions at hand should not be used. There is no point in leaving flies in trouts' mouths. Judgment as to what the particular conditions require calls for experience and experimenting. The size lure being used and the type water being fished are the governing factors.

Consider the contrast in size between the leader and the lure. A 1X leader on a size 8 fly would not be conspicuous while, even in the same water, a 1X leader on a size 20 midge would look like a cable. In still, clear water a fine leader is essential on any size fly, however. In fast water, a much heavier leader can be used for the simple reason that the trout does not have time to scrutinize the offering. He must make up his mind in a hurry. And with a very conspicuous lure, like a spinner, which is traveling rather rapidly in fast water, the leader is even less likely to be noticed.

Where conditions require very delicate work, I prefer to lengthen my leader before going to the extremes of 4X and 5X tippets. I was once given some 6-foot, 4X leaders. To my mind, this combination is entirely inconsistent. A 9-foot, 2X leader would present a dry fly better and fool more fish than a 6-foot, 4X leader, and it would be twice as strong. About the only conceivable use for a 6-foot, 4X leader would be for dabbling a fly on a small, brushy brook.

A leader 9 feet long tapered from 5/5 to 3X is about right for all-round dry-fly fishing. When necessary to cast into a brisk wind, a short, sharply tapered leader, such as a 7½-foot leader tapered from 4/5 to 3X, may be necessary. On the other hand, for working over skittish fish on flat water, a 12-foot leader tapered to 3X will take fish that would be put down by the 9-foot one. Although it is rarely necessary to go to greater extremes than this, a long leader can make up for a lot of careless casts by keeping the line away from the fish. A long leader also allows the fly to float to the water more gently than does a short one. I never use a leader shorter than my fly rod for any kind of trout fishing and often use one longer. A long leader may prove a little more difficult to handle, especially if there is any head wind, but it is worth the extra effort.

The color of a leader is cause for endless discussion. I have never completely satisfied myself on this subject, so I'll say little about it. With a deeply sunk fly, a dark-colored leader may be a good idea. However, most often a trout comes from beneath to take a fly, so transparency seems to me the most important factor. Of course we are deluding ourselves if we think that a trout can't see a leader—any leader. The best we can do is to try to make it as inconspicuous as possible. A floating leader of any size is very conspicuous, and glint also may be a factor.

IMPROVED CLINCH KNOT ... for joining line to lure

IMPROVED BLOOD KNOT ... for joining two lines

IMPROVED END LOOP ... for forming a loop

Three basic knots. The tensile strength of any monofilament, whether used as a casting line or as a fly leader, is materially reduced where knotted. Some knots, such as a simple overhand knot, will reduce the strength of the monofilament by more than half. With the use of the proper knot, however, this loss can be effectively controlled; that is, the monofilament where joined together or where tied to a lure or fly will maintain its rated strength. Also, most monofilaments, such as Stren, resist being tied and may slip if improperly knotted. The above three knots, being both strong and slip resistant, are the most effective with modern monofilaments, and they will cover all the trout fisherman's requirements, including making up one's own tapered leaders.

There are several stunts for removing glint and making a leader sink. Some fisherman recommend pulling the leader between a fold in a rubber boot. Others use the juice from the young leaves of an alder or underwater weeds. I've had some success by scouring a leader lightly with a handful of mud or other fine stream sediment. There is no good leader-sink dope made commercially to my knowledge.

Knots: Granted that it is an unusual person who can look at a knot diagram, then sit down and tie the knot, it is nevertheless necessary to include such diagrams in a book on trout fishing. If a man is to get any pleasure out of trout fishing, he must learn to tie three or four leader knots as easily as he ties his shoelaces. Although pages of knots could be included, only one knot for each basic operation will be shown. Most fishermen have their own pet knots for each purpose, but the following will serve.

First, in order to understand the importance of the proper knot, take a small-diameter strand of gut and pull on it to determine its strength unknotted. Now tie a simple overhand knot in it

and pull again. With such a knot it has less than half its former strength. When a man uses the wrong knots, or ties an overhand knot in his leader inadvertently while casting, he's throwing away flies and fish.

Next, take a piece of Stren and tie it to the swivel of a casting spoon or anything handy with an ordinary square knot—or anything else you think might be suitable. Now pull on it. Watch it slowly worm its way out of the knot and let go, and picture this happening with a four-pound trout on the end of your line. Then sit down and learn these three basic knots. They are the ones recommended by Du Pont to hold best with Stren, and if they will hold Stren they will hold anything.

The first is the *improved clinch knot*, used for tying flies and lures to a leader or to a monofilament spinning line. Look at the diagram and follow these four steps:

1. Thread the leader through the eye of the fly or swivel.

2. Double back and take at least five turns around the standing part of the leader. Knot strength drops off sharply with less than five

turns; with only three turns as much as 41 per cent.

3. Thrust the end between the eye and the first loop then back through the big loop so formed.

4. Slowly pull the knot up as tight as possible and cut off the end.

The second knot is the one used to tie two strands of leader together. Or, if an overhand knot should be thrown in the leader inadvertently, it should be broken immediately and re-tied. This knot, as can be seen, has the same principle as the clinch knot above. It is merely done twice. This is the *blood knot:*

1. Lap the ends of the strands to be joined. Twist one end about the standing part of the other strand at least five times. Bend the end back over turns and place between strands.

2. Turn about and repeat procedure with the opposite strand, winding five turns in the same direction and same manner. Push the end through the same center hole as the first except from the opposite side.

3. Pull the knot slowly and tight, allowing the turns to gather, and cut off ends.

The third and final basic knot involves forming a loop on the line end of the leader (if a line-tip eyelet is used, this knot isn't necessary; the clinch knot will serve). This *improved end loop knot* is tied as follows:

1. Form a double strand by bending back about four to six inches of the end in a tight "U" shape.

2. Fold this "U"-bend back and spiral around itself five times.

3. Insert the bottom of the "U" (which is to become the loop) through the hole made by the backward bend in step 2.

4. Pull up as tight as possible without breaking.

Although anyone will be all thumbs the first few times he attempts these, they will become simple and automatic after a bit of practice. Then, if he carries a few coils of leader material in his pocket, he can tie up any leader to suit the situation in hardly more time than it would require to unwrap a store-bought leader.

Chapter 10

FLY CASTING

Learning to cast sufficiently well to catch trout is really a simple thing. To become a perfectionist —to arrive at that point of mastery where casting and the placing of the fly can be almost as exciting a sport as fishing itself—takes time and practice.

Some young fishermen may be awed by the prospect of learning to cast a fly because they have heard that it is difficult, or because it may appear difficult when they see someone doing it. It is not difficult, and remember this as an example: a good fly caster can take a properly balanced fly line and with his two hands alone— with no rod—he can actually lay out forty or fifty feet of line as neatly as you wish. If this is possible without a rod, it should be easy with a rod. It is.

The first rule to learn in fly casting is that the wrist and forearm deliver the power to the cast. The upper arm is used little, the less at first the better.

The second rule is that a forward cast can be only as good and no better than the backcast. To counterbalance the fact that we only see the forward cast, we must continually concentrate— keep the mind's eye, so to speak—on the backcast. A high, well-extended backcast is essential.

You should realize that it is easier to learn the right rules first than to unlearn bad ones later. Therefore, in learning to cast, it is best from the very start to use as good a rod and line as possible. Poor tackle can teach a person bad rules just as can a poor instructor. After a fisherman has become proficient at casting with a good outfit, he can pick up poor tackle and get the most out of it; but the reverse is not true.

Overhead Cast

The first cast a person should master is the direct overhead cast. This is used in 90 per cent of fishing. Once it has been conquered, the various specialized casts, most of which are merely variations from this standard, will come easily.

In the old school for fly casters, the practicing pupil was told to stand in rapidly moving water and to clamp a five-dollar bill between his upper arm and side. This made him concentrate on using his forearm and wrist and not his upper arm, or else. It was a good stunt, worth remembering but not worth practicing because no part of the arm should be rigid. The caster must be relaxed.

The whole secret to fly casting lies in timing and in co-ordinated movement of the forearm and wrist. The forearm moves backward and forward at moderate speed in order to "cock" the wrist; and, just before the end of each stroke of the forearm, the wrist suddenly delivers the power to the rod. In making the forward cast, for instance, the forearm may move through an arc of fifty or sixty degrees, down almost to the horizontal, and just prior to the end of this stroke the wrist, which has been cocked back in the process, swings sharply forward. This puts a deep bend in the rod, the spring of which shoots the line ahead. It is possible to cock the wrist and rod for a forward cast, however, only if there is a good backcast in the air, the inertia of which provides something solid to pull against. Therefore, the backcast must be mastered before the forward cast can be attempted.

In order to drill into the mind of a beginner the necessity for keeping the backcast up in the air, another stunt used in casting instruction is to stand the pupil with his back against a wall higher than his head. This prevents his carrying the rod back past the perpendicular, and thus the backcast is necessarily shot high in the air. A lot can be learned from such a restriction in the casting arc, but it is a little drastic. In actual casting practice, it is true that the power to the backcast must be delivered prior to the perpendicular and the wrist snap stopped at this point; however, before the forward cast and during the process of cocking the wrist, the rod is allowed to ease back with the pull of the line before "taking hold" of the backcast for the forward thrust.

It is sometimes suggested that a beginner should learn to cast on dry land because by having things as difficult as possible he will be forced to learn the right rules quicker. This is probably true, but I learned to cast on water, and the incentive was a trout. I like this idea better. As a starting place, my suggestion is that the pupil stand in six inches to a foot of moderately moving water and face downstream. The area behind him should be clear. His rod should be fully rigged with a floating fly line, short leader, and small fly.

He must not attempt to handle too much line at first, but should use a line heavy enough to bring out the action of the rod. Twenty to twenty-five feet including the short leader is enough. The line must float, of course. As a start, he will allow the line and fly to extend directly downstream with the current, then will pick it up, extend it into a backcast and finally complete the cast, each in its turn. It is accomplished in these four simple steps:

1. *Position.* Assume a comfortable stance, as though you were going to shoot a rifle or shotgun at a target in the direction of your intended cast; that is, with the feet spread and the left foot ahead of the right. With the upper arm hanging alongside the body, hold the rod horizontal to the water surface with the tip pointed in the direction of the fly and, with the left hand, take hold of the line between the reel and first guide.

2. *Pickup.* The important thing in the pickup is to put the line in motion gradually and increase the tempo to the point of step three, the backcast. This initial action is a combination of two things: the right forearm is drawn up and the left hand holding the line is pulled down. The combined effect is to start the line in motion and to bend both the wrist and the rod tip down slightly—in effect to cock them forward.

3. *Backcast.* At this point the power is applied to the backcast. As with a baseball batter, golfer or tennis player, this power comes from the wrist. The feeling should be that the line is being tossed up in the air rather than directly back. With a low or weak backcast a forward cast is impossible. The line should be shot high and be well-extended to afford something for the wrist and rod to pull against in making the forward cast. To emphasize this action, an attempt should be made to stop the backward motion of the rod at the perpendicular. After a high backcast has been mastered, feel free to ease the rod back a bit farther to get a long forward stroke.

4. *Forward cast.* If the backcast is good, the forward cast will almost take care of itself. It merely requires proper timing. If it is made too soon, the line will pop like a whip; if too late, the backcast will have fallen too low. The tendency is to rush it.

The power of the forward stroke is also applied gradually, although not as deliberately as in the pickup since the line in the air is more responsive than it was on the water. The rod is thrust forward and down to a position about thirty degrees above the horizontal to complete the forward cast. This forward cast is not aimed at the water but at about eye level above the point where the fly is intended to land. This gives the line the opportunity to extend before dropping to the surface. As it drops, the rod is lowered with it.

In action, these four steps are all as one of course, but the beginner will do best to work on each one in its turn. He shouldn't attempt a forward cast until the backcast has been taken care of. Good practice is to turn the head with the backcast to watch it. If it isn't high, toss it higher. If it doesn't extend all the line, put more power in it. By watching the backcast, a person will see that there is no great rush to make the forward cast. This is where most beginners fail the first few times: they are in too much of a hurry to get the forward cast under way.

As we recall, part of the action which gave power to the backcast was the pull on the line

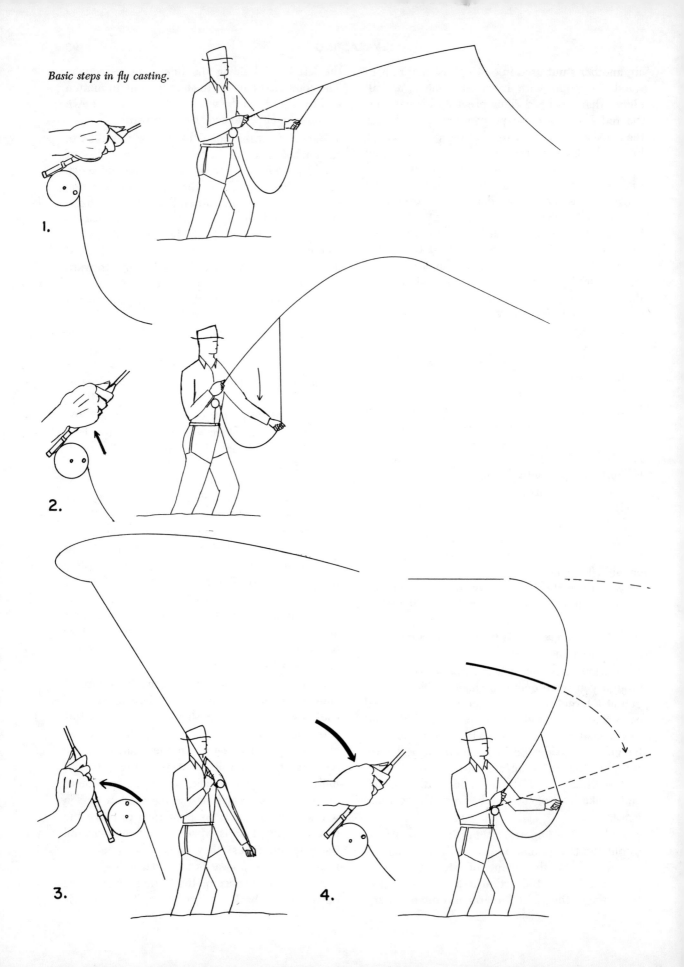

Basic steps in fly casting.

1.

2.

3.

4.

with the left hand. In order to reach for distance, later on, a double pull is used: the one on the backcast and a similar one to cock the rod sharply at the start of the forward cast. For normal stream fly fishing, however, this double haul is not necessary.

False Casting

Finally, the beginner will learn to keep the line in the air by continuous false casting, back and forth. The line must be held high on the forward stroke as well as the backcast. Consequently the movement of the forearm is limited, and the lighter the rod the less it moves. The movement of the dry-fly fisherman's forearm while false casting may be barely perceptible, his wrist putting the rod through the necessary arc. The bigger and stiffer the rod, and the longer the line being held in the air, the more the forearm must move, until the distance caster uses not only his wrist and his arm but his body as well.

During false casts with a stiff rod, the fisherman may wish to continue the down pull on the line with the left hand to start the backcast, then return the hand to the rod again at the end of the forward stroke. This gives the visual effect of the hands continuously coming together during the forward thrust and separating widely during the backward thrust.

This same motion of the hands is used in working out line from scratch to make the first cast. To start each false cast backward, the line is grasped by the left hand near the reel, and as the hands are separated, two or three feet of line are pulled from the reel. This slack is released into the forward false cast, and on the next backcast another few feet are pulled from the reel in the same manner.

In working out line, the motion is rapid at first because so little line is in the air, but as more and more line is put into the false casts, an increasing amount of time is required to allow the line to extend, and the tempo becomes slower.

When the caster has learned to hold thirty feet of line and leader in the air with ease by continuous false casting, he knows enough about handling a rod for fishing success, and there is no reason why this cannot be accomplished in a morning's practice. From then on, if he keeps his mind on the principles and concentrates on his casting as much as on his fishing, he will become increasingly adept.

Once a man has learned to cast with the forearm-and-wrist motion, he shouldn't feel that the upper arm must be kept motionless along his side. Actually, it is used to considerable extent in fishing, principally as a means of extending the casting hand to a convenient location. In starting a long line up off the water, he may stretch his hand over his head; in shooting up under a headwind, he may lower the hand and rod near the water. The wrist will still deliver the power to the cast, however.

A stiff-wrist cast can be made. Since it is impossible for the whole arm to travel through as great an arc as the wrist in as short a space of time, the sudden power cannot be delivered to the rod with a stiff wrist. This, then, is a much softer method of casting. A fly fisherman would wear himself down using a stiff wrist all day because he instead of the rod would be doing the work. However, there are times when a soft motion is desirable. When a man is using a hard-action fly rod with a heavy lure, such as a spinner, it is necessary to use an easy cast. Heavy spinners must be put into motion very gently to keep from breaking a leader or rod tip. And with bait, which is easily snapped off the hook, a stiff-wrist cast—a lobbing motion—must be used.

The manner of stripping in line after a cast has been made is simple and should be learned from the start. The left hand reaches forward and grasps the line near the first guide; then, as the line is brought back, it is hooked through the middle finger of the right hand which is holding the rod. Whenever it becomes necessary to hold the line securely, such as in reaching forward to grasp the line again with the left hand, the middle finger of the right hand merely clamps down on it. Continue to hold the line at the same point in your left hand and reach forward with your left hand to grasp the line a second time near the guide. As you do this, drop the line from your right hand, thus forming a loop of line held in the left hand. In the process of stripping the line from a cast, the fisherman will have four or five such loops, or coils, of line in his left hand; these are then released one at a time into each forward cast while working out line again in false casts.

This business of keeping the stripped line in coils in the left hand and of clamping the line with the middle finger of the right hand is essential. In this way the line is always under complete control, both for giving motion to the fly and for responding to a strike whenever it might come.

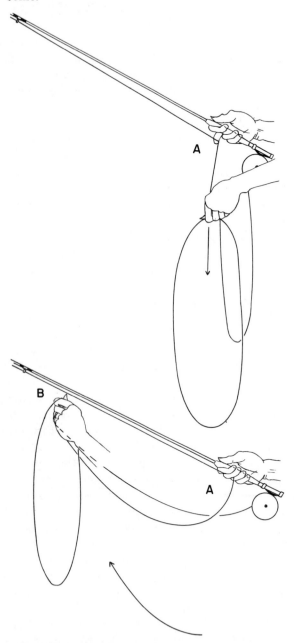

Retrieve a fly line by pulling down over middle finger of right hand (A), as shown in top figure. Then, as shown in bottom figure, hold at point A, reach forward with left hand, grasp line between thumb and forefinger at point B and release at A, thus forming a new loop in left hand. These coils of slack are released as needed in making next cast.

In making this basic overhead cast, the rod moves forward and backward in an almost perpendicular plane. However, there is a very slight rotation given the rod in order that the rod and line will clear themselves during the forward and backward motion of the false casts. In looking up at the rod tip, the fisherman will see that it travels in a slightly oval path. The motion I use, and I believe most right-handed fishermen use, is counterclockwise as the rod tip is viewed from beneath; that is, the line is picked up with the rod canted off the right shoulder, then shot forward directly overhead. After an hour or two of steady casting, as when fishing upsteam, this continuous rotation will twist the line. Therefore, it is a good idea consciously to change the direction of this rotation occasionally.

The position of the right hand as it grasps the rod does not seem to me to be of great importance. I believe most casting instructors tell their pupils to lay the thumb on top of the rod grip and in line with the rod itself, and this is probably best. But no matter how a fisherman consciously starts out, his hand will soon work into the most comfortable position, and as the muscles tire he will occasionally shift position. Actually there is less danger of the beginner's carrying the rod too far back on the backcast if he holds his thumb a bit on one side of the grip rather than directly on top, but it really makes little difference.

Side Cast

As mentioned earlier, almost all specialized casts are merely variations of the basic overhead cast. The side cast definitely is. The cast is the same, but the rod is shifted from a perpendicular plane to a horizontal plane; that is, the rod moves back and forth along the caster's side almost parallel with the water.

This cast can be very handy in shooting the line up under willows or any overhanging branch. It is effective, too, in keeping the line low to get under a head wind. Also, if at the point where the angler is standing in the stream there are branches directly overhead, the fly may still be put out by means of the side cast. It can be useful, too, in keeping the rod tip down out of sight of a shy trout.

The rotary motion imparted to the rod tip is

more pronounced in the side cast than in the direct overhead cast, and the motion will be counterclockwise for a right-handed fisherman. The rod is drawn back in the backcast almost parallel with the water's surface, but up a bit at the end; then the forward cast is arced up somewhat to keep the line off the water and to give the line just enough altitude to extend the fly before dropping. It requires excellent wrist action and timing to handle much line and keep it from striking the water during a side cast. It has an advantage, however, in that the fisherman can turn his body with his left side in the direction he wishes to cast, and then he can watch the line comfortably throughout its entire course.

A fisherman can also effect a side cast on his left if, for instance, his right side is up against brush or overhanging branches. The method of accomplishing this backhand cast is to extend his right arm across the front of his body and to work the rod over his left shoulder, or even down parallel with the water if necessary. Then, of course, the rotary motion of the rod tip will be clockwise; that is, the line will be returned on the backcast close to the water and arced up and forward on the front cast.

Tower Cast

The fly fisherman will find each stream an obstacle course, with unfriendly bushes which suddenly appear from nowhere to grab his fly and versatile rocks that can reach up and flick the barb off a hook. If nature weren't forever conniving against a man by interfering with his backcast or by blowing a wind in his face, casting would be a simple business: the direct overhead cast could be used all the time. But the best fish is often in the most difficult place to reach; so we must learn tricky casts, like the side casts described above, or the tower cast.

A fisherman who is a real master of the tower cast can stand with his back against a building and shoot the line forty feet ahead. The backcast is short and made to tower directly overhead without going behind the fisherman at all. It is a difficult cast and requires a powerful wrist motion and perfect timing, but it is a valuable one to know.

This cast follows the same principle as the overhead cast, the difference lying in the greatly exaggerated backcast action. When the line is picked up, the arm is extended forward, the right hand held high, the rod tip dropped, and then the line shot as directly up in the air as possible. This should be attempted with a short line only. After the knack of shooting the backcast directly overhead has been acquired, the fisherman will have to time the moment of the forward cast perfectly. The first few attempts will result in the line's striking the water smartly right in front of the caster. The forward cast must be short and sharp, and the feeling will be that he is attempting to cast up in the air ahead of him. If he aims at a point just a yard above the surface, as he might normally do, the line will certainly crash to the surface before it reaches its goal; but by aiming high, he can deliver the cast in an effective manner. This cast should not be attempted by a beginner, but a seasoned caster can master it in short order.

Hook Cast

The hook cast, or shepherd's crook as it is sometimes called, comes under the category of a trick cast. It is so rarely necessary that there are few who can execute it flawlessly when the proper time comes.

If a shy rising trout can be approached only from directly below, it would seem wise to cast the line a few feet to one side or the other of him, rather than directly over his position, and hook the fly around so that it will float to him. Actually in practice most fishermen find there is far less chance of frightening the trout by dropping a light leader on him than by making a botch out of an attempted hook cast.

Another, more practical, use of the hook cast is to hook the fly around on the far side of brush or another obstacle in a stream. This may be used often enough along a deep, meandering meadow stream that you acquire considerable accuracy before the day is out. Not only is it used to get around clumps of willows and points of land, but it is especially useful for dropping a fly tight up under the near cut bank on which the fisherman is standing or kneeling.

The method I use of throwing a hook involves a side cast, described above. In hooking the fly to the left, I use a side cast and deliver more power to the cast than necessary to straighten the line: that is, I deliver power enough for a long cast then stop it abruptly. This excessive momentum carries the fly on around and hooks it to the left. In fact, when anyone is learning a side cast, he will discover at first that he either doesn't deliver enough power and the line falls to the water in an incomplete cast, with the line and leader hooked to the right, or he delivers too much power and the fly carries beyond its objective to the left.

In hooking to the right in open water, I sometimes use the incomplete side cast, mentioned above. However, this is not practicable in hooking the fly around an obstacle, unless it is low to the water, as the belly of the line must travel over the obstacle. The best method of hooking to the right is the direct opposite of the left hook; that is, the backhand cast is used and delivered with enough power to carry the fly on around to the right.

Such hook casts are easier to execute with a heavy wet fly or spinner, which develop some momentum of their own, than with a fluffy dry fly. A heavily hackled dry fly follows the pull of

the line unwillingly at best, and it is difficult to make it carry on around.

Roll Cast

The roll cast has the advantage of the tower cast in that the fly never goes behind the fisherman but can be placed a considerable distance ahead. The fly can be cast farther with the roll cast than with the tower cast. Either one is useful when the fisherman has a solid obstruction at his back which will not allow a normal backcast. In such a situation, if you are fishing with a dry fly, the tower cast should be used; if fishing with a wet fly, the roll cast should be used.

The roll cast is useful in wet-fly or nymph fishing quite often regardless of the presence or absence of obstructions behind the fisherman. It has the advantage that the fly is out of the water for a moment only and it will not be whipped dry as in working out line by the usual false-cast method. It is an especially nice cast if there is a breeze behind the fisherman. It has the disad-

A high, extended backcast is the key to fly casting. From the point shown in this illustration, the fisherman has complete control on the forward cast, enabling him to spot a fly neatly and accurately.

vantage that it disturbs the water considerably and may put down a shy trout.

When you are making a roll cast, the line is never picked up clear of the water. A powerful, good-sized rod is an advantage. The right hand is raised to a level with the head and a little forward, and the tip of the rod allowed to point back slightly beyond the perpendicular. The line will drop from the rod tip in a belly alongside the fisherman and forward to the water. The timing of the moment when this belly is properly formed for a cast is the most important thing in making a good roll cast. At that moment the rod is cut forward and down sharply. This action forms a loop which appears to roll out to the end of the line, where the fly is picked up, rolled out and dropped eight or ten feet farther away. Enough line is stripped from the reel to form another such belly, then this is rolled out in the same manner to extend the fly another ten feet. The line must float nicely, of course, so that as the loop rolls out it will pick up off the water easily, and it should be a conventional double-tapered line. The heavy belly of the distance-taper resists being picked from the water by the roll.

The roll cast can also be used with a dry fly to a limited extent, usually when you wish to reach a spot that could not be reached with a direct cast. For instance, a fish might be rising in a protected spot under a bush, and obstructions behind the fisherman prevent his making a side cast directly to the fish. A cast can be made alongside the bush; then, at the proper moment, with practice, a roll cast can be made on a bias —that is, with an oblique cut of the rod—which will pull the fly over under the obstacle. In such a case, the roll is made just once. Repeated roll casts will make a dry fly soggy. For best results, a dry fly should be whipped free of water between casts so that it will sit high on the water.

Diverting a Cast

Many times a fisherman will have only a narrow opening behind him through which he can put his backcast. Using a direct overhead cast, the fisherman is thus afforded only a small field in which to cast ahead of him. However, an overhead cast can be diverted quite successfully to one side or the other.

The fisherman will false cast until he has the right amount of line in the air and until he has the proper feel of it. Then on the final forward cast, if he wants to send the fly to his left, he will arc the rod out to the right, around in front of him and make the final thrust across his body to the left. The opposite technique would be used to divert the fly to the right. When you are making such a cast, great care must be taken that the backcast is kept direct into the opening behind. The natural tendency is to divert the backcast slightly to one side or the other just prior to the forward cast.

Reverse Cast

If there is a very narrow opening behind the caster for his backcast, a good idea is for him to reverse his position; that is, turn his back on the intended casting direction. By facing the obstacle, the fisherman will find it an easy matter to direct his false casts through the opening and the line can be shot backward for the final cast. If much line is being held in the air during the false casts, there will be ample time to do an about face after the line has been directed through the opening on the final false cast and shoot the line while facing forward.

The fly fisherman as he goes along will learn the casts described here, along with other slight variations, and he will lose a lot of flies and his temper in the learning. But that's all part of the game, and on any heavily fished streams, the man who has learned to place a fly in spots the other fellows can't reach will get results. The trout whose feeding station is in a well-protected spot is generally not a suspicious type.

Strip Casting

Strip casting is in effect spinning (see Chapter 16) with a fly rod. It has limited use to the trout fisherman, although the minnow fisherman could use the technique to great advantage. Also, a man with a fly rod might conceivably want to present a small spoon or small plug to a large trout, and he could do it by strip casting.

In strip casting, the lure must have weight, as the principle of the cast is the same as in spinning. The line is stripped in and held in coils in the left hand or piled neatly on the ground. The minnow or other lure is pulled to within six inches of the rod tip, just as a plug is reeled up to the tip of a bait-casting rod. The casting motion is the same as with a bait-casting or spinning rod: back a short distance to cock the wrist and rod, then ahead sharply to cast the bait or lure. The line is allowed to flow loosely through the guides.

Naturally a heavy fly line cannot be pulled through the small guides of a fly rod as easily as a small, braided line. If a man were setting out to do strip fishing exclusively, he would use a much lighter line than the ordinary fly line. Continuous monofilament spinning line would be ideal, of course.

Wind

Several other little fly-rod casting tricks are worth knowing. For instance, in trying to make distance with the wind behind one's back, a few rules are broken. Ordinarily, the fisherman is continually striving to keep his backcast high. With a tail wind and no obstructions behind, he may purposely shoot the rod back considerably beyond the perpendicular in order to send the backcast under the wind in a tight, low loop; then the forward cast is aimed higher than usual to catch the wind. Any strong wind is a nuisance, and a tail wind can be almost as aggravating as a head wind. The backcast must be delivered with even more than usual power because without an extended backcast there's no forward cast.

When you are casting into a head wind or cross wind, the forward cast is the one that is shot low so that it will get under the wind as well as possible. With a strong side wind from the left, a right-handed fisherman may find it helpful to lower the rod from the direct overhead-cast position to a modified side cast; and if the wind is strong from the right, a backhand cast may be easier than the overhead.

Throwing Slack

Then there's the matter of throwing slack in order to get a natural drift. A dry fly, and usually a nymph, must float naturally with the current. Except in a few specialized cases treated later, drag is disastrous. Often a fish will be rising on the far side of a current. In a normally extended cast, the line will be swept along by this current and the fly will begin to drag the instant it touches the water. The way to beat this problem is to throw a lot of slack to drop the line on the water in snake fashion. There are two methods of doing this.

One method of throwing slack is to shoot a hard cast, one which would normally carry far beyond the objective, then stop the flow of line abruptly. For an even more pronounced effect the tip of the rod can be raised slightly at the moment the line is stopped.

The other method of throwing slack is to shoot a very high cast ahead, rather in the manner of a tower cast in front of the fisherman. The line will then drop to the water in S-shaped coils.

Another method of floating a fly in a slow spot across a current is to use the hook cast described earlier in this chapter. If the current is flowing to the right as the fisherman faces it, the fly is hooked to the right so it will have a lead on the line and will have a moment to float free before the line is bellied downstream. This is usually referred to as mending a cast. A cast can also be mended after the line is on the water by tossing a loop of slack up into the current.

Occasionally a fish will be seen to rise at a point directly downstream from the dry-fly fisherman, and his only opportunity to present a fly would be to float it to him from above. Generally one float only can be made to such a fish without putting him down when the line is picked up, so it should be good. The same system of throwing slack described above is used in order to drop the line on the water in S-shaped coils. The fly then will be given a free float downstream until the coils are extended. If there is a long stretch of potentially good water downstream beyond casting distance, it is possible to continue working out slack by twitching the rod tip and obtain a single float as long as your line.

The thing for a beginner at fly fishing to concentrate on is the direct overhead cast with a high, well-extended backcast. Once he has mastered this basic cast, the other tricky casts described here will evolve naturally as he continues to try for fish in difficult spots. There's no casting instructor like a rising trout.

The rise to a dry fly on a Montana meadow stream.

Chapter 11

DRY-FLY FISHING

An old fishing adage says that when the leaf of the elm is as large as a squirrel's ear, the trout will rise to a floating fly; and that's a glorious time of year. Heaven comes down close to a trout stream on a May morning.

The man who has discovered the enchantment of a rising trout is lucky. Any trout fisherman is lucky. He has the insight and imagination to fathom the mysteries which lie beneath the surface of a stream. He is privileged merely to be a fisherman and so be a part of the complex and fascinating stream of life in and about a trout brook. But somehow I feel that the dry-fly fisherman has an edge even on his fellow fishermen.

Tackle

Good tools come first. Since the fisherman is dealing with the same general problem no matter where in North America he offers a dry fly to a rising trout, the same outfit is universally acceptable. The rod must be light, and therefore should be of good quality and have plenty of punch, or "backbone," for its weight. My bamboo dry-fly rod is 8 feet long and weighs 4½ ounces. Many enthusiasts use lighter rods, some as small as 7 feet and 2¼ ounces. For the average man, however, a rod around 8 feet in length and 4 ounces in weight would be about right. Eight-and-one-half feet and 4½ ounces would be about the maximum for pleasure and results.

The reason for keeping the rod light is twofold. First, a man is casting almost continuously while dry-fly fishing, and the rod must be kept light to prevent arm strain. (Although rods made of graphite are much lighter, it is the weight of line being carried which matters.) The other reason is that the terminal tackle is so delicate—the leader so fine and the hook often so small—especially in smooth-water dry-fly fishing, that it would be disastrous to have a large and harsh rod. Occasionally a heavy trout is hooked on a dry fly, but it would be more of a handicap than a benefit to have a stiff 6-ounce rod at such a time if the fish were on the end of a 3X leader.

Since distance is not a prerequisite to stream dry-fly fishing, the various distance-taper lines are neither necessary nor advisable. These special tapers are generally too bulky forward for delicate work. A direct taper, as in the double taper, is best. The line should be kept as light as possible and still bring out the action of the rod. Most dry-fly rods in the 8-foot, 3½- to 4-ounce delicate work. A direct taper, as in the double tapered line, although some stiff ones may require a DT7F. The line should be soft and pliable and float well.

The leader is important. The minimum for most fishing is 8 or 9 feet, and when conditions require particular finesse it is well to have coils of tip-section monofilament handy to lengthen the leader as necessary. In broken water a fisherman can get by with a leader tapered down to 2X, although the more common rule is 3X; that is, about four-pound-test in nylon or Stren. I try not to go much lighter than this and get around it when conditions are demanding simply by adding more three- or four-pound-test monofilament to lengthen the leader. A 5X or 6X leader hardly has the strength where knotted to set the hook in a big fellow. However, the leader size should be reduced as the size of the fly is reduced. A 4X leader would be suitable on a size 16 fly or smaller, and a 5X on a size 20 midge.

Just as the fly line should always float, the leader should sink. This is especially true of the terminal end. A floating leader distorts the smooth surface of the water and thus becomes very evident to the trout. In bright sunlight, notice the shadow a floating leader casts on the stream bottom and it will be obvious how this distortion acts and why it is such a handicap. After a leader has been handled, it should be wiped as free of grease as possible. Anything adhering to the fisherman's hands is easily transferred to the leader. As a very temporary remedy, saliva will usually put a leader under. Another streamside stunt is to rub the leader through mud or fine silt. This will scour off the grease and has the added advantage of removing some of the leader's glint. Soap or detergent is the surest way of removing grease. Still another good trick is to run the leader through a piece of typewriter carbon paper. The juice of the young leaves of streamside shrubs or those of underwater plants will also help.

I mention this long list because the difference between a floating leader and a sinking leader in still water is usually the difference between putting a big trout down or raising him, and because there is no good commercial leader-sinking dope available to my knowledge.

Then comes the fly, the business end of the outfit. This subject has been treated fully in the chapter on flies. About all that will be said here is that the successful fisherman must have at hand a variety in size, shape, and color. On any one stream or area, the thorough fisherman may get a good idea through the seasons just what insects make up the bulk of the trout food, as well as when and under what water conditions they hatch. He will also discover what patterns are the most successful imitations and will outfit his fly box accordingly. I had one southern New York stream figured out so well that if I could locate a rising fish I was fairly certain of getting a strike. My flies were nondescript because most of them were original concoctions, but they worked. Some were odd-looking. The most extreme was a No. 16 short shank made solely from the very sparse hackle-like feathers which cover the ear of a ruffed grouse, by name a Grouse Louse.

But the fisherman who takes his fishing here and there and who must fish where and when he can without a previous knowledge of the water must depend on a variety of sizes, shapes, and hues to imitate the natural fly being taken. And if he is more provident than I am, he will have at least two or three of each size and pattern. If I am using a particularly effective fly and lose it, it is invariably the only one I have.

Many fishermen apply oil to their dry flies regularly to insure their floating. I never use any dressing on a fly. A fly tied with good hackles on a light-wire hook will float high without help. Fly oil seems to me to gum the hackles and bunch them together, and I much prefer a fly with hackles as evenly spaced as possible. There are prepared silicon dressings available which do not gum up the hackles too much, and another trick used by some fishermen is to dab a bit of line grease on the head of the fly, then with a forceps to hold it in the live steam of a kettle. The steam melts the grease and distributes it in a thin coat over the fly, waterproofing each whisk of hackle.

An old brown trout in his role of playing hard to get.

By the way, flies which have been used and put away wet, or which have been kept too long in cramped quarters, are usually misshapen. A simple and effective way to rejuvenate them is to hold them for an instant in live steam. They immediately regain their natural shape. On the stream it will usually pay to wet such a misshapen fly, snap the water out, and blow on it from behind until dry before using it. A fly with straight, evenly spaced hackles is most effective.

Where

The dry fly is commonly used in the East and Midwest, less often in the West. However, some of the finest dry-fly fishing I have ever experienced has been on western streams. It is true that many of the big Rocky Mountain rivers are too heavy for good dry-fly work and they contain such a variety of food that the largest trout seldom bother with floating food; but size of a river alone is no limitation to the use of a dry fly. I have taken trout on a dry fly in the Colorado River in Arizona below Hoover Dam, as large a trout river as any. The North Fork of the Snake in Idaho for years was one of the country's finest dry-fly streams; yet, where it grows up, there are flatwater stretches so big and deep that they wouldn't be waded with less than a diving suit.

The Yellowstone River between Yellowstone Lake and the falls flows flat and smooth and although it is a big river the cutthroats are surface feeders. Where the river takes a U-bend the current is somewhat faster against the outside of the bend and the feeding trout gather there for food. It makes ideal fishing from the bank. Two other fellows who were fine dry-fly fishermen and I got so much action fishing such a bend in the Yellowstone near the main highway that we tied up the tourist traffic in knots. Many park tourists are fishermen at heart, but most of them come equipped with spinners, plugs, trolling spoons, and the like, and a rising smooth-water trout won't have much truck with such gear. The dry-fly fisherman has every possible advantage.

Some of the finest dry-fly fishing in the West is in the mountain meadow streams. These clear, cold creeks which meander through the mountain parks are full of trout and they offer an ideal opportunity for the man who can float a fly. Again, the majority of fisherman use wet flies, spinners, and salmon eggs; and the dry-fly man can have things his own way. The dry-fly fisherman in the West sees a lot that others miss. He often stands so quietly working a good spot that he is soon taken for granted by the wild life. His persistence, mistaken by many for patience, may keep him rooted to one spot until he becomes part of the scenery. Nervous ground squirrels come out, scold for a moment, then go about their busy way until startled by something about as dangerous as a butterfly. The dumpy little water ouzel may start fishing almost around the fisherman's feet. I remember the first time I ever saw one of these strange, thrushlike birds in Colorado years ago. It occurred to me that the silly thing was bobbing around the rocks too close to the white water for his own good and I expected him to be washed away any moment. Then he calmly waded into the water out of sight under the current and nonchalantly picked nymphs off the bottom. I've never worried about one since.

Although some spots offer more delightful dry-fly conditions than others, there is absolutely no limit to where a floating fly can be used. My dry-fly rod gets first priority no matter where I go, even if to the mighty rivers of western Alaska or to the salmon rivers of eastern Canada. Some of the finest fishing is found in the most surprising places. The most exciting few moments I ever experienced with a rod in my hand was late one evening on a long, deep, slick stretch of Gods River, which is considerably larger than the average Atlantic salmon river. In two weeks' time I hadn't seen a single rise, but on this particular evening the caddis flies hatched by the millions and towered in great swarms up and down the banks. Needless to say, every trout in the river came to the surface and gorged himself. If only there had been more time! There never is when a fellow is fishing. At that I took two brookies which topped six pounds on a No. 12 Tups, the two largest trout I have ever landed on a dry-fly, and with luck—or more time—there was no reason for not taking a ten-pounder. It was simply a matter of finding the biggest one before dark, but it takes time to land two six-pounders on a little rod.

The location or size of the river makes no difference in the tackle outlined. Nothing alters the fact that the tackle is chosen to present the fly in the most lifelike manner. This is the preliminary step to raising and hooking a good one, and the size of the water or the size of the fish is of no consideration.

When

From the time that the first trout or two has been seen to rise in the spring right up to the end of the season, the dry fly is generally as good a way to take trout as any. Early in the year the heat of midday is the time to try a floating fly. After that it will be effective throughout the fishing day, although mornings and evenings will provide the most concentrated fishing. I like late summer when the streams are so low and clear that coarser methods won't tempt trout; then the dry-fly fisherman is in a league by himself. In states that allow fall fishing, midday may again become the best time as cool weather sets in, but the dry fly will remain effective right up until the winter rains commence.

Successful dry-fly fishing depends on two things: first, the presence of mature insects, either land- or waterborne, in numbers sufficient to tempt a trout to feed on them; and, second, stream condition. Winged insects are usually numerous enough by May in the East and June in the Rockies. An unusually warm spring will occasionally present dry-fly conditions on opening day, but generally for the first few weeks of the season the air is either too cold or the streams too high and roily to use a floating fly. Other than this beginning of the season, and those occasions throughout the year when a cloudburst or concentrated rain has put the stream out of its banks, the dry fly is good any time.

Fishing the Rise

Dry-fly fishing falls into two general divisions: fishing for rising fish and fishing the water. The majority of dry-fly fisherman work on specific rising fish. This gives them a very distinct advantage over all other fishermen. Beyond a cer-

Striking the rise. Notice that the line has sprung from the water in an S-shaped pattern, evidence that the fisherman deliberately cast a loose line so that the fast water between him and the fish couldn't drag the fly before it reached the crucial point. This is the Albany River in Ontario.

A mountain meadow creek is as delightful a place as a man ever floated a fly. There are many such creeks throughout the western mountains, this particular one being high in the Sierras of California.

tain proficiency in handling tackle, fishing to a rising trout is easy; and by proficiency with tackle I don't mean that the fisherman must know how to handle a lot of line, for this is not so. A long cast, one over fifty feet, is seldom necessary and rarely productive with a dry fly. If a man can handle thirty feet of line with ease, delicacy, and accuracy, this is enough.

Fishing the rise is easy because it is visual: a man can see exactly what he is doing. He can see where the fish is feeding, what it is feeding on, and where his own fly floats in relation to the fish. There is no guesswork. Other fishermen must operate on subtle indications of what is actually happening. The underwater fisherman doesn't see the trout; he sees only the water surface and must determine from this the fish's likely position. A nymph fisherman doesn't see the nymphs rising from the bottom preparatory to hatching; if he's lucky he may see the first empty case floating down and gathers from that what type nymph to use. Again if he's lucky, the nymph fisherman may see trout bulging and tailing and know they are feeding on nymphs, but he doesn't know what kind.

These indications are important to the fisher-

man. It is like piecing together the tracks of a deer in the snow and determining what he has done, or is about to do. Even the man who fishes the rise may get a hint of what is to come if he sees the swallows and swifts dipping and swooping along the water surface. They seem to know when a hatch is due.

Another reason that dry-fly fishing has its advantages is that the fisherman invariably approaches from behind the trout. A feeding trout faces the current and is concentrating on the area ahead of him for any food coming his way. The dry-fly fisherman, since he works upstream, benefits by approaching the trout from his blind quarter. If he makes no quick moves, he should find it easy to approach within twenty-five or thirty feet of the feeding fish. It is generally advisable to sneak within fairly close range rather than attempt a long cast. Experience will tell the fisherman just about how close he dare approach under various conditions.

Fishing the rise has the disadvantage, on the other hand, that it is generally carried out on smooth water. Smooth-water dry-fly fishing is the most exacting, most fascinating, and sometimes the most exasperating, of all forms of trout fishing. The problem is presented to the fisherman clearly and openly, and he is challenged to solve it. His ability to solve the problem depends on his keenness in identifying the insect food of the trout, his judgment and ability in imitating it, and his skill in presenting the imitation in a lifelike manner.

This problem is the same on a heavily fished metropolitan stream as on a seldom-visited mountain meadow brook. A trout feeding on an insect hatch is selective to the extreme. During a plentiful hatch, his single-track mind narrows his menu down to one delectable item. And trout lying out in the open and near the surface, as is generally the case when feeding on floating food, are invariably shy. This is just as true on Anan Creek in Alaska as it is on the Beaverkill in New York. It makes no difference where he is found; this is a trout's nature.

Selecting the Fly: During the major part of the day when there is no concentrated hatch on, rising fish may be feeding on a variety of surface food, including both water-born insects and land insects that have fallen on the water. At such times the problem of fly selection is an easy one. Any lifelike, buggy-looking pattern in a reasonable size may tempt the trout. A number of such patterns, which just naturally seem to look like food to the trout, are listed in the chapter on flies.

If several fish are rising steadily, they are probably feeding on a specific hatch. This is especially true toward evening when the big hatches come on. During a very heavy hatch, the largest fish in the stream may turn to surface food, but when there is no great concentration of surface food, the lunkers will probably look for something that will fill the belly more rapidly than the floating flies.

The problem in fly selection, then, arises during a hatch; the fish are focusing their attention on one form of food only, and the larger and wiser fish are on the prod. The first thing to do is to identify the hatch. Since many of the standard dry-fly patterns which were designed to imitate specific hatches were created to copy English insects, not American, we cannot merely identify a hatch of iron-blue duns, for instance, and select a fly accordingly. The English dry-fly patterns work well in America, but even if they had been designed for specific American insects,

most of us ordinary folk wouldn't have a sufficiently intimate knowledge of buggy critters to call each one by name and select its proper imitation. We must follow whatever course our judgment dictates.

In making the selection we must recall the trout's view of the fly and the manner in which he sees it. Before it actually enters his window, he sees the impression it makes on the mirrored surface of the water. This is why a fish will often rush expectantly at a floating fly only to turn back at the last moment. The impression on the water shows him that an object is floating, but his window is so small when he is near the surface that he can't actually see what is on top until he swims under it. When the trout does see the fly itself, he sees it from underneath, and the bright light of the sky is behind it. Even in the late evening, what little light there is comes from the sky, so the fly as seen by the trout is always backlighted.

To understand the effectiveness of a dry fly it is necessary to bear in mind the distortion caused by the impression on the water surface by the hackle points. The light rays are bent when passing through the uneven water surface dented by the fly, much as they would be when reflected from an uneven mirror. This distortion is the saving grace in dry-fly fishing and it explains why a high-floating fly will take fish when a soggy, semisubmerged one will not. When floating properly, the stiff hackle points dent the surface much as do the legs of the insect, and if the distorted image of the fly above is of the same general size, color, and bulk of the natural insect by backlighting, then the imitation is a success. Comparative bulk is the most important consideration. Consider this, the trout's view, as well as it can be visualized rather than your own above-surface view in selecting a fly.

If a fisherman is careful, he may float a fly over a feeding fish several times without disturbing him and putting him down. If just slightly annoyed, the fish may merely move to another location a few feet away. During a heavy hatch, a fish is not so prone to take shelter as he is normally. A heavy hatch is his time to gorge himself, and he doesn't want to miss any more food than he can help. Therefore, if the fisherman's first selection fails, he may have the opportunity to try several other patterns on the same fish. If the presentation of the fly has been good, the fly cocked nicely, and if it was obviously seen by the trout, three or four floats with any one pattern are sufficient. He either wants it or he doesn't. The idea is to keep trying different flies to give him a look at as many selections as possible before a false move puts him down. Once the proper fly is found, it will generally serve for all other fish feeding on the same hatch.

One of the most satisfying trout I ever took finally rose to the seventh fly I showed him. It was early in the dry-fly season on the Ammonoosuc in New Hampshire, and the trout were rising in midafternoon to a caddis-fly hatch. It was obvious by the broad nose of this one as he deliberately took in the floating insects that he was by far the largest fish in the pool. The seventh fly I tried, and the one which apparently looked like a caddis to him, was a No. 12 Light Cahill. By that time I had my leader pretty well extended with tippets to make the presentation more deceptive and I had to handle him as gently as he would permit. I cast to him for an hour and landed him fifty-five minutes later at the foot of a rapids a quarter-mile downstream. He was a nineteen-and-a-half-inch rainbow that did some plain and fancy jumping. Landing him was important, but what pleased me most was that I succeeded in showing him seven flies on slick water without arousing his suspicions.

Occasionally, when all attempts to imitate the natural insect fail, a large, contrasting fly may make a trout strike. If so, he will generally hit it with a terrific splash as though out of annoyance. When the trout is rising to No. 16 naturals, show him a No. 8 Fanwing. This subterfuge usually doesn't work, but it is worth an attempt as a parting gesture; and the results, if they come, will be surprising.

Presenting the Fly: A good dry-fly fisherman in action is a beautiful thing to watch. There's grace and rhythm in every movement of his rod and line; and, when the line is shot forward to present the fly, the cast is made with just enough power to roll the leader out smoothly and allow the fly to float to the surface like so much thistledown.

His greatest problem is drag. A dry fly must float across a fish in an entirely natural manner, in perfect tune with the current. If the line floats faster or is pulled faster than the fly and thus drags the leader and fly unnaturally across the fish, the game is up. The fisherman might as well reel in and go look for another trout. Therefore, before he makes the first cast to a rising fish, the angler sizes up the situation and determines how to place the fly so that it will float a natural course over the trout. Sometimes this calls for a bit of maneuvering to get in proper position, or it may necessitate throwing slack into the cast. When he is lucky, the surface current around the rising fish will be generally uniform and no problem is presented. Because of the vagaries of the current and the disastrous effect of drag, the casting of a perfectly straight line and leader is not good form in dry-fly fishing.

When the fly has been selected and the current judged for drag, the first cast is made. The fly is never dropped directly on the trout, on purpose at least. The trout should be led by dropping the fly five or six feet upstream and placing it in the current so that it will float directly over the proper spot. Also, where possible, it is best to fish quartering across current rather than directly upstream so that in making the cast the leader or line will not fall over the trout. Where a cast must be made from directly below, it may be best to attempt a hook cast to drop the line to one side or the other of the fish.

When a fisherman is confident in his accuracy, he won't waste much time on preliminaries, but will work out line and drop the fly where it will do the most good. Where a big fish is concerned, however, he will make a practice cast or two to one side to check that his distance and presentation are as planned. The actual cast to the fish is aimed upcurrent and at an imaginary target in the air a yard or so above the stream's surface. A line cast directly at the water would strike hard, but one aimed high will extend and give the fly the opportunity to float down like a parachute. This aerial descent gives a winged fly the opportunity to cock itself and land erect, an important piece of strategy. Of course, as in all fly casting, the heavy part of the line drops to the water first, then the taper and leader unfold and the fly descends last of all.

As the fly floats downstream, the fisherman strips in line to pick up the excess slack. Stripping too rapidly might drag the fly, so it is better to err on the side of stripping too slowly. However, a great deal of slack between the rod and the fly will delay the hooking of a striking

The upper Yellowstone River appears almost as calm as a mill pond, but it has a strong, uniform flow. A rising cutthroat can be spotted from a distance, and the insect hatch is not difficult to identify. This makes an ideal situation for the dry-fly fisherman.

trout. If the fly is not taken by the trout, it should not be picked up until it has floated well clear of the fish.

When the current is moving the fly toward the fisherman rapidly, keeping him busy stripping in slack, a convenient way of picking up the line to start a new cast is by use of the roll cast motion. Instead of stripping in the last few feet of slack during the fly's course, allow it to float down alongside; then, by raising the rod, a belly is formed in the line. Finally, the rod is cut sharply ahead and down. This will roll the line out and extend it ahead, from which position it can be drawn back into a backcast.

If a cast is bad—if the fly is not cocked or is half submerged—it should always be allowed to float through regardless. A line and fly being picked from the water causes quite a commotion which is all right several feet behind the trout, but not ahead where he is looking.

Also, if there's reason to believe that a wary trout might have had his suspicions aroused by an imperfect cast, it is best to cast elsewhere, or stop casting altogether, until the trout rises

again. When he rises naturally, he's over his fright sufficiently to be caught, but in the meantime another cast over him might put him down for good.

Fishing the Water

In contrast to casting to specific rising trout, the dry-fly fisherman sometimes fishes the water at random. When the trout are rising, especially in smooth water, the dry-fly fisherman has it all over anyone trying other methods. Fishing the water regardless of rises, he may or may not be able to take more trout than an undersurface angler. It depends on which fisherman knows the most about where trout lie and feed.

During the season of big evening hatches, the dry-fly fisherman will concentrate on the big pools and flat water toward dusk, but during the day he will fish the shallower water and runs. The fish will be lying at various feeding stations taking whatever comes along. Occasionally they will take a floating bug off the top; otherwise

In playing and landing a fish the upstream fisherman often has an advantage. If he can keep the trout above him, it is fighting tackle and current both rather than having the current work to its advantage. This is a pasture stream in lower New York.

they are taking nymphs and miscellaneous food brought down underwater.

A trout lying in deep water can rarely be tempted up unless he is already rising. A deep-water trout will be lying or cruising just under the surface when concentrating on a hatch; otherwise he will be down near the bottom where the current will bring his fare to him. In a small stream, a trout can be brought to the surface almost any time by a good fly, but not so in the deep parts of the big rivers.

Typical spots to float a fly when fishing the water are those places discussed under habits of the trout: the tongues of current at the foot of a rapids or those entering the head of a pool, the corners of rocks and boulders protruding through a steady current, the race of water tight up against a cut bank, the spot where the water swirls around the bole of a tree, and similar feeding stations.

The man fishing the rise may spend a couple of hours on one pool, but the man fishing the water covers a lot of ground. He rarely floats his fly twice over the same spot, but keeps moving until he gets action. Like all fishermen, he goes

on the theory that there's no telling what is waiting around the next bend.

In fishing the rise, it's possible to concentrate on the best fish in the pool; so the fish taken at such a time average better than those taken when there is no particular rise on. Nevertheless, fishing the water during midsummer, clear-water conditions, a man sometimes gets quite a surprise from the size of the fish he raises on a dry when all else fails.

Since there is no pronounced hatch to imitate, and since on rough water deception is not so difficult as on smooth, there is little problem of fly selection. Two of my favorites for this random dry-fishing are a No. 12 Brown Hackle Bivisible and a No. 16 Brown Spider Bivisible, the former for rough water and the latter for water not so turbulent. An outstanding virtue of such flies for this type of fishing is that they never become waterlogged. They may be doused a hundred times by rough water, yet will float as high as ever after being flipped out in a false cast or two.

Deliberate Drag: In a few special cases a dry fly is deliberately moved—not so much dragged as

This is the moment when most are lost. Lead the fish to the net; never move the net toward the fish. This big brown (which was lifted high and dry a moment later, and which measured 19½ inches) was taken on a dry fly.

twitched. On a lake or pond, when the surface is still, this is an effective and exciting method of fishing. A high-floating fly twitched or dragged slightly creates a commotion on the glassy surface which can attract trout from a considerable distance.

And on a very still pool in a stream—such as above a beaver dam—this technique will bring a big trout when nothing else will tempt him. The important thing is not to overdo it. It is far easier to dampen a trout's enthusiasm by over-playing a trick than to make him eager by teasing him. After the cast, the fly should remain motionless for some time. Don't worry about the trout seeing it. He didn't get big and fat with poor eyesight. He knows it's there, but he's not interested. Then twitch it ever so slightly, to give it life. If that doesn't have any effect, wait awhile and twitch it once or twice again.

I knew one such pool where there was one huge old brown and a bunch of sprats. The little ones would snatch a small fly the instant it touched the water, then splash around and kill any chances of hooking the big one. One day I sneaked up to it, tied on a big No. 8 Brown Vari-

ant, which looked so out of place on the quiet pool that the little ones didn't touch it; then I twitched it a couple of times.

That came close to being the largest trout I ever landed on a dry fly. One reason it wasn't is that I didn't land him. He took the twitched fly all right, and it was fun while it lasted.

The leader must sink for such an operation, of course; otherwise its drag on the surface would put every trout under the bank.

So much for the floating fly. This was my first love in trout fishing, and will surely continue to be my first choice wherever I am; yet I am not a purist. I am a flexible fisherman who at one time or another has been known to resort to almost every legal lure that fish were in a mood to accept. In fact flexible is hardly the word. When there was nothing else at hand, I have been known to jig with a handline for cod and halibut, simply because I like to catch fish. But although I am a long way from being a dry-fly purist I admire the man who is one. He's a dreamer and an idealist. He will accept nothing but the best of anything—and dry-fly fishing is the best of everything.

Chapter 12

WET-FLY FISHING

Wet-fly fishing is the most common method of trout fishing. This is true on a nationwide basis —from Maine to Arizona, and from the Smokies to Alaska—and on a stream-wide basis. A greater and more efficient coverage of any one stream is possible with the wet fly than with any other type of trout lure. This form of trout fishing has been practiced for five hundred years, and it is still out in front in popularity.

The fly-fishing ·beginner should commence with the wet fly. Wet-fly fishing is the easiest and best method he can use. As most commonly practiced, it does not require the casting skill and precision of some of the more specialized forms of fly fishing. The stream currents, which have spoiled the chances of many a dry-fly cast by causing drag, more often work to the advantage of the wet-fly fisherman than against him. An intimate knowledge of the ways of trout, their like and dislikes, is not essential at the start. Fine rods and delicate terminal tackle are not necessary to success. The wet fly is not limited to particular conditions: it is applicable to all waters in all seasons and all weather. And what's most important, it's almost as good a way as any to take trout.

Most fly fisherman start out wet-fly fishing. Many stick with it exclusively as the most satisfactory way to catch trout, and with experience become better and better at the game. Others, as they master the casting technique and learn more of the ways of trout, like to branch out and specialize in certain forms of fly fishing, like dry-fly, nymph, or streamer and bucktail fishing. Few, however, abandon wet-fly fishing altogether.

Nymph, streamer, and bucktail fishing are actually specialized forms of wet-fly fishing. Since they are flies fished wet—under the surface— they belong in the same category. Wet flies, as commonly fished, imitate both underwater insect forms and minnows. The nymph fisherman specializes in imitating only certain aquatic insects, and the streamer and bucktail fisherman concentrates on the minnows. Since these are such specialized forms of wet-fly fishing with a technique of their own, they are treated individually in other chapters.

The basic difference between wet-fly and dry-fly fishing is not in the fly itself but in the manner of fishing. A dry fly always floats on top of the water and it floats naturally with the current, seldom with any influence on its action from the fisherman. A wet fly is fished beneath the surface, most of the time under tension and with action imparted to it by the fisherman. Occasionally it may be fished on or near the surface, but under action, as in skittering. A fly designed for dry-fly fishing can be fished downstream under water in wet-fly fashion; and conversely, it is conceivably possible to dry-fly fish a fly designed for wet-fly fishing. The manner of fishing is the true distinction.

Most wet flies are tied with the feathers and hairs lying back along the hook in a streamlined fashion so that the fly will slide through the water easily. The hackles are soft in order that they will conform with the current and also will absorb and hold water. The hackles of the dry fly, as described, are tied at right angles to the hook shank and should be stiff and not hold moisture.

Wet flies are tied in unlimited varieties and patterns but, as explained in the chapter on flies, in a very general way of classification there are two basic types: the natural-colored flies designed to imitate certain insects, and the bright flies which represent nothing under the sun but trout flies. In dark or cloudy water the bright flies often work better than the natural. Eastern brook trout certainly prefer the bright patterns most of the time, and browns and rainbows do on occasion.

When fishing two flies on a leader, as is common practice in wet-fly fishing, I like to use a bright fly on the dropper as an attractor if nothing else. It is conspicuous, and a trout will fall in behind it curiously. That's when he sees the stretcher fly that looks like food to him. At least that's the theory, and it seems to work.

A trout probably strikes a bright-colored fly mistaking it for a small minnow. Sunlight is refracted into the spectrum of the rainbow when it passes obliquely through water, and it's likely that the silvery sides of a minnow reflect these many colors. Whether this is actually the answer or not, it is certain that a trout can see and be attracted to a bright fly from a greater distance than he would be to a somber-hued one.

A wet fly often retains an air bubble in its feathers or furry body when it is being fished, and just as often a bubble trails from the bend of the hook. In fast water, the fly may even pick up an air bubble by cavitation. This air bubble, I believe, may be quite an advantage on a wet fly fished to imitate a minnow. An air bubble underwater glistens like quicksilver.

The reflecting qualities of an air bubble underwater are as good as if not better than those of a spinner or spoon. The bubble shines just like the silvery sides of a minnow. On occasions such an air bubble held by a wet fly may very well be responsible for the strike of a trout. However, this has little to do with the way the fly is fished.

In cloudy or heavy water, or anywhere that the trout are not too particular, it is all right to use snelled flies—that is, flies which are attached permanently to short, looped leaders, or snells. These have a certain advantage in that they can be slipped on and off leader loops with ease. However, they have more disadvantages than advantages. In the first place, the snells are usually too coarse and the loops too conspicuous for many conditions. Also, unless eyed as well as snelled, once the snell becomes cracked or worn, the fly is useless. By far the better method is to use eyed flies. These are tied directly to the end of the leader and to strands of dropper gut tied into the leader; or, if preferred, looped snells of the size monofilament required can be tied individually to the eyed flies.

Using two or three flies at once probably doesn't increase one's trout-catching chances materially over using one fly. For precise work and feeling out certain limited holes, one fly may be better. But the use of one or two droppers has a psychological effect on the fisherman: at least he can hope he will catch twice as many fish. Personally I am in favor of two flies in most wet-fly fishing.

One method of fishing in which a pair of flies definitely pays off is to keep the trailer fly deep in the current, raise the rod tip and dap the dropper fly along the surface in a teasing manner.

Nothing special in the way of fly tackle is needed for wet-fly fishing. Any good rod will serve, glass rods being good enough for most such fishing and less expensive than bamboo. I like one about 4½ ounces in weight and 8½ feet long, but have used everything from 3½ to 8 ounces. Most western wet-fly fishermen like a good-sized rod 9 feet long and 5 or 6 ounces in weight. The action should be similar to any good fly rod. The idea of a "wet-fly action" is antiquated. Old-fashioned rods were soft toward the butt and reacted slowly, much like solid glass compared to hollow glass. The modern design which is progressively more powerful toward the butt—and is thereby faster in action and has reserve power for long casts—came in about the same time that dry-fly fishing became popular, and the two were associated with each other. The old-fashioned rod was retained as a wet-fly rod. The ease with which a line could be cast with the newer rod action had much to do with making dry-fly fishing practicable, but the rod isn't limited to dry-fly fishing any more than a new radio is limited to receiving just one kind of music. A rod that is soft in the middle or butt can conceivably be an aid in fishing only with live bait or a heavy spinner.

The use of a level line is not prohibitive to success with a wet fly. Many fine fishermen use a level line. However, as in all fly casting, a little smoother and more delicate work can be accomplished with a tapered fly line. A double taper is ideal. Only on large rivers, such as in steelhead fishing, and on some lakes would a distance taper be preferable. A seven-foot leader is probably long enough for heavy water, although I never use a leader less than nine feet in any kind

(ABOVE) *Brook trout from the Broadback River, Quebec.*

(LEFT) *Five shots showing proper casting technique. (A) Position. (B) Pick up. (C) Start of backcast. The power has been delivered before rod reaches the perpendicular. (D) Backcast. Rod eases back with line to cock the wrist for forward cast. (E) Forward cast. For more on casting, see chapter 10.*

of trout fly fishing. The taper need not be lighter than 2X; that is, about 4-pound test in nylon.

The conventional method of wet-fly fishing is to cast the pair of flies across current or quartering downcurrent; then, while allowing the stream to swing them around and below, to impart action to the flies with rhythmic jerks of the rod tip. The beginner will find this as good a method as any. He should start in a rapids or

fast water. A trout's vision is more limited in broken water than in smooth; he does not have the opportunity to inspect the fly leisurely and, therefore, is less choosy; and when he strikes in fast water on a taut line, he hooks himself. When the flies have swung below the fisherman he can strip in and make another cast, working carefully downstream so as to cover new water. Between casts the flies should be false cast as seldom as possible since they should remain wet and sink the moment they touch the water. Forty feet of line is ample to handle unless there is a likely looking spot which cannot be reached by any means other than a longer cast. There is a much better chance of hooking the fish on a short line than on a long one.

Some wet-fly fishermen use no technique other than this, but there are variations that are sometimes helpful. A fly in action is more evident to a trout and will probably have more chance of attracting him than one floating naturally. A wet fly, we know, can represent any one of a host of trout foods: the nymphs and larvae of the numerous varieties of aquatic insects, the many forms of land insects fallen in the water, freshwater shrimp and other crustaceans, and minnows. Most of these, except the minnows, are weak swimmers at best and are helpless in a current. Therefore, a rapidly moving fly can mean only one thing to a trout, and that is a minnow. Yet nine out of ten times a trout swallows, he is making a meal out of an insect, not a minnow. This is worth remembering.

When you make the cast across stream, instead of bringing the line up taut immediately and giving the flies action from the start, you can allow them to float naturally with the current for ten feet or so. The line should be barely taut. This not only allows the flies to be swept naturally with the current, like free-floating nymphs, but it has the advantage of giving them the opportunity to sink a foot or so below the surface where most feeding trout lie. The remainder of the cast can be brought around in the conventional manner under action. Then when the fisherman works down a few feet for the next cast, the free float will be over the area in which the flies were given action on the previous cast. This way all the water is covered by both action flies representing minnows and free-floating flies representing nymphs.

A moving fly with action imparted by the rod

tip is best for trout that are not too suspicious, but a wise old trout that is selective in his feeding habits may demand a perfect nymph imitation with a natural drift. This knowledge is what brought about the development of precise nymph fishing. Such nymph technique may be essential to success on some of the heavily fished eastern streams, but it is neither so practicable nor so productive as standard wet-fly methods on large western streams. On many of these large western rivers which are not overfished and so have a normal proportion of small and large fish, I have found that a small wet fly means small trout and a big one, big trout. Of course, the vast majority of trout in any natural stream are small; only a tiny percentage survive long enough to be called big. A stream which has enough food to support a good number of large trout has just that many more small ones. A good nymph fisherman or the man using small wet flies would be busy all day taking off the little fellows. One of the best flies I have discovered for the very productive large trout rivers of Wyoming and Montana is a No. 6 Jock Scott salmon fly.

An exaggeration of the natural float described above should be used in deep water if the fish fail to rise to flies fished in the normal manner. Often the trout are deep and refuse to come up. To get the flies down, cast them quartering upstream to give them time to sink; or, the moment that they strike the water, several feet of slack can be stripped out. By the time the stream takes up the slack, the flies may be deep enough to attract attention.

The successful fisherman will always be ready to experiment. If the trout are not taking flies fished in one manner, it doesn't necessarily mean that they are not feeding. Fish them shallow and fish them deep. Try dancing the dropper on the surface, or skitter the whole cast along the top. When the flies are directly below, raise the rod tip high and let it drop sharply to allow the flies to sink loosely. Try working the flies in slow sweeps with long rests in between instead of in short, sharp jerks. Retrieving the flies across a pool as slowly as possible, merely by working them in with the fingers of the left hand, will often bring results when all else fails. A sinking fly line will help in using this technique on big water.

Sometimes flies fed downstream around a rock, slowly, as a worm fisherman would present his bait, will bring a strike. The same system can be used to feed the flies downstream under overhanging willows or under a cut bank. Since trout in well-protected spots, such as in a hole completely covered by brush, are not so suspicious as those in the open, the man who manages to get a fly to them will usually get a strike. A wet-fly fisherman should be ready to change his attack at any time, and he should try to cover all types of water. He has a great advantage in that he can fish many places well that other fishermen must pass by.

Along little meadow streams, and even along the banks of larger streams, especially where he is protected by a lot of brush, the wet-fly fisherman can often do well by dabbling a fly. This is practiced with a short leader and single fly. The English call it bushing, which is a fairly descriptive term. It amounts to little more than bait fishing with a fly. It is productive because it puts the fly where it could not be placed by casting. The fisherman takes advantage of the brush by making it his blind and he eases the rod, leader, and fly through whatever hole is available and dabbles the fly in the water. Generally no more than the leader need enter the water. Sometimes when a fisherman is after a trout lying back under a cut bank or ledge beneath him, he can dabble a fly without the necessity for a brush or rock blind. Then he can watch his fly and dabble it along the bottom in such a way that no trout could resist. If the fly is allowed to sink to the bottom directly in front of the ledge, then is lifted occasionally just enough to allow the current to carry it a few inches along the bottom before settling again, any trout under the ledge will soon be out after it. If the same technique could be developed out in the middle of a pool at the end of a forty-foot cast, the fisherman could take practically all the fish in the place.

A wet fly can be fished just about every conceivable way. It can be dabbled, and it can be fished downstream, across stream, and upstream. A nymph is fished up or across stream on a slack line, but the wet-fly fisherman can also fish upstream on a taut line effectively, working the fly with the tip as in downstream fishing while he strips in.

Chapter 13

NYMPH FISHING

A surface artificial, a dry fly, should not be an exact imitation of the natural, but rather an object which when viewed through the distorted surface on which it floats creates a reasonable impression of the natural; however, an underwater artificial, such as a nymph, should be as exact a duplication of the natural as possible. This is especially true in slow and clear water where a trout has the opportunity to scrutinize the offering and less true in fast-moving or murky water where a trout must strike fast.

A wet fly, although it is fished underwater, is usually not an exact imitation. Wet flies are normally fished in fast water, for one thing, and against the current so that they move rapidly in relation to the water. Some wet flies, especially those with furry bodies, retain an air bubble, and almost all wet flies when retrieved rapidly or against a heavy current trail an air bubble. The refractory quality of this air bubble gives the fish an entirely different impression of the fly from the way we see it in air.

A nymph, however, should not retain an air bubble and should not move rapidly in relation to the water. It is most useful in water so slow and clear that the trout will not give the standard wet fly a tumble. Therefore, it can be viewed as clearly, distinctly, and leisurely by the fish in his medium as by us in ours. A nymph floating naturally with the current in clear water can be seen as minutely by the fish as we can see a spider dangling before our face. There is no distortion. Distortion is caused only by the passage of light rays through a surface, whether it is the surface of the stream or the surface of an air bubble. Reflection is caused by the inability of light to pass through the surface at an oblique angle whether that surface is likewise on the stream itself or on an air bubble.

A trout can see a nymph well because it is in his medium and also because he can view it leisurely. He has leisure because the nymph floats naturally with the current as does a dry fly. The reason for this, of course, is that most nymphs have little swimming power of their own. They have legs and can walk and crawl around the rocks, grasses, and mud, but can swim very feebly. Therefore, when they are washed downstream or when they are rising to the surface preparatory to hatching, they are practically helpless. Trout know this, and any May-fly, caddis-fly, or stone-fly nymph that is swimming about madly is something to avoid.

The obvious exception to this is the dragonfly nymph which is a comparatively strong swimmer. The dragonfly nymph is the original jet propulsion job. He moves forward in spurts by ejecting water through an orifice in the end of his abdomen. A dragonfly nymph, then, can be fished either naturally or in slow jerks regardless of the current. A hellgrammite can swim feebly by rolling his tail under, somewhat in the manner of a crawfish. A very limited number of May-fly nymphs are free swimmers. But the majority of underwater insects move with the current.

Nymph fishing, then, is the most difficult form of trout fishing. It requires the most precise imitation of the natural and it also requires the ability to present the lure in a natural manner. In return, when mastered, it is by far the most deadly form of trout fishing. Any lengthy stomach-contents analysis of trout will show that the vast majority of the food of these fish is made up of underwater insect life. Of course individual trout concentrate on the type of food that is most prevalent and easiest to consume at the time, but for the tribe as a whole the nymphs and larvae of aquatic insects are the meat and potatoes of their diet.

The moment of truth—a big one in the bag.

Better than any commercial nymphs are certain amateur creations, the following stone flies being a good example. These are made by cementing a small aluminum form to a long-shank No. 10 hook, then the nymph is built up by wrapping a strip of thin rubber, like a toy balloon rubber, around this form. This strip is wrapped in overlapping fashion, as World War I leggings were wrapped on, and this gives the appearance of the segmentation of the body. The proper colored brown or dark green rubber is used of course. A wider strip humps over the forward part of the body where the wing case is found on the natural insect. The striped quills of small Plymouth Rock hackles are tied in for the setae at the tail and for the six legs. A darker strip of rubber is placed lengthwise along the top of the nymph, and thread bound tightly over this rubber accentuates the segmentation and gives the proper bulge to any desired section, like the wing case. The hook is turned up over the back of the nymph rather than under so that it can actually sit naturally on the bottom without fouling. Such a stone-fly nymph made properly looks as though it might crawl away.

The lure itself is of the utmost importance in successful nymph fishing, especially where the water is slow and clear, and next comes the presentation. A nymph should be presented as is a dry fly except, of course, underwater. In other words, it is cast upstream above the waiting fish and allowed to float down to him underwater. This is a more difficult procedure than with a dry fly because the nymph is not visible to the fisherman except under very unusual conditions. Both a nymph and a dry fly are fished with the current on a slack line, but dry-fly fishing is easy because the lure is always visible and so is the fish when he takes it, and nymph fishing is difficult for the opposite reason: the lure can't be watched by the fisherman and he doesn't see the fish take.

This raises the most difficult of many difficult questions in nymph fishing: When does the fisherman know to set the hook? The lure is floating on a slack line, the lure cannot be seen and, being an artificial, the trout will not mouth it long before ejecting it.

In clear water a careful nymph fisherman wearing Polaroid glasses may at times see his quarry before casting to him. Under these conditions he has a tangible hold on the problem.

Probably he cannot see the nymph itself but by watching the fish he can often tell by the trout's actions whether he gets any response. He knows where he casts the nymph and can judge fairly accurately when it will arrive at the trout's feeding position. Then if the trout darts to one side or the other or makes any motion to indicate he has taken the lure, the fisherman sets the hook. It's easy to be wrong at such a time but it's better to set the hook than not. A dry fly drawn sharply across the surface of still water can have a very disturbing effect, but a small nymph underwater on a long, fine leader may be jerked past a fish without disastrous results. That is, there may be no harm in hooking with a nymph prematurely or when the fish has darted to the side to take some object other than the fisherman's lure.

As we know, many nymphs preparatory to hatching rise slowly to the stream's surface and float barely submerged for some time before the nymph shell splits down the back and the mature insect emerges. This is a favorite time for trout to be nymphing and the easiest time for a nymph fisherman to do business. When the trout are merely humping or bulging the surface with their backs, they are feeding on nymphs in this stage of their development. This form of rise is very characteristic and with a little experience can be spotted easily. This condition makes nymph fishing simple because the trout's act of striking is visible, as it is in dry-fly fishing. A lightweight nymph that will not sink rapidly can be used and the nymphing trout should be led by only a few feet so that the lure will not have time to sink much below the surface. Then if the trout takes the nymph, he can be seen to bulge the surface.

Many times, however, the nymph fisherman must fish "blind." He neither sees the trout humping for nymphs, nor because of conditions can he see the trout lying beneath the surface. He merely works upstream dropping his lure in likely spots for trout as he goes. But even here when he doesn't see the trout or a sign of him before casting, he should watch the water carefully in the location where his nymph is floating, and Polaroid glasses are a definite help. Often

This could be a photograph by Brady taken a hundred years ago, but it's a "modern" fishing camp in the Rockies.

The Beaverkill River in New York State is a fine trout stream, though heavily fished. This brown trout was taken with a stone fly. PHOTO BY JOHN SKEITH

the fisherman will see a flash beneath the water as the fish turns to take his lure, and this is his sign of a strike.

The most experienced nymph fishermen can read much into the action of their floating line. As in almost all fly fishing, the leader should sink, but the line float. A good man will notice even the slightest hesitation in the tip of his free-floating line and with perfect reflexes can hook in time to get the trout. Some nymph fishermen give themselves the advantage of tying a fluffy, well-oiled dry fly at the head of the leader where it joins the line and this serves as an indicator of what is going on at the terminal end of the leader, much in the fashion of the bait fisherman's bobber.

If a trout takes a lure with assurance and there is no drag on it to give him immediate warning, he is quite slow about ejecting it. I have experimented along these lines and know it is true, and anyone can prove it to himself without much trouble. Sneak up on a trout that is feeding in clear water where you can observe him clearly. A trout feeds by opening his mouth and drawing considerable water into the mouth cavity along with the item of food. This excess of water is then forced out through the gills, the gill rakers seining the bit of food out of the

water as it passes through. After the water has been emptied out of the mouth cavity, the food is swallowed—or ejected if it is not food. If you watch such a trout long enough you will see that he mouths a considerable number of things that are not food and ejects them slowly. And if you wish to prove to your complete satisfaction how leisurely this action is, drop a lifelike nymph to him, unattached to a leader. If he has no reason to be suspicious, he will take it enthusiastically and discard it reluctantly. After all, we don't give up on a rubber-tough steak without a fight.

When a nymph fisherman has observed this trait of trout to his satisfaction, his confidence in being able to hook the fish will rise considerably even though he is fishing blind. If his presentation is proper and his leader sufficiently fine not to arouse suspicion nor to be obvious as the lure is taken, the fisherman has plenty of time to set the hook. A coarse leader may become obvious to the fish the moment he takes the fly, or it may actually prevent the fly from entering the trout's mouth.

The tackle used is precisely the same for nymph fishing as for dry-fly fishing under the same conditions. The rod should be light for two reasons: one, the fisherman is fishing upstream against the current and must cast constantly;

and, two, he is using a fine leader, and a man simply cannot hook and play a fish with the combination of a fine leader and a harsh rod. The two must be matched.

The line should be a soft, pliable fly line. For best results it should be tapered, as then the nymph can be presented properly and gently. A double-taper is as good as or better than any of the distance tapers, since most nymph fishing to be successful must be comparatively short range. The line should float at all times in normal stream fishing. On deep streams and lakes, though, a fly line designed to sink rapidly may be used. It is cast, given a moment to sink, then retrieved very slowly—and very effectively, I might add.

The leader should sink and be as fine as in dry-fly fishing. A nine-foot leader is normally long enough, especially if the casting line is tapered gradually to a small size, such as H. I rarely use a leader smaller than 3X, as I find it difficult to handle, but under very exacting conditions a smaller size is called for in nymph fishing. The very best of nymph fishermen often taper their leaders down to 5X. Such extremely fine tackle is deceiving to the trout and allows the fisherman ample time to set the hook, but it also requires the utmost finesse in order to set the hook and play the fish.

Successful nymph fishing requires the ultimate in ability and trout sense. It calls for keen deception, faultless presentation, and perfect timing. We have a lot to learn about this form of fishing, but we do know that nine-tenths of the average trout's food is made up of underwater insect life. There are few masters at taking advantage of this fact, but those who have arrived need never worry about an empty creel.

Chapter 14

STREAMER AND BUCKTAIL FISHING

Any and all trout are minnow eaters by desire just as most men are filet mignon eaters by preference. Some trout live in a place where they can gorge themselves on solid food regularly; others may rarely realize such a treat, but the instinct is there. This works two ways: a trout which habitually feeds on other fish will grow large as a result, and a large trout requires a substantial diet in return. The man who is interested in taking only big trout might fish with nothing but minnow imitations or with live minnows themselves. He wouldn't take as many trout as a more versatile fisherman, but his average on large trout would be high.

Bucktails and streamers are the fly fisherman's answer to the large trout's desire for solid food. Live-bait fishermen and those who use spinning tackle and bait-casting tackle are constantly taking advantage of this side of a trout's nature, but many fly fishermen get no pleasure from these types of angling. They'll fish with a long rod and a fly or not at all; so in the early spring, or whenever the water is high and murky, or wherever there is a preponderance of minnow food in the water, the fly fisherman turns to streamers and bucktails.

There is a considerable variety available. All such flies are intended to represent small fish and minnows and are designed for this purpose only. This should be kept in mind in selecting patterns. However, the fact that we think of most minnows as being rather neutral in color does not eliminate bright flies. Many minnows actually are very colorful in their iridescence, and an injured one is inclined to show his red gills.

An important argument in favor of colorful streamers is based on the behavior of refracted light. Any schoolboy has witnessed the demonstration that shows how a ray of sunlight which is bent by passing it through a prism of glass is broken into the color of the spectrum. The same thing, to a lesser degree, occurs when light passes obliquely into water. A spectrum so formed would be reflected from the shiny sides of a minnow.

Also, in discolored water, where the trout's vision is necessarily limited, anything that will attract his attention, such as bright colors or a tinsel body, is advisable. And in fast water where a trout must see the lure soon enough to catch it before it is swept away, bright colors are in order.

My own theory is that bright colors should be used in high or murky water, in heavy water, and in big water where the fisherman is covering a lot of ground and hopes to attract fish from a considerable distance. The latter applies to lakes as well as rivers. On the other hand, where a fish is spotted and the water is confined and clear, I am in favor of using a pattern that imitates the minnow in shape and color as nearly as possible.

Something else to consider in selecting patterns is the appearance of the fly when wet. A maribou-feather streamer, for instance, looks like a miniature dust mop when dry, but when wet it streams into a perfect minnow shape. Because of this shape and because of its willowy swimming action, this nondescript-looking fly becomes one of the deadliest of all streamers. Where color is appropriate, the Yellow Maribou with red feather at the head is a good choice; where precise imitation is in order, the White Maribou with jungle-cock eye and peacock herl stripe down each side is a good bet. The maribous are excellent for big squaretails.

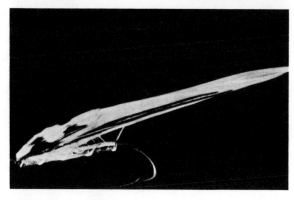

White Maribou Streamer, Dry and Wet.

The Gray Ghost when dry appears to be an intricate but meaningless assortment of feathers, but when wet it takes on a minnow shape, with a dark back, light belly, eyes, gill covers, and a stripe down the side. It's a killer.

Of all the natural flies, the bucktail heads the list in popularity. This long-time favorite has probably accounted for more large trout than any other one fly. As the name implies, it is made from the coarse hairs on the tail of a buck deer, or even a doe or fawn. The brown hairs on the upper side of the tail are used for the top of the fly, the white hairs from the underside are used for the belly. Deer hair is tubular, stiff, and water resistant. Consequently a wet bucktail appears no different from a dry one. This being the case, it should not be tied too bulkily so that it flares out. The best ones are rather sparse and minnow-shaped to start with. Large flies, such as bucktails, are good for evening and night use.

The addition of eyes to a bucktail is a big help. This can be accomplished by any one of the various methods described in the chapter on fly tying. In clear water where a trout has the opportunity to take a good look at the fly, this optic effect is deadly.

Some fishermen prefer the squirrel tail to the bucktail. Squirrel hair is finer and conforms to the water current more than does deer hair. However, it is not so inclined to retain an air bubble as is deer hair, which may be one of the reasons for a bucktail's effectiveness.

The deadliest of all streamer flies for low, clear water and educated trout, as far as I am concerned, is called the Uncle Dudley, although that's not its name—if it has a name.

I haven't fished the Uncle Dudley for several years now, and I doubt if anyone else has. For a while it took fish wherever and whenever I used it; then gradually over the years it seemed to lose some of its charm. The last two or three times I fished with it there was little noticeable difference between it and any other good fly. I have experienced this same cycle with other lures on trout, on bass, and even on salt-water

Gray Ghost Streamer, Dry and Wet.

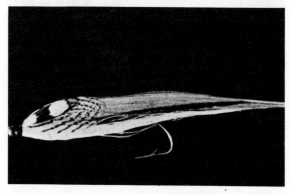

fish, and certainly other fishermen have done the same. Considered logically, the lure doesn't change and it's doubtful if the fish change, so it must be the fisherman himself who changes. Probably a favorite lure takes more fish because of the fisherman's complete confidence in it, with the result that, consciously or not, he uses it often and with great care and under the best conditions.

The Uncle Dudley Streamer, twice natural size.

The Uncle Dudley, then, may be no more than a very good fly, with no magical qualities whatsoever; and having arrived at this conclusion I can foresee no disastrous consequences to the trout population if I describe it. The fly is tied on a No. 12 long-shank hook. The hook should not be offset as this has a tendency to make it rotate. The body is black silk ribbed with a strip of silver tinsel, and a thin whisk of red feather no more than a half-inch long is whipped in at the tail. Two well-matched gold-red cock neck hackles about an inch in length over-all are tied in at the head so that they extend back parallel with the hook, one on each side. Finally, the smallest size jungle-cock eye is tied in on each side of the head, and the fly is complete, as you can see in the sketch above.

The selection of a good fly, like the Uncle Dudley, is important in streamer and bucktail fishing, but the knowledge of where and how to fish it is more important. I am in favor of two principles in this type of fishing: a slow retrieve and a deep retrieve. From watching other bucktail fishermen I feel I am somewhat in the minority in taking this stand, but I am nonetheless confident that it produces results. Most fly fishermen who turn to minnow-imitating lures are looking for big trout, and big trout lie deeper and are slower swimmers than small trout.

Every bucktail fisherman has been bothered by "short strikes." He'll see the water boil behind his fly or feel the merest tick on the fly rather than a solid strike. And if he is wearing Polaroid glasses he will often see a fish turn or flash behind his fly. Many of these are fish that are suspicious of the imitation and turn away at the last moment, but there are others, especially in fast water, that have tried but are unable to catch the lure. Usually when a large trout misses, no matter whether it is his fault or the fisherman's, he won't try for the same lure again immediately. Either he gets a mouthful or he wants nothing to do with it. In such a case, if the fisherman marks the spot where he has had a short strike and tries later with a much slower-moving lure, he'll take the fish. Also, if a fisherman experiencing short strikes is sufficiently alert, he may see a trout start after his lure and slack his line quickly enough to allow the fish to catch it.

There are some who would discount the theory that a trout could unintentionally miss a lure, but I have experimented enough to prove to my own satisfaction that such is the case. One day I fed a handful of grasshoppers to eight or ten breeder trout in a hatchery pool. I dropped the hoppers in the fast water where it entered the pool, and often as many as four trout would miss the insect before one got it. These trout were big and sluggish, of course, and not accustomed to foraging for their own food, but there could be no doubt as to their intentions. They liked grasshoppers and they were doing their level best to get them. The chances are that small- and medium-sized trout will hit anything of reasonable speed that they start after, but a large trout does not have the acceleration of a small one, nor is his aim so sharp. That's why I fish a bucktail as slowly as the current will allow, and often cast quartering upstream to defeat the speed of the current.

Also, a fly on fairly slack line, as when cast upstream, has an opportunity to travel deeper. In the model stream big trout will commonly seek the fairly calm water afforded by big pools. They will rest in the depths where they are safe and feed in the heavy runs at the head of the pool or cruise in the shallows in the evening or at night. Many good streams, however, don't have pools. Their flow—on the surface, at least—is fairly uniform throughout. Here the trout must lie along the bank far up under the willows where they are difficult to reach or they must lie deep and take advantage of the slow water caused by the friction of the rough bottom.

In any case, large trout are rarely found far from the refuge of deep water, and the fisherman who is looking for them will learn to make his fly travel deep. Aside from casting upcurrent to give the fly an opportunity to sink, there are other means of accomplishing this. One of the best is by using a weighted fly. Some streamers are weighted by putting lead on the hook before whipping on the body of the fly. Also, some are weighted by means of BB or buckshot, split and clamped on for a head in an optic fly. Flies can be weighted on the spur of the moment by winding strip lead about the shank of the hook or, if preferred, some distance up the leader. The appropriate amount of lead can be wound on spiral fashion and cut off. This should not be placed on the leader immediately ahead of the fly as it is conspicuous and also because it has a tendency to dampen the darting motion imparted to the fly by the current, making the action less interesting.

The accepted way to fish a bucktail or streamer is in short jerks. The resilient character of bucktail gives it a breathing action when retrieved in this manner. A weighted fly will also dip between jerks. This erratic motion may suggest an injured minnow to the trout. There is no doubt as to its effectiveness. For variety, however, the fisherman should try retrieving in long, steady sweeps occasionally. Sometimes I will stop and reel in the line when I have no idea of quitting, just to give the fly a long, slow, and steady movement. I learned this by the many strikes I have had when actually reeling in at quitting time. Now I never leave a pool without working out as much line as possible on the final cast prior to reeling in.

And a good rule wherever practicable is to make the current do the work. Keep the streamer in the water and and let the stream sweep it in and out and around. It is the current which brings a trout his food, so let it take your fly to the fish. For this type fishing a limp leader material, such as Stren, is preferable to a stiff nylon monofilament since it permits the fly that much more motion. Working out a lot of line by means of the current into a big pool is a likely way to latch onto a good one.

A small stream can sometimes produce surprising results. Notice the size of the streamer which enticed this big brown from under the bank.

Chapter 15

SPINNER FISHING

A beat-up tobacco tin on a path bordering a trout stream prevented my becoming a dry-fly purist. I was twelve years old when I stumbled on it and was a much better student of tapered leaders, model-perfect hooks, and insect forms than I was of my school subjects. I had started to tie my own dry flies, to the dismay of stray chickens; and in addition, being sharp-eyed and as agile as a squirrel, I managed to keep myself supplied with an amazing variety of tackle by retrieving it from trees, bushes, and snags along the well-fished stream. Luckily, many of the local fishermen used a dry fly, so they left behind the tackle I wanted. Then I happened across the tobacco tin. I kicked it aside at first, but with the curiosity of a twelve-year-old turned and picked it up to see if it was full of dead worms as expected.

Instead it contained two dozen brand-new Colorado spinners, size 4/0. This was on an eastern metropolitan stream where the spinner was not popular. I wasn't sure just what to make of my find.

During the next few weeks I played with my new spinners curiously to get the feel of them, and actually caught a trout or two. Then in a swirling pool below a little mill dam I sunk one deep and hooked and landed a 2¼-pound trout. That did it. It was the biggest trout I had hooked or even seen up to that point, and it took third prize in a local fishing contest.

Catching that trout spoiled my chances of becoming a purist, although I wasn't prepared to admit it. This led to considerable confusion. I was morally and ethically a dry-fly man, but instinctively a spinner fisherman. The two didn't jibe. I was sure that the taking of trout on anything other than a floating fly was hardly fair, yet I couldn't resist the knowledge of the spinner's power. In those days I kept a detailed fishing log, complete from the time of day each and every fish was caught to what he had eaten for breakfast, lunch, and tea. Entries for each day followed the same general pattern: during the morning and evening there might be indicated the taking of small trout on a dry fly, then toward the end of the day would be noted a nice keeper or two followed by the inevitable admission, "spinner." At the height of this battle between that which I felt was right and that which paid off, I made a notation, written obviously by my conscience, that in spite of the appearance of the log I really fished a dry fly most of the time and only after an unsuccessful day resorted to a spinner. Fortunately, about this time we went to fish in the Rockies where the spinner was socially accepted, and this discovery that spinner fishing wasn't quite in a class with robbing the church poor box was a great relief. I took up spinner fishing in earnest.

The fisherman who lost that batch of spinners which I found knew a lot about trout, and I'm grateful to him. He taught me the most important lesson in spinner fishing: use the correct type and size lure. Anyone starting out spinner fishing on his own would be beset by the almost endless variety of types, such as the kidney, fluted, June bug, willow leaf, Indiana, and Colorado. Each has its purpose and is appropriate in its own field, but to start with, the fly-rod fisherman should forget all but two. These are the Indiana and the Colorado. Each has a specific and well-defined use. The Indiana, a spinner which revolves about a shaft, is designed to be used in combination with another lure—a fly, worm, or minnow—and is never used by itself. The Colorado spinner, which turns on swivels, is designed to be used by itself. It should never be combined with any other lure and its action should not be impeded by the addition of any bait on

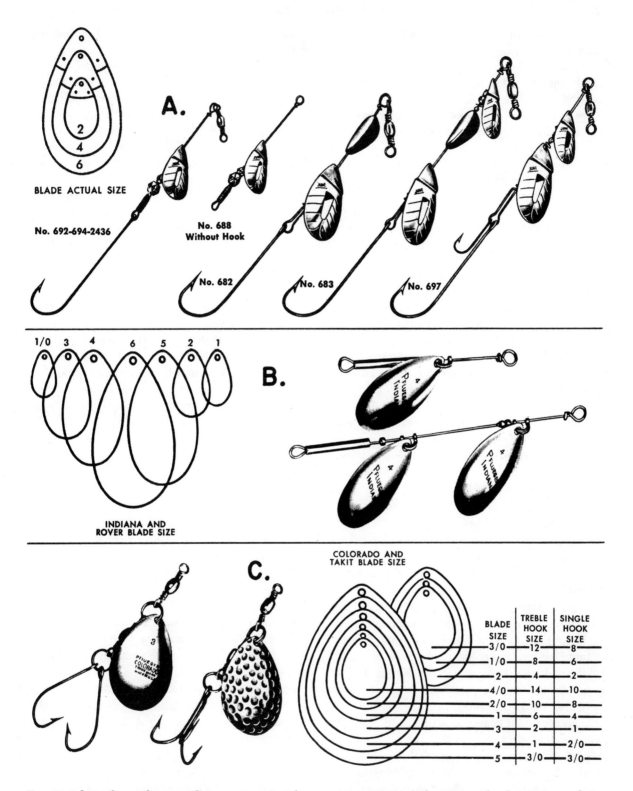

BLADE ACTUAL SIZE

2
4
6

No. 692-694-2436

No. 688
Without Hook

No. 682

No. 683

No. 697

A.

1/0   3   4   6   5   2   1

**INDIANA AND
ROVER BLADE SIZE**

B.

Pflueger Indian 4

Pflueger Indian 4

Pflueger Indian 4

**COLORADO AND
TAKIT BLADE SIZE**

C.

3

Pflueger COLORADO

BLADE SIZE	TREBLE HOOK SIZE	SINGLE HOOK SIZE
3/0	12	8
1/0	8	6
2	4	2
4/0	14	10
2/0	10	8
1	6	4
3	2	1
4	1	2/0
5	3/0	3/0

Few trout have the wisdom or will power to resist taking a pass at a pretty little spinner. The three spinners shown here are the types most applicable to trout fishing. (A) The June bug, is primarily a bait spinner and is used in combination with a worm or minnow. (B) The Indiana, is also a combination spinner, being used with bait, wet fly, streamer, or even lure. These two are best suited to spinning or trolling. (C) The Colorado, is most effective as a fly-rod spinner, being cast and fished as is a bucktail. The Colorado is complete in itself and should never be dampened by addition of fly or bait. It is most deadly in the smallest size (4/0) fished slowly on a light leader.

the hooks. So much as a single salmon egg on the hooks of a Colorado will dampen its action and hamper its effectiveness. The Colorado, fished without any such impediment on the hooks, is the subject of this chapter.

There are many different makes of Colorado spinners. Some are made much more durable than others, but forget about durability when selecting a trout lure. The object is to catch fish, and it's the action that counts. Pick out the make that has the lightest and most delicate construction. This is very important. These light spinners do not last long. One that is allowed to touch a rock on the backcast will fly in several directions at once. But as long as a light one lasts it will take fish. The important thing in spinner fishing is to use a lure that will turn and glitter in the slowest current. The more action it has, even at very slow speeds, the better.

As to size, use the smallest possible for the water conditions at hand. On eastern trout waters there is rarely any reason to use a spinner larger than the smallest size made, the 4/o. Many a time when the water was low and bright I have wished that a spinner even smaller and daintier than the 4/o were made. I have gone so far as to try to make one myself, but without much success. However, for most conditions the 4/o is small enough for results. It is large enough to be an appealing mouthful to the largest trout found in eastern streams; yet its small size gives it the desired action and allows it to be used on a light leader.

On western streams where the water is heavy or cloudy, a size 3/o or 2/o may be necessary to attract the trout, but even on large rivers the size should be kept as small as practicable. All the biggest trout I have taken on a spinner, even on large western rivers, have been on a size 4/o. Anything larger than a 2/o is out as far as fly-rod fishing is concerned. Big spinners strike the water too hard, don't have the delicate action, require too heavy a leader and, besides that, are uncomfortable to cast.

Spinners are finished in copper, bronze, brass, or nickel, and sometimes in a combination of two. Others may be enameled red. My own preference is for the brass finish, although I have never been fully convinced that this is necessarily the best. A silver finish works almost as well, if not equally well. And on occasions where bullhead minnows are prevalent, a bronzed one may be a good choice.

The type, size, and finish of a spinner are important. More important is the way it is fished. Catching fish on a spinner is not very difficult, certainly not in comparison with nymph and dry-fly fishing. With the right outfit it can be mastered well enough for success in a day or two; but, as with everything worthwhile, perfection takes time. There are quite a few tricks to learn about spinner fishing before a man can get the most out of it.

The first difficulty for the fly fisherman will be learning how to cast a spinner smoothly. A *fly* in being cast has no momentum of its own, only resistance to being pulled by the momentum of the fly line. Without direction and power of its own, it is completely at the mercy of the pull of the line. A *spinner* on the other hand, having considerable weight for its size, does have considerable momentum of its own. Once energy has been imparted to it through the rod and line, it tends to continue on its course. It does not follow the pull of the fly line willingly. There's the rub in casting a spinner smoothly.

The best form in *fly* casting, of course, is to deliver the power of the cast to the rod with the wrist and forearm only. The wrist can be moved through more of an arc more quickly—with more snap—than can the extended arm, and therefore a sudden burst of power can be delivered to the rod. With a *spinner* the cast must be tempered—the power must not be delivered suddenly—and the obvious way to accomplish this is to work in reverse; that is, the entire arm should be extended and brought into play. This will tend to soften the cast. In making false casts especially, it is necessary to soften the action. The spinner's momentum must be overcome gently and its direction changed before the wrist snap delivers the power. The gentle movement of the extended arm is the means of reversing the spinner's course, and the wrist still does the casting.

A soft-action fly rod—that is, one with the action continuing well down into the middle section—will be a help in spinner casting. Some of the inexpensive glass rods are too soft—have too slow an action—for satisfying fly fishing, but are well adapted to spinner fishing. They temper the sharp wrist thrust and tend to make a smooth instead of a jerky cast. Too sharp a jerk against a fast-traveling spinner may part the leader. Once the fisherman masters the timing necessary in false casting with a spinner, he can cast a small spinner comfortably even on a dry-fly rod. A rod with a dry-fly action has more power and can account for more distance, but with more snap it has a harsher movement. The fisherman must allow the spinner to extend itself and must start it on the reverse course gently with the extended arm before snapping the wrist.

As far as casting is concerned, another thing on which to concentrate in spinner fishing is the pick up. The harder the pull against a spinner underwater, the faster it will spin and the more resistance it will put up against the pull. Therefore it is vital that the spinner be on the surface of the water before the wrist snap is delivered to shoot it into a backcast. If the spinner is sunk, the wrist snap may be enough to break a rod tip. After the line has been stripped in at the end of a cast, the arm should be lifted high to bring the spinner to the top and skitter it along the surface before the backcast is attempted. Also, since the weight of a spinner tends to make it drop, the fisherman must be even more attentive than usual to keeping his backcast high.

All this sounds complicated, but it needn't be of too much concern at first. The way to learn to cast smoothly with any type of lure is to practice, and the best way to practice is to get out and fish. The way to fish with a spinner without knowing much about casting is to make the current do the work. This is good advice even for anyone who is a master at casting. A trout can't catch a spinner flying through the air. The idea is to get it in the water and keep it there as much of the time as possible.

The best place to learn with a spinner is at the head of a pool where there's a strong central current to carry out a lot of line. Little actual casting is necessary in such a place. From a stand a little to one side of the main current, the fisherman can toss the spinner in or over the current and then feed slack as fast as the stream will take it. On the first try, only twenty or twenty-five feet should be extended, then this can be stripped back slowly along the edge of the current. Each succeeding time a little more line should be used until a point is reached that the current will take no more. The spinner should be allowed to weave around in the cur-

rent for a few moments each time before the line is stripped back in. Often it is possible without picking up the spinner from the pool below to lift the rod high, toss a loop of slack across the main current, and thus drag the spinner over to the far side of the pool.

By playing with a spinner in the current—by stripping, by feeding slack, by swinging it back and forth, and simply by allowing the current to whip it around—a fisherman who doesn't know the first thing about casting can catch fish all day. Gradually as he discovers the necessity for tossing the spinner into heavy currents a bit farther and farther away, he will learn all there is to know about casting; then he can enter into the fine stages of spinner fishing.

As indicated, I was fortunate in my introduction to spinner fishing. I was presented by Lady Luck with the proper kind and size spinner. On top of that, since I was fishing a dry fly most of the time, through luck or laziness I used the correct terminal tackle. Instead of bothering to set up a new outfit and soak a heavy spinner leader, I took the immediate path of tying the tiny spinner on a nine-foot, 3X leader in place of the dry fly. Casting was difficult with such a light leader and a small dry-fly rod, so I resorted to making the current do most of the work as described above. My failure to change to a heavy leader, such as is generally accepted for spinner fishing, worked to my advantage. Most fishermen, I am thoroughly convinced, not only try to use a spinner that is too large, but they use a leader far too heavy. A fine leader is not only completely deceptive on a conspicuous lure like a spinner, but it allows the spinner complete freedom to whip about in the current. Today in rigging a rod especially for spinner fishing, even in heavy water, I never use a leader less than nine feet long or heavier than a 1X taper. For most fishing I choose a nine-foot leader, tapered to 2X. For very fine, clear conditions I may even go so far as a twelve-foot, 3X leader. It's mean to play a trick like that on a trout, but fishermen are that way.

When spinner casting is fairly well mastered, the fisherman will begin to help out the current in presenting the spinner to the fish, and he will begin to take trout in spots where otherwise the current might be a hindrance rather than a help. Also, of course, there are many good trout in still water that can be reached in no way but casting.

A fair caster with a 4½-ounce rod will soon learn to lay out a spinner forty or fifty feet with ease.

From the start when he allowed the current to do the work for him, the spinner fisherman will discover that a spinner is most effective when fished deeply and slowly. Often it is best when opposing a current with just enough force that the blade barely turns, and against a fast current the spinner need no more than creep along.

There are two ways of taking a spinner deep and one way not to take it down. The way not to is with a sinker. With a sinker, even split shot, the chances of results are cut down. In the first place, a sinker and a spinner on the same leader are easy to tangle and difficult to cast. In the second place, the inertia of a sinker destroys the weaving motion of the leader which can be very important in spinner success. And for other reasons not necessary to mention, a sinker of any kind is inadvisable.

A spinner of itself doesn't have much sinking weight, and when it is spinning hard it tends to work itself toward the top. However, if allowed to float with the current in such a way that it is not working, it will sink quite rapidly, much faster than a streamer or bucktail. The idea, then, is to cast in the current well above the spot where a trout is expected. The spinner is allowed to float down on an almost slack line until it has arrived at the desired depth or location, then it is brought into action. A good spinner fisherman in a fast stream will be casting or quartering upcurrent a good deal of the time in order to get the lure down under the current. Somewhat the same effect can be obtained in fishing directly downstream by feeding slack rapidly, but if a fish should strike while the spinner is tumbling, the fisherman in this position does not have quite the control that he does when fishing across current or slightly upcurrent.

Another method of getting the spinner down is to drop it in an undercutting current; that is, a current dropping over a boulder, bedrock ledge, or spillway that cuts under the water below, sometimes forming a backwater on the surface. Such a current often digs deep into a pool and a spinner or fly which can be placed in it accurately will be pulled far under where the big ones live.

This is a good way to lose a spinner. But the spinner fisherman who doesn't hook bottom fairly often doesn't catch any big trout. A snagged spinner can often be worked loose with a little patience. Try to avoid coming up on it hard until all else has failed. It may have run afoul of a sunken log or may be wedged in a crevice between rocks. Pulling would only drive it in deeper. Instead work out as much slack line as you can handle, lift the rod high and back, as in a roll-cast position, and throw a loop of line on the far side of the snag. Then come up on the rod to give the line a pull from the far side. In other words, work the line around in such a position that the pull will be from the direction that the spinner hit the snag. If it becomes fouled when retrieving it against the current simply feed out a sizable belly of line in the current below the snag and pull sharply. Without the current, roll cast a belly beyond the snag, allow it to sink momentarily and pull sharply. This will generally do it, although spinner fishing admittedly is hard on tackle. The little 4/o spinners wear out and break easily, and others are lost on the bottom. But it's worth it.

When a man learns to cast a little spinner with the ease and accuracy of a dry fly, he begins to learn what spinner fishing is all about. He'll fish the tough places in a manner the unsuspecting trout know nothing about. He'll learn how to drop it so that it tumbles around the very edge of a rock. He'll hit the head of a tiny eddy with bull's-eye accuracy, and he'll flip it far up under a cut bank. He'll cast upstream and down with equal abandon, depending on what the currents demand, and he'll learn to drop it in still water with barely a splash. Then he has arrived, and the Lord help the poor little fishes. They're due for a bad time.

Spinner fishing is a lot of fun, especially in clear-water conditions when the generally accepted rule says to steer clear of such tactics. Spinner fishing is commonly considered a coarse manner of trout fishing, and when practiced as such it is a waste of time. A good man with flies can outfish the fellow with a larger spinner and heavy leader any day. But spinner fishing can be an art. When properly handled, there are few if any trout so shy or particular that they can't be fooled by a 4/o Colorado on a long, fine leader.

There is nothing in trout fishing quite so satisfying as tempting a hard-to-please trout up to a well-conceived dry fly but there are times when a dry fly doesn't look like food to a trout, especially to an old lunker lying deep. Yet he might become pretty excited about a pert little spinner. This is most true during the bright hours of the day; it's in the sunlight that a spinner is at its best. With the same rod, line, and leader a fellow can fish a dry in the mornings and evenings when the hatches are on and a spinner during the heat of the day. That's as good a way as I know to have a lot of fun.

The beautiful El Serrano (the Mountaineer) River in southern Chile.

Chapter 16

SPINNING

Trout fishing is for everyone. Although its greatest rewards lie in the field of fly fishing, this approach not only takes time to master but it may be too much to ask of the arms of some youngsters and women. My wife, for instance, simply is not built to cast a hundred feet of fly line. Yet, for what she may lack in punching power, she compensates with enthusiasm. No one could get more of a thrill from a trout than she can. It matters not if it is big or small, if it takes an artificial or bait, if the hook is a No. 6 or 16, or if it is summer or winter, she gets excited! When she pulls a foot-long trout through a hole in the ice, everyone from one end of the lake to the other knows it. Her enthusiasm is so genuine and contagious that everyone around her is happy. But the fact remains that she is not a fly fisherman, and I wouldn't encourage her to be one since this method does not suit her particular abilities and disposition. She also claims that she doesn't want to be a fly fisherman because she doesn't want to show me up. But she has no qualms about showing me up at trolling, ice fishing, or spinning. And when she gets one, no trout could ever be more appreciated on the line, in the kitchen, or on the table; and this is the name of the game. Fishing is for fun.

For her and the hundreds of thousands like her who don't have the time to learn the intricacies of fly fishing, or who don't have the physical aptitude for it, or who may be beginners at trout fishing, or who don't even care one whit about anything but results, spinning is a blessing.

In trout fishing generally the fish does not come to the fisherman, rather the fisherman goes to the fish. In so doing he must be able to present a lure from a sufficient distance and with sufficient finesse that the trout will remain at ease and accept it as food. Aside from trolling,

there are three basic methods of accomplishing this, each demanding its own particular tackle. The most appropriate and productive is, of course, fly fishing. The second is spinning. The third, and least effective, is bait casting.

Each of these different methods carries an unusual name when analyzed. Fly fishing sounds like fishing for flies rather than with them. Spinning as we practice it today is a misnomer—almost a contradiction—in that the crucial element of the equipment, the reel, has no spinning part. And a "bait" casting outfit is rarely used to cast bait, but the essential reel does spin when the cast is made.

The inappropriate names of the latter two, as a matter of interest, stem from the early days of their evolution. Spinning in its original meaning has been practiced for well over three centuries, whereas our spinning reel was invented in England sixty-five years ago. Traditional spinning involves fishing a minnow hooked or arranged in a bait harness in such a manner that it spins in the current or as it is retrieved through still water.

Similarly, the bait-casting reel, which is an American invention of the early 1800s, was designed to cast frogs, minnows, and the like for bass. Soon this natural bait was replaced by artificial plugs and casting spoons, but the name "bait" casting has remained.

Reels

Spinning reels have changed little in operation since the first Illingworth was developed years ago. The principle of the reel, well known to most fishermen, is exactly the same today as it was in the prototype. It is best described as a stationary-drum reel. The axis of this line-holding drum lies parallel with the rod instead of at right angles as in the American casting reel, and the drum does not revolve. The line peels off the end of the drum in a frictionless manner just as thread can be pulled from the end of a spool.

The effectiveness of the reel stems from the fact that there are no moving parts when the cast is made. Only the line and lure move, and since there are no mechanical parts there is no resistance to the cast. Also, since there are no moving parts, there can be no overrun and no backlash. It is the apple-on-a-stick method of casting in its simplest form. However, though simple, it is not all wine and roses. For each coil pulled off the reel there is one complete twist in the monofilament. This constant twisting with each cast will weaken the line in time, and if the lure spins in a manner to compound it, the monofilament will ball into an unsolvable bird's nest the results of which are unfortunately evident wherever there have been spinning fishermen.

Though the operation of the spinning reel has changed little, its appearance has undergone some evolution. The original type spinning reel hangs under the rod and looks more like a pencil sharpener than fishing gear. In such a spinning reel a wire finger or guide geared to the reel handle is used to pick up the line as it is being reeled in and to distribute the line evenly over the spool. This is a fairly ingenious level-wind mechanism, but it gives the reel an odd look. American manufacturers have attempted to make the spinning reel with a more conventional appearance, such as designing it in the form of a fly reel or placing it on top of the rod in the position of a bait-casting reel. No matter what may have been done, it's the same reel basically, and none casts better or looks worse than the original English type.

Another feature of spinning reels is the friction clutch. This clutch operates as does the star drag on salt-water reels; that is, if the fish exerts a pull greater than the breaking strength of the line, the clutch slips and allows line to flow out backward regardless of which way the fisherman is reeling. Some fresh-water fishermen have ridiculed big-game fishing, suggesting that no skill is necessary, only brute strength and ignorance, because of such a clutch arrangement. But of course the star drag is not incorporated in a large reel to relieve the fisherman of the judgment of when to allow a fish to run; a mechani-

Trout fishing is for everyone. My wife demonstrates that trout can be caught without expensive tackle or cumbersome gear.

cal clutch is necessary simply because it would be impracticable to thumb such a large reel manually. The same in general is true of a spinning reel. It would be impossible to thumb it manually, and the friction clutch is the only way to release line as necessary in such a reel design. This might rob the fisherman of some satisfaction in the skillful playing of a large fish, but it can't be helped.

Rods

There are both one-handed and two-handed spinning rods. The reel is hung in English fashion beneath the handle on the two-handed rod. A pair of sliding rings allows the reel to be seated anywhere along the handle for convenience, the usual position being a little forward of midway for a two-handed cast and six or eight inches from the butt for a one-handed cast. One-

This sequence of pictures needs little explanation. Spinning tackle has brought this smile of success to many thousands who might otherwise never have known what a two-pound trout looks like.

handed rods are made for top-mounted reels. They are similar to bait-casting rods except that they are longer and softer in action.

Conventional spinning rods fall between fly rods and bait-casting rods in size and vary in length from 6 to 8 feet. Seven feet is a popular trout length. The action of the rod should be limber and supple in order to handle the lures with which the spinning reel is so effective, and the action should continue well down into the butt. In comparison with most modern fly and bait-casting rods, the tip should be relatively stiff in action and the butt section pliable. The soft action thus provided puts the lure into motion gently and has the effect of tossing or lobbing it, which is advisable with a dense lure and essential with live bait. Glass, which makes the top grade as fly-rod material only when expertly designed (since it is essentially a softer fiber in

its action than either bamboo or graphite), is the ideal spinning-rod material for this very reason.

Lines

A light line is the answer to smooth operation with a spinning reel. A six-pound-test line is fine for trout fishing. Some enthusiasts prefer to use three- or four-pound-test line. Eight pound test is about the top limit for satisfactory performance with light lures. Monofilament is much preferable to braided lines in these light weights. It has great strength for its size, it sinks readily, and since it is almost invisible in the water it has the advantage of being a continuous leader.

A typical spinning reel on the English design holds 120 yards of six-pound-test line. This may not sound very strong to the beginner, but it is about twice as strong as the leader used by most fly fishermen. With the large reel capacity, the line doesn't have to be very strong to wear down a large fish. And for the steelhead fisherman, if he thinks this isn't sufficient, he can get a supplementary drum which will hold 250 yards of six-pound line. In fact, there's a spinning reel and drum with a capacity to suit anyone's tastes. Also, a convenience in most good reels is that the drums are interchangeable, which means that a fisherman can have one filled with six-pound line for stream fishing and another with ten- or twelve-pound line for trolling.

Leaders

A leader as such is rarely necessary in spinning. The lines are necessarily small and the lures are all large by comparison. And there is no advantage in tapering the end of a spinning line as is done with a fly line and leader.

Since many of the lures used in this type fishing do spin when fished, the use of swivels is important to prevent the line from becoming badly twisted. With very light spinners which will not cast well of their own weight or which will not travel deep in the water, place a small keel sinker on the line ahead of the front swivel. This will serve the double purpose of providing casting weight and preventing the line from twisting. Some men overcome the line-twisting problem by regularly alternating lures, one with a right-hand twist, the other with a left-hand twist.

Lures

Among its many attributes a spinning outfit is the ideal bait-fishing rig. The advantage of spinning is the ease and gentleness with which it will cast light lures, those a bit heavy for the fly rod and a bit light for the bait-casting rod. A minnow can be cast accurately and easily on a spinning rod with no danger of flipping it off. The same is true of a worm. Most natural bait is a little delicate to be cast on a fly rod, except by strip casting, and is too light to be cast on a bait-casting rod. The spinning outfit is what the bait fisherman has always been looking for.

Still the deadliest spinning bait for large trout is a natural minnow rigged in the fashion which gave spinning its name. Sometimes these minnow tackles are weighted—which is not necessary for casting, as a minnow can be handled easily and accurately under its own weight—but the extra weight does serve to take the minnow deep under the current where the big ones are found. Any other natural trout bait can be handled well on a spinning outfit. A worm alone is not too light to be cast. A worm is effective when preceded by a pair of small Indiana spinners.

The English-type spinning lures are the deadliest of the artificials on trout. These include the various devon minnows and phantoms. Some of the phantoms have so many hooks hung on them, however, that a fisherman with a conscience wouldn't be caught using one. With two out of every three hooks snipped off, they're still effective. They're wicked meat getters.

The original red-and-white Dardevle, the most successful and most imitated all-round bait-casting and spinning lure. It comes in a number of sizes. In selecting the size of any such lure, the type water to be fished is more important than the size of the trout it contains. In the security of a lake or big river, a ten inch trout might have the courage to attack the standard 3⅝" Dardevle while in a clear, still pool the splash of even the tiny "Skeeter" might put a five-pounder under the bank. ILLUSTRATION COURTESY OF LOU. J. EPPINGER, DEARBORN, MICHIGAN.

Spinners are more typically American. Colorado spinners in size 4/0 and 3/0 are so light that they require a small sinker to be cast any distance. Larger sizes will cast under their own weight. If weight is used with a Colorado spinner it must be placed far enough ahead, at least one foot up the leader, that the action of the spinner will not be materially impaired. For use with bait of any kind, the Indiana rather than the Colorado should be used. No weight other than the bait and the spinner need be used.

Spoons are particularly useful, especially in

the smaller sizes. There is a great variety of patterns of spoons. The lightweight ones which will rotate and act easily even at slow speeds are good for spinning. The best ones for trout are two inches or less in length. Not all lures used on a modern spinning outfit spin. Some of the good nonspinning trout lures include small wooden plugs weighing a quarter of an ounce and less, light composition minnows, weighted streamer flies, and a multitude of other gadgets designed especially for this type fishing. In fact there is such a number and variety of effective spinning lures that it proves without doubt some trout are both curious and adventuresome creatures.

Of course most of these artificials can be fished as well on either a fly rod or a bait-casting rod by a man with experience, but the spinning fisherman can use them all, along with bait, on the same outfit. In other words, he can use a spinner for a while, which would ordinarily require a fly rod, and he can shift immediately to a three-eighths-ounce plug, which otherwise would require a bait-casting rod.

Casting

The European spinning cast is an easy side sweep with a dipping motion so that the rod tip is higher at the start and finish of the cast than in the middle; that is, the rod tip travels through an open-U arc. Another cast, more accurate but slightly harsh if you are using bait, is an underhand flip. The rod is pointed toward the target, dipped sharply to cock the rod, and flipped up, at which point the line is released. Most American fishermen, since we have become accustomed to bait-casting tackle for a century and a half, prefer a direct overhead cast. The variations will depend on the obstacles around the fisherman. Casting with a spinning outfit really requires little explanation. It can be mastered in almost any form in a matter of minutes. The only difficulty at first will be a matter of timing, i.e., when to release the bait or lure so that it will not travel in too high an arc. This can be conquered rapidly.

When you make a cast with the typical two-handed rod on which the reel is hung beneath, the left hand is placed near the butt of the rod and the right hand grips the handle around the reel seat. The forefinger of the right hand controls the cast by releasing the line at the proper moment. At the end of the cast, the right hand remains in the same position, the butt of the rod is moved in against the body, and the left hand does the reeling. If desired, the cast can be stopped before the momentum of the lure is spent by engaging the line with the pick-up bail. This is accomplished simply by turning the reel handle. This is an aid to accuracy, and the pinpoint accuracy which can be developed with spinning tackle will come in very useful on a brushy, willow-lined stream.

On a single-handed rod with the reel seated on top in the position of a bait-casting reel, the principle of operation is similar. The difference is that the right thumb controls the cast by operating a conveniently placed lever, and the cast is retrieved with the right hand, not the left.

Fishing the Lure

Casting is easy with a spinning reel; it can be learned well enough in thirty minutes. But casting simplicity has nothing to do with fishing ability. Lures do have something to do with success. Almost all spinning lures are designed with sufficient density for easy casting, and being of high density, spinning lures run deep.

Good trout in many waters are either up or they are down. There's not much in between. When they are up it is because insect food has brought them up. Otherwise they are down, taking advantage of the slower water caused by the friction over the rough bottom. And, of course, much of their food comes to them deep. Foreign matter in water either floats or it sinks.

Successful fly fishermen have long known this. When the trout weren't rising, they have worked their flies deep by drifting them with the current long enough to allow them to settle before starting the retrieve. This is a good way to foul the bottom, but often it's a case of no snags, no fish. But although this has long been a successful technique, it has been difficult advice to pass along. It seems to be one of those things a fisherman must discover for himself. The fast-sinking spinning lures have proved good teachers for many.

But sometimes things can come too easily. The effortless casting and the effectiveness of the type lure demanded by spinning tackle have lulled some fishermen. They accept this bounty and fail to progress beyond the initial stage. They cast and reel in, cast and reel in, with no variation. If something happens, that's good, if it doesn't, that's bad luck. But this does not have to be the case. Those bad days are not necessarily due to bad luck. Making your fishing days successful requires a moment's observation of the natural world about us.

This natural world is cruelly harsh by human standards. It is always the weak or disabled prey which is first attacked by a predator—even its own kind at times. Any animal born malformed or feeble is not around long; a quail left wounded is the first picked off by a hawk or owl; a diseased rabbit is the first caught by a coyote; an injured fish is the first eaten by a larger one. All predators have an instinct to spot unusual behavior in prey which indicates any weakness, and they take advantage of it immediately.

An injured minnow often spins crazily, which is why spinning in its original form has always been successful. Manufacturers often try to build erratic motion into their lures to make them look like vulnerable prey. Even if this is not the case, many such lures are attacked simply because they appear strange. However, a good fisherman doesn't depend on this; he gives his lure an erratic action through his own manipulation. Read in the next chapter ("Bait Casting") how to tumble a spoon. Admittedly, imparting this motion is not as easy with spinning tackle as with a bait-casting reel since with the latter a spoon can be spun or tumbled in the current as desired by mere thumb pressure, but it can be done well enough. At the very least a spinning-tackle fisherman must get out of the rut of automatically casting and reeling directly in over and over again.

In some ways fishermen are no different from other people. We have our likes and dislikes, our preferences and prejudices; so when I conclude that spinning is not my favorite method of angling—that it somehow does not afford me the fascination and satisfaction of bringing trout to a fly—I am not detracting from it. I am only making an admission. Spinning has proven its great value to the trout fisherman, especially the beginner. If a newcomer to the game should ask me what was the surest way for him, short of dynamite, to catch a basket of trout, I would nominate for the job a gold-finish devon minnow in a size from one to two inches, depending upon the nature of the particular stream, fished on a spinning outfit with a four-pound-test line. A devon can make an otter look silly when it comes to catching trout. It goes down where they live.

But I would also advise that the beginner not start and stop in the same place. Spinning has been of enormous service in introducing hopeful fishermen to the wonders of trout fishing. Those who were on hand to try it ten or fifteen years ago were particularly rewarded. They found a vast new assortment of flashing, glittering lures new both to themselves and the trout, and they realized success they never thought possible. Spinning will continue to do fine service under a great many conditions, but the fisherman shouldn't stop here.

In the open water of a lake, no trout has much of a chance against the relentless mechanical efficiency of spinning tackle. Among the hazards of a stream, however, a big trout's first rush will likely result in a parting of the ways.

With all honesty I must say this: spinning has come as an even greater blessing to the fly fisherman. Spinning, along with being effective, is also a simple means of fishing, and it is human to pursue the path of least resistance. As a result, our streams are crowded with spinning-tackle fishermen today in comparison to fly fishermen. Where trout were once gullible to a spinning lure, they are now becoming pushovers to a well-presented fly. The flashing, whirling lures that left many a trout gaping a few years ago are now old stuff.

Therefore, my advice to young fishermen is to explore the next step. Spinning, while excellent in the field for which it was designed, is far too confining for a full measure of trout-fishing enjoyment. After a man becomes acquainted with a fly rod, there is no limit to the developments, intricacies, and explorations which lie ahead. And, as long as trout continue to eat for a living, they can be taken by a good man with a fly rod. It is the most deceptive means of fishing, and a trout's various natural foods—no matter what time of year or day—can be most closely represented by fly-rod lures.

Spinners, trolling spoons, most spinning-tackle lures, and bait-casting spoons are usually one-shots. That is, a trout either strikes a large, flashy lure impulsively or he is frightened by it. A trout is not alarmed by a small fly presented properly. He either accepts it as food or he ignores it. In the latter case, he is still susceptible to the correct fly fished in the correct manner. This is the distinction. Anyone using large lures should cover a lot of ground in order to reach new fish continually. A competent man with a fly, on the other hand, can cast to a solitary fish for an hour or more and still stand a chance of taking him if he eventually comes up with the correct combination. One of the most fascinating phases of the sport is attempting to tease such a hard-to-please trout into striking by showing him exactly the right fly or nymph in exactly the right manner.

Chapter 17

BAIT CASTING

The term "bait" casting is a holdover from many years ago. This type tackle is strictly an American product, which got its start with the invention of the multiplying reel by a jeweler named George Snyder in 1810 in the bluegrass country of Kentucky. Other Kentucky jeweler-fishermen, the Meeks, Talbots, Milans, and Gaylords, further developed this novel reel which was the first to make possible the casting of natural bait, such as frogs and minnows, directly from the free-running reel. Today, artificial lures, such as plugs and spoons, are used universally on this type tackle, but the original name "bait" casting is retained.

Before going into the bait-casting outfit in detail, I shall describe my own favorite outfit. The rod is the lightest commercial weight, five-foot, one-piece bait-casting rod with detachable handle. The reel is the best grade bait-casting reel on which I remove the level-wind mechanism to make it as free-running as possible. The line is ten-pound-test oval monofilament. The lure is the all-important item of any outfit. My favorite is the standard red-and-white "shoehorn" casting spoon popular for pike and other game fish for many years. This spoon comes in the original pike size plus one outsize for muskies and two smaller sizes. For anyone using this method regularly on all waters, the small two-inch model would be the best, but when I start dredging, I'm after big fish. This calls for the standard three-inch model.

In general, rods may be of many sizes and actions. In addition to the five-footer, I have a specially designed, extra-light 6¼-foot rod for trout fishing. It is really a delight to fish with. It is sufficiently long and limber to have a lot of play in it. However, being in one piece, it is a bit cumbersome to carry about. I also use a four-foot light rod on occasions. It is handy on a very brushy stream where there isn't room to swing a longer one. It is short enough to flip out a spoon underhand.

The length of the rod is up to the fisherman's own preference. Whatever he is accustomed to, he will like best. A comparatively long rod, however, has several advantages. The increased leverage makes it possible to cast lighter lures where trout don't want a heavy spoon. Also, it has more give to it when playing a fish; and, since a trout's mouth tears easily, a long rod may make the difference between landing or losing an old lunker. Regardless of length, keep it light, the lighter the better. The normally slower action of glass lends itself well to a bait-casting rod.

In bait casting, no matter whether for trout, bass, or tarpon, the reel is the vital part of the equipment. Get a good one even if it means skimping on the rod. Make sure it spins easily and freely. No matter how good a man is, if the line won't flow freely from the reel he can't attain any distance. The reel I use seemed extravagant when I got it years ago, but it is still going strong and has paid for itself many times. Although I remove the level-wind mechanism and anti-backlash tension, fishermen who learned to cast with a level-wind reel would probably find this refinement more of a handicap than an advantage.

As far as the line is concerned, there's no excuse for using one heavier than ten-pound test. A light line will cast farther than a heavy one, and often it is the hard-to-reach pockets in the middle of a river or along the far bank that hold the good ones. A nine- or ten-pound line is heavy enough to hold any trout that swims and it's small enough to be inconspicuous in the water.

If a heavier line is used, especially a braided

one, about six feet of monofilament should be tied on the end as a leader. The two can be secured by means of a blood knot, which will run through the guides smoothly.

Lures are legion. There's an endless number of spoon designs alone. I have had good luck with the smaller sizes of various trolling spoons, like those designed for lake trout and for Pacific salmon. The action of these spoons is perfect. Their light weight gives them the enticing motion in the water—but also makes them difficult to cast. The heavier casting spoon mentioned earlier may not have as deadly an action as some others, but it has advantages that outweigh this. It has the weight to give ease and accuracy to the cast and also to carry it deep in the water—a very important feature. Big trout lie deep.

There are a number of small-mouth bass plugs which will take trout. The best—a small, diving, wiggling, plastic affair—happens to be the most popular of the bass plugs. It's a fish killer on almost any kind of game fish. Personally, though, I don't like the way a plug handles in fast water as well as I do a spoon, and it always seemed too bad to me to put so many hooks in a trout's mouth, no matter how big he might be.

Many light lures—spinners, small spoons, and even flies—can be used on a bait-casting rod effectively by placing a half-ounce dipsey or bell sinker on a dropper about two feet ahead of the lure. This serves a double purpose. First, it gives the necessary weight to cast the small lure; second, it carries the lure deep in the hole or pool where it will do the most good, and where the fly fisherman has difficulty fishing.

Where

There are really only two excuses for using the bait-casting rod on trout: one is to take large, cannibal trout, the other is to reach trout unavailable to the fly-rod fisherman. Only in rare instances will a bait-casting rod be advisable in the eastern United States. With the obvious exception of the Sault Sainte Marie Rapids in Michigan, there are no trout rivers in the eastern United States so large that they cannot be covered satisfactorily with a fly rod. I do know of a few Maine lakes where the squaretails would be quite susceptible to a casting spoon, but I also know that on certain calm evenings in June these same squaretails cruise and feed heavily on floating May flies. It would be little short of criminal to kill trout with a casting rod that could be taken so delightfully on a dry fly.

The where of bait casting for trout is the West —in the Rockies, the Northwest, British Columbia, and Alaska where there are many waters suited to little else than bait-casting or spinning tackle; where some rivers are completely brush lined and others are simply too big, fast, and deep for delicate fly work; and where, also, in many large lakes and reservoirs the trout feed almost entirely on smaller fish of one kind or another and are therefore of limited interest to the fly fisherman. Bait casting in lakes, along with other forms of lake fishing, will be covered in a later chapter. Here we are concerned with taking trout in mighty western rivers where both the water and the fish are too rough for fly-rod results.

How

Bait casting is an incidental method of taking trout compared to fly fishing, and a basic knowledge of the principles of bait casting is assumed to be possessed by anyone planning to give it a try; therefore, the only point to be stressed along these lines is the matter of accuracy. Pin-point accuracy is often very important to success on trout. Nothing will make a trout lose his appetite so quickly as a casting spoon or plug splashing in calm water alongside him. In no time he'll be under the nearest rock wondering what missed him. Yet the same plug or spoon dropped a couple of feet away in broken water and tumbled into the calm water of the trout's haven might be his undoing. Accuracy and a certain amount of finesse must be mastered.

The most accurate cast is a direct overhead cast. The cast is started with the rod pointed in the direction of the intended target; then, in an almost continuous motion, the forearm and wrist are brought back rather sharply to cock the rod over the shoulder and snapped forward to the original position to make the cast. As in fly casting, the cast is made with the wrist and forearm. If the overhead cast is made in a true perpendicular plane, as it should be, there will be no lateral error in the cast. The only remaining factor to be controlled for bull's-eye accuracy is distance. This is the most accurate cast and will be

This fine rainbow was taken in the Andes of South America. The bait-casting outfit shown here should be reserved for big meat-eating trout in deep water and for the occasional inaccessible spot out of casting reach of other equipment, as was the case in this instance.

used wherever possible, but the trout fisherman working along a brushy stream will also become proficient at a variety of other casting forms, such as the sidearm, backhand, underhand, and even slingshot cast.

Distance can also be important. In some western canyons where the fisherman might have access to one side of the river only, a man who can sling a spoon like a major league outfielder can work some seldom-fished spots. With a free-running reel, a light line, and a heavy spoon, a fifty-yard cast is not unreasonable. Such a fishing range gives the bait caster a great advantage over other fishermen. On some rivers too turbulent for boats and too heavy for wading I feel

quite certain that on many occasions I have fished virgin water, simply by casting a spoon beyond the limits of range of the fly fisherman and bait fisherman. The response of the trout in such out-of-the-way spots would seem to bear out the hunch. In a stream of moderate width, the bait caster with both distance and accuracy will find that he can work the holes along the far bank more effectively than those on his own side of the stream, and in many such cases the far shore is seldom fished by others.

The efficient bait caster must learn to pick his spots. A spoon or plug is not effective over nearly so wide a variety of water as is the fly or the spinner. The bait caster will look for deep holes. Large, deep pools are ideal, but there are also numerous likely holes throughout the broken water. The deep holes often appear slick on top and they are found behind boulders, behind shore projections, in eddies and backwaters, along swift runs, under cut banks, and below sharp breaks in the stream. The calm spots behind rocks may fill up with gravel in certain streams with the result that there is a bar where a hole might be expected. In the big rivers of northern Canada, the point where two currents join in a big pool, the point of the V they form, is a likely spot to look for a big brookie.

It takes experience to pick out such productive spots, and even then it is easy to miss some of the best ones. I recall a perfect hole under a slick no more than six feet long and a couple of feet wide that I stumbled on—in fact, almost stumbled into—quite by accident. It was on the near side of a heavy run and I was attempting to wade as close to the run as possible in order to hold my line in the air over the fast water while fishing the far side with a dry fly. When I was close enough to see that the water under the slick was five or six feet deep instead of the expected two, it was too late to fish it. I returned in the evening a couple of days later, approached it properly and took a 4½-pound brown.

A good spoon hole does not have to be big, but it must be deep. Three feet of water is the minimum for consistent results, and five or six feet is best. This does not mean that large trout do not feed in shallow water, because they often do, but a fish lying or cruising in shoal water will shy much more readily than one in deep water. A spoon cast in shallow water might give a trout the jitters, whereas the same trout in the security of a deep hole could be tempted into striking.

Controlled fishing—the efficient selection of spots to fish and a planned and methodical approach—will pay off many times against hasty, random fishing. After choosing a likely hole it is well worth several moments' consideration as to the best possible cast and, if necessary, is worth all the time devoted to maneuvering to the best place from which to make the cast. The first cast is worth as much as the next nine put together.

A 31¼″ rainbow from the Newalen River, Alaska. On the racks are split salmon drying at an Indian camp.

Bait casters who are accustomed to working the still water of lakes will find stream fishing a bit difficult at first. What appears to be a well-placed lure may be grabbed out of position almost immediately when the current takes hold of the belly in the line. The current can easily take the play away from the fisherman and race the lure at a speed beyond all possibility of getting a strike. When the fisherman no longer has control over the speed and action of his lure, he's had it. He might as well retrieve as quickly as possible and try somewhere else. With a little study, however, he can often make the current work for him rather than against him. If this is impossible, often he can keep control if he spans a heavy current with his line by holding the rod tip high.

The greatest secret to success with a spoon is the ability to make it tumble. The spoon should come to a trout—preferably from upcurrent—in a tumbling, falling-leaf manner, as though it were helpless. It must be kept in mind constantly that a trout is a shy creature and that a casting spoon is a large lure. From the very start of things for a trout, it's eat or be eaten, and anything as startling as a vigorously moving spoon can easily make him take shelter. Never rush a spoon directly at a trout; he'll think it's after him.

The ability to tumble a spoon calls for accuracy in casting and complete control. If the current can be made to work for the fisherman so that he can keep control over a long stretch, it is advisable to lead the trout's station by a wide margin so that there is no danger of startling him when the spoon hits the water. If the intervening currents are such that a controlled float can be maintained for a few feet only, pin-point casting accuracy is essential. The fisherman might as well not cast at all if he drops the spoon in the slick itself, so he must hit the boiling water at the far edge of the slick and tumble the spoon into the hole. Often when a trout is lying along a rock, ledge, or bank, it is possible to hit the spoon against the object just above the water line so that it will slip into the water quietly.

When a spoon is tumbling correctly into a current, the line is barely taut. There's no danger of missing a strike because a trout hits the spoon hard, and you either have him or you don't. No finesse is required in the hooking. Sometimes a controlled, tumbling float can be extended by allowing line to flow from the reel under a light thumb pressure. In order to get the proper action I generally cast directly across stream or quartering up. The best brown I ever took on a spoon was from a position that forced me to cast directly upstream.

When the spoon is cast across stream, it is allowed to tumble with the current under light tension as far as possible; then, of course, it is allowed to swing across the stream and it is retrieved from below. If it is being retrieved through likely water, it is advisable to continue the tumbling operation by alternately raising the rod tip and allowing it to drop while reeling in. This is especially productive when retrieving a spoon across a deep, still pool.

When the current has taken charge by sweeping the belly of the line downstream, as is the case a good percentage of the time in a heavy stream, many trout will be seen flashing and turning behind the spoon. Whether they are wary of the spoon because of its vigorous action or whether they are actually attempting to hit the spoon but cannot because of its speed, I do not know; however, one is rarely hooked at such a time. I have sometimes seen as many as forty or fifty trout in a half mile of stream behave in this fashion, and have certainly not hooked more than one in ten. I almost feel that I'm conducting a stream survey. Occasionally I have spotted a big trout in such a way and have returned at a later date and caught him by a more careful approach.

All this may sound as though a good fisherman with a bait-casting outfit and a spoon can play havoc with a stream, and it's true. The one thing I can say in defense of my using such an outfit and in defense of fishing companions who have worked out similar tactics is that we release the majority of trout taken. I have never carried a creel when using a casting rod and never intend to. If I take a trout big enough that I must keep him, I certainly don't mind stopping fishing and carrying him back to the car.

A while back on the Big Hole in Montana I met a doubtful fisherman. He asked what luck, and I replied that I had taken a few. He saw I had no creel and asked where they were. The attitude he took when I told him I had returned them was rather disrespectful to say the least. Then I started fishing in earnest. I picked out a perfect hole, studied the currents for several minutes before making a cast and fortunately dropped the spoon just right. The trout was a big one and by the time I landed him the character was alongside me as excited as a ten-year-old at the circus. By the way he acted I gathered that it was a bigger trout than he had ever seen caught, and when I eased him off the hook and slipped him back in the water his eyes bugged out so that they could have been knocked off with a stick. Under any other condition I admit I might have kept that trout. I hope I taught the gentleman some manners.

That also happened to be a brown; however, in my experience, the casting spoon has been far more effective on rainbows and big brookies than on brown trout. Most of the good browns I have been fortunate to take have been on a fly rod and a relatively small fly. I have accounted for only one big one—over five pounds—on a spoon. On the other hand, I have taken a number of larger brookies—although I don't enjoy the admission of treating as beautiful a fish as a brook trout in such a manner—and by far the majority of the big rainbows I have taken, many over ten pounds, have come via a spoon.

If I have approached this subject of bait casting rather apologetically, it is because I realize that it is a deadly and not particularly sporting method of taking trout. I believe that most sportsmen will instinctively realize this. The trout is primarily a fish to be caught by casting with a fly. Bait casting may be more rewarding to the stomach but less rewarding to the soul. The trout has certain incomparable attributes when played on light fly tackle. These are speed, grace, and endurance. He is a relatively delicate game fish, however, and when hooked on harsh and stubborn tackle or when his mouth is gagged open by a spoon or plug, his performance is poor. Some fish, such as pike, which fight with rushing, savage, head-shaking tactics, put on a better show against the short rod than the fly rod, but not so trout. Therefore, the fisherman who takes trout on coarse tackle inevitably loses some of the charm of trout fishing. The man who fishes by this method indiscriminately must have the ability to use some discretion in the size and number of fish he keeps.

Chapter 18

FLOATING, TUBING, AND ICE FISHING

Ever since Noah pulled the first pair of Caspian catfish aboard, the idea of fishing from a boat has gained in popularity. Some people wouldn't consider fishing by any other means, but most trout fishermen find a boat either too restrictive or too much of a burden to buy and keep. This does not mean that they cannot enjoy its advantages occasionally by renting a boat on a lake or floating with a guide. Even more appealing to the trout-fishing enthusiast (and within the pocketbook range of almost everyone) is tubing.

Floating and tubing are two comparatively recent developments in the age-old history of boat fishing. The term "floating" refers to drifting down a stream or river for trout, generally on one of our larger western rivers and under the conduct of a licensed guide. Tubing, in contrast, is strictly an individual effort, practiced on ponds and lakes from just what the name indicates, an inflated inner tube. Don't be misled by the primitive transport; tubing can be great fun!

Floating

Floating, in its broad meaning, is an old practice. Rivers have been floated for trout in Maine and Canada by canoe for many generations, but the canoe has been used primarily as a means of transportation to reach areas remote from road or trail. Some fishing may be done from the canoe, but only one member of the party can fish at a time, and for the most part, both members have to handle paddles to get from one camping or fishing spot to the next.

Chilean rivers have been floated for trout for many years also, and there the fishing is done from the boat. It is a relaxed way of fishing since the hired guide does all the work at the oars and in effect does most of the fishing itself. It is an unusual and very effective method. The oarsman keeps the prow of the boat headed upstream all day while one or two fishermen sit in the stern facing downstream with flies trailing in the water below. The oarsman rows just hard enough into the current to keep the lines and flies extended downcurrent while the boat drifts slowly down, stern first. And more than just rowing constantly all day, he moves the boat back and forth around the river to sweep or drop the flies into the best trout lies. The fishermen just sit there and admire the scenery, as in trolling on a lake, until the oarsman puts a fly into a trout's mouth—something which occurs with considerable regularity.

Only a few Chilean rivers in total are floated because there are not enough roads to the rivers, and of course such a float trip requires both a starting and a pick-up spot on the river accessible by road. The area between these terminals where the float is made is generally remote country inaccessible by other means. It makes for a beautiful and bountiful trip even if the fisherman is left with somewhat less than a feeling of accomplishment.

In contrast to much of Canada and Chile, if there is anything we in the United States have, it is roads, and too many of them! Where there may not be enough to suit an individual, we are even inclined to permit the unchecked use of all-terrain vehicles to make their own tracks wherever they please.

I have been a lifelong advocate of using one's own legs. The rewards in life are often directly related to the commitment and effort expended to attain them. Should a non-fisherman be trolled around a lake and land a four-pound trout, he couldn't possibly appreciate it as would a dry-fly fisherman who has struggled at length with a recalcitrant trout. By effort, I don't mean that one should waste energy, say by walking down a road to the river, but where the road ends a fisherman's opportunities should commence. If I am willing to walk a mile farther than others, I expect the fishing to justify it; and if the next fellow outwalks me, he should reap his reward. This philosophy becomes ever more important since fewer and fewer places remain, outside wilderness areas, where the trout fisherman can be rewarded by the solitude, the purity, and the calm of the unfrequented spot.

For this and other reasons, I am not enthusiastic about the organized floating popular on some of the best western trout rivers. In many cases, the areas fished by this method could easily be reached by a pair of healthy legs. Floating destroys the desire or even the inclination of the most enthusiastic fisherman to do much more than get out of his own tracks. Why walk an hour if boat after boat of fishermen hit the same spot more effectively and with no effort? Since floating is so effective, sections of some rivers are occasionally given a rest for a year, but this action is not taken for the benefit of the foot fisherman; it merely permits that section to recover sufficiently for the next floating season.

This is my prejudice, but, viewed with less bias, floating has unquestionably diminished the quality of fishing on many rivers in heavily fished areas readily available by road. Trout exercise territorial rights, or "pecking orders," just as do other animals from chipmunks to bears. The best trout in a pool claims the best feeding spot. If he is taken from there by a fisherman, another trout almost his match is ready to fill his fins immediately. Then he rules the hole. If good trout are to continue in such prime spots, they must come from somewhere—and they do not come from the hatchery! In an unfloated river, good trout from the unfrequented sections of the same river continuously reoccupy these lies in the overfished sections. And no matter how many enthusiastic, two-legged fishermen there may be on these larger western trout rivers, there are always such unfrequented areas unavailable to them. But virtually nothing is unavailable to floating fishermen, so this natural restocking of the sections most heavily fished is to a large extent eliminated through steady floating.

Having said that, I will try to present some of the good aspects of floating, and there are a number of them.

First, where conducted as an individual effort rather than a commercial enterprise, it will not be overdone to the point of depleting a stream. Individuals in canoes or small boats are usually in pairs rather than in parties, as is the case in a larger boat controlled by a guide. At least one of these fishermen is constantly preoccupied with the craft while the other fishes. Far more of a handicap than that, such an operation generally calls for a third person to drive down the river after the launch to pick up the fishermen at their destination—and such third parties are difficult to find! When it can be worked out, it is an enjoyable experience for all but the third man, who not only couldn't participate but who has to listen to the tall stories of the other two all the way home.

There are also some good things to be said about commercial floating. As we have said, floating is an extremely effective method of fishing—as long as the particular river is floated with some discretion. Not only does the fisherman reach all of the river with ease but his approach from the river toward shore is more effective than casting from shore out. Second, as in the Chilean float trips, it provides an opportunity for an inexperienced, unskilled fisherman to get trout. Third, it almost always makes for an enjoyable scenic ride with the possibility of viewing river wildlife better than the foot fisherman can. Wild creatures respect and fear man when he approaches them on his two feet, but man in the disguise of the constant traffic on roads or in a parade of boats on a river is much less threatening. Animals must accept his presence or die of starvation in hiding.

Generally two types of boats are used in commercial floating, and the use of one or the other depends on the nature of the water being floated. One is the inflatable raft, which is easy to transport and can handle rough water safely as well as float over shallows. The second is a specially designed river boat. It is heavy and a bother to transport, but it is the better of the two for the fisherman since he sits high enough to see and cast comfortably.

Tubing

I would like to know the man who first rigged a saddle inside a truck inner tube, took a rod in hand, and launched his unlikely craft in search of new horizons. From this imaginative, adventurous individual's crude beginning has evolved a safe and delightful new approach to trout fishing in ponds and lakes.

No one has to make up his own tubing outfit today; many models are available in tackle stores ready to launch except for the air. It begins with the tube, which has a protective cover as well as the saddle, or seat, and the cover which has pockets for tackle and even for a spare tube in some models. This is the complete "boat," hundreds or thousands of dollars less expensive than other fishing boats. However, tubing equipment doesn't end there. Trout thrive only in cold water; so stocking-foot waders are worn to keep the water out, and insulated long underwear and heavy socks are worn to keep the warmth in. Swim fins for the feet complete the outfit. The tube is easily transported to the lake, where it must be pumped up. To facilitate this, a small compressor electrically powered from a car's cigarette lighter is available.

Although some fishermen float slow streams, tubing any moving water is definitely not recommended since it could prove dangerous or even disastrous if the fisherman were to get his feet tangled in weeds or among rocks. Beyond that, such streams are not large enough to accommodate both tubers and waders. The tubers wouldn't give themselves any real advantage, but they would disturb the fishing of others. Even on a pond or lake a tuber should remain well beyond the casting range of shore fishermen. Just as no one should usurp a pool or run already occupied by another fisherman, anyone in a boat or tube should respect the domain of those on shore. This is just plain courtesy.

Except when it is done on moving water, tubing is a much healthier activity than it might at first appear to the observer. Precaution is necessary only in shallow water, as when getting launched. As clear a bottom as possible should be chosen; then the proper method of entering the water is to back in, something which any skin diver who wears flippers knows. Flippers are a delight in the water and a misery underfoot, which is exactly where they are when a

A tube fisherman is so much a part of the scenery that he doesn't even stretch the necks of nearby teal and mallards.

person tries to take a step forward. In fact, I think ducks might do better walking backward, but that is their problem. There is no question about tubers. They should always enter the water slowly and backward to avoid tripping, and they should remember to do the same when returning to shore.

Aside from these considerations, all experienced tubers agree that their method is safer than boating. You cannot fall overboard; the tuber is already overboard comfortably surrounded by his individual life raft. Also, a tuber has his center of gravity below waterline, so his

A tuber goes to the action wherever it may be.

One in the bag for a tube fisherman.

is a stable craft which will outride many small boats on rough water. And he is not about to run out of gasoline or lose his paddle, and neither is there any way that he can take on water and swamp.

Nevertheless, it is advisable for tubers to carry inflatable life jackets and to fish in pairs. Help is usually needed in either launching or landing, but even when safely afloat, a tuber should have a companion. Should anything go amiss, one of the two tubes is ample to float two people. Besides that, it is always more enjoyable to share an adventure. Fortunately, my wife is every bit as enthusiastic a fisherman as I am, so I have no problems. Being conservative, we prefer ponds and smaller lakes, ideally those which have relatively shallow water and weed beds extending some distance out from shore, but many tubers take on the largest lakes they can find. The only thing to beware of, really, would be a severe squall with lightning, but this obvious precaution applies equally to all open-boat fishing.

There is nothing special about the manner of fishing. Almost all tubers are fly fishermen, but this is true only because they are the most advanced of trout fishermen and they are open to new ideas. Tubing is equally adapted to spinning and even bait fishing, for that matter. It is the manner of transportation which is special and effective. Anyone who has done any scuba diving knows how effortless his maneuverability becomes after short acquaintance, and the same is true of tubing. Moving about as one fishes becomes as free and automatic as walking, and fishing from within the tube makes lake fishing take on an entirely new and exciting perspective.

Ice Fishing

A trout is the superb game fish he is because of his essential qualities of awareness, caution, and discernment before he takes a fly or lure, and his speed, grace, and endurance after he has taken one. None of these fine attributes plays any role whatsoever when a trout is taken through the ice. However, a trout has other characteristics which lend themselves to this manner of fishing. Number one is that he is a cold-water fish, active and feeding to some degree in the coldest of water. Number two is that a trout is a delicious fish to eat, and he cannot be firmer of flesh or more succulent than when taken from the coldest of water. Third, at any place and at any time of year, a trout is a beautiful fish to behold.

Ice fishing is permitted only at limited locations, usually on a lake which is amply populated or even overpopulated to the degree that the fish might become stunted. Some ice fishing is practiced in lakes or reservoirs where there is no natural spawning and which are stocked regularly with fingerlings. An abundant food supply will permit year-round fishing with no possible

Ice fisherman and fish, auger to left. Note the fresh coyote tracks, lower right.

danger of harming the natural or fut
pects of the water. When such a situa
exist, anyone who likes fresh air an
should take advantage of it. It is tota
any other trout fishing and it cannot
too seriously, which is one of its best as

In fact, ice fishing is not only unlike
trout fishing, it is outlandish! One of
popular baits is whole-kernel cann
Imagine it! It's a disgrace to trout as a
even to the entire fishing fraternity.
wife tells me, don't fight it. That's the
so relax and enjoy it.

Other baits are salmon eggs and wo
specialists combine a delicacy consi
small bit of worm together with one s
I forget which item is placed on the
and as this is an essential part of the
blown it. Otherwise, the mechanics o
are not too complex.

iggles.

An important item of equipmen
auger which will drill a hole six or
in diameter, although some optimist
or chain saw to cut a hole large en
out a seal. Another requirement is a
folding chair in order not to strai

a bucket in which to build
t one's delicate fingers don't
oves to keep the same from
lace of the gloves, a scooper
ce chips. Finally, and by far
is a big lunch and a bottle
unimportant, though I do
ellent ice-fishing outfits. I
ete—rod, reel, and line—for

There's no better excuse to get out in the ... *n Holland in action.*

$4.98 plus sales tax. It was on sale, however. The other outfit, perhaps a little too fancy for the purpose, cost $7.97 complete. In fact, judging solely from the number of nibbles I miss, I am convinced that trout in the daze of winter prefer split shot to either salmon eggs or corn.

Just for the fun of it—and that is exactly what ice fishing is—I have caught trout by jigging a lead minnow pounded and shaped from a one-inch sinker and also by jigging a small spoon, but trout are so sluggish in such cold water that they can barely tap a lure, much less strike it. Twenty such gentle taps are missed for every one hooked. Since it is impossible for me to sit still and hope something will happen, I am either foolishly jigging or I am drilling new and better holes until the lake is a hazard.

Trout are obviously attracted to bait in ice fishing solely by odor. It is impossible to imagine who could possibly have been so ignorant as to try a kernel of canned corn for the first time. No trout ever saw, tasted, or envisioned in wild dreams any such thing, but corn smells like food, evidently. Worms smell right, too, and salmon eggs are doctored to smell particularly appetizing, but nothing has the allure of canned corn. My wife Jean, who is a master at preparing trout and who therefore will stoop to almost anything to bring home a pair, goes Niblets one better. Izaak Walton three hundred years ago knew that the oil of anise attracted trout, but maybe it cost only a few pence in his time. Today it ranks with Parisian perfume. This discovery didn't dismay Jean. She went from the bad news at the pharmacy directly to the market and bought a cheap bottle of anise extract. She marinates the corn in this, and it works.

When dinner is on ice, it's time to relax and enjoy it all. Jean Holland at rest.

All other considerations aside, getting out on a high mountain lake in the sharp, clear air of midwinter is food for the soul. Our favorite little ice-fishing lake neighbors another on which there is always some open water due to hot springs, and a few Canadian geese winter there. We often hear coyotes sing as well as the geese honking, and there is no music to match these two wild sounds. And, thanks to my scheming and remorseless wife, we always bring home at least a couple of fat trout for her to stuff and bake for a banquet money could not buy. Ice fishing can be fun and filling.

Chapter 19

LAKE FISHING

Lake fishing for trout is a distinct field of sport in itself, about as different from stream fishing as big-game hunting is from upland hunting, and so it must be treated separately. The lake habitat results in a difference not only in the tackle and technique employed but in the behavior of the trout themselves.

The one most universal and singular characteristic of the trout is his shyness, but even this trait varies with the water in which he lives. He is most retiring in shallow, clear water, and the less confining his surroundings the bolder he becomes. In an open lake he remains cautious, but with the haven of deep water close at hand he is considerably less wary than when living in a stream.

All creatures—not man alone—have a native curiosity. Nova Scotia duck hunters use a small dog, called a tolling dog, which runs up and down a beach in front of the blind and actually decoys the curious birds from off the bay. Caribou can occasionally be brought up within easy range simply by the sporadic flicking of a white handkerchief. Certainly many of the most successful bass lures operate solely on the principle of arousing the fish's curiosity and pugnacity, for they look like nothing the good Lord ever let live. And this inquisitiveness is no less true of most other fish. I recall swimming deep underwater in a clear Pacific lagoon and opening my eyes to behold a semicircle of small, pop-eyed golden fish inspecting me curiously a foot from my face. My immediate reaction was to get back in my own element.

Under normal stream conditions, however, a trout's shyness overcomes his curiosity. He is prompted to pursue and strike a lure by one motive, and that is the lure's reasonable imitation of a natural food. But in the safety of deep lake waters a trout's curiosity may come to the fore. I have carelessly dropped a heavy lure, like a spinner, too close to a cruising trout in a lake and startled him into dashing off, only to have him turn about at the end of his run, return curiously to the scene of the splash and take the lure. Such a thing would never happen in shallow stream surroundings. A startled trout there remains startled for several minutes.

A trout living in a small, clear pond or mountain lake will behave quite similarly to a stream trout because his habitat, except for the lack of running water, is much the same, but the larger the lake or reservoir, the more unique become his actions. In some large lakes with an abundance of school fish for food, such as the Great Lakes or Pend Oreille Lake in Idaho, the trout take up an existence almost identical to that of their migratory cousins living in the ocean. Their entire existence centers around the pursuit and consumption of the sawbellies, smelt, little redfish, or whatever the school fish may be. These trout attain very large size and can be compared only with steelhead and salmon while in the sea, and not with ordinary stream trout as we know them. Lake fishing, and each form of lake fishing, requires its own peculiar approach.

Dry Fly

The dry fly is of very limited use in lake fishing, and as a rule the larger the lake the less the opportunity for the floating fly. I say this in spite of the fact that some of the most delightful fishing I have ever known was on a lake and with a dry fly, specifically, on a calm day when a cruising trout's speed and direction can be gauged—and anticipated!—by his sporadic rises as he approaches.

I have taken a number of trout on a dry fly in small, clear lakes where the movements and reactions of the fish could be observed clearly, and I have taken a few by casting hopefully into a heavy hatch where the trout of a large lake were feeding freely. Sometimes along the windy shore during such a heavy hatch, trout will gather and feed on the windrows of insects. I've seen western lakes at such a time when it looked as if a thousand trout were rising, but casting a dry fly into such a melee and allowing it to sit is like shooting into the middle of a covey: it rarely seems to connect.

A dry fly should be allowed to float free and unmolested. The best way in the world to put down a feeding stream trout is to drag a dry fly across him unnaturally. But since trout in lakes, especially in large lakes, are bolder than stream trout, they are often victims of the unorthodox. When nothing else succeeds, a dragged fly on a calm lake surface often works. This is especially true just about dusk when the visibility is failing. This maneuver is most effective if the leader is sunk and so is not made conspicuous by being dragged along the surface, and the fly should not be moved rapidly but little more than twitched occasionally to attract the attention of a neighboring trout.

Dapping: British fishermen developed a method of fishing a dry fly on the Scottish lochs which overcomes this static quality of a floating fly on still waters. It is known as dapping. I have never succeeded in applying the system successfully in this country, but I am sure that it has possibilities.

Dapping is practiced from a boat where there are rising trout and a fairly brisk breeze. The line is very light and the leader long. The fly and line are allowed to be carried down wind from the boat by the strength of the wind alone; and, as a flag flaps in the wind, the line will wave in the breeze and bounce the fly here and there along the surface. The fly thus covers a lot of ground, like a female May fly depositing her eggs and, instead of dragging along the surface, it hops from spot to spot.

In dry-fly fishing a stream, I have often succeeded in making a fly hop by sending a snake-hump down the line with a twist of the wrist just before the fly touches the surface. This wave in the line reaches the fly just after it drops to the surface, picks it up again and bounces it along for a foot or two. When timed perfectly, such a fly behaves momentarily as a dapping fly

does, and it's deadly effective; so I am sure that anyone who can learn to dap a fly in the breeze among the rising trout of a lake will make a killing. Many open western lakes where a breeze springs up just after sunset, when the hatch is at its heaviest, would be ideal for dapping.

For the most part, however, and certainly for all random fishing, the dry fly has little place in lake fishing. The reason is obvious: too little ground can be covered with it. In a stream the current floats the fly past the waiting trout; in a lake it gets nowhere. Unless a dry fly is fished unnaturally and dragged on the surface, in the manner of a bass bug, or unless it is dapped, it just sits on the spot where it is cast. The fisherman must have good reason to believe that that particular spot contains a surface-feeding trout which might fancy just such a dry fly, or he's wasting his time.

Wet Fly

The wet fly is the fly-rod fisherman's best method of taking trout in a lake. Some men are good at it, some aren't. I don't claim to belong to the first group. With perseverance and variety I can eventually take my share, but the results are so inconsistent that I continually realize I have a lot to learn. Hank Doremus and I were helping out during a roundup on the Grand Mesa in Colorado some years ago, and after a week's steady diet of salt pork we figured some trout might go well. Of course we had trout tackle with us. That's a habit of ours. And although we probably hadn't been too helpful at rounding up cattle, we did think we knew something about catching trout. We started out at dawn for the nearby Mesa Lakes whose water is so clear that the numerous trout appeared almost to be floating in air. By noon our confidence in taking a big mess of trout had waned, and by late afternoon we were satisfied to return with one trout for each man in the roundup gang.

Years ago when I first fished with Ted Trueblood, he told me all about lake fishing, but I didn't listen. I had to dub around and try to learn for myself. I guess I doubted that he or anyone else could catch trout consistently in a lake; then, when he told me it was easy, I was all the more suspicious. I knew different. At least I was polite enough to ask how. He used a long leader and a small fly, he told me, and he laid

Lake fishing is a specialty. Finding the spots feeding trout frequent is not as easy as reading a stream. A man needs considerable experience on any one lake. On certain calm evenings when fish are rising, however, as here on Meadow Lake, Montana, the stranger is in luck.

This scene is Lake Maule in far-off Chile, but trout follow definite patterns according to conditions wherever they are found. In lake fishing, for instance, the reef just off a rocky point is often a hot spot, as two men in this boat can testify. In fact, the fisherman in the middle is about to be pulled flat on his face by a charging rainbow.

out a long line. That much I knew was true because I had done a lot of stream fishing with him. I had seen him work out so much line that I looked around for witnesses. Then he said that he gave the leader and fly ample time to sink, and he retrieved the fly ever so slowly, not by conventional stripping but by an alternate weaving motion of the left hand. The first part of this technique I eventually learned for myself on the little Quebec lake, but the second part—even though he had described it to me in plain English—I never did master on my own.

For some reason it was about fifteen years before I happened to do any lake fishing for trout with Ted. Now I've seen him operate on two greatly contrasting types of trout lakes. One was a series of high mountain lakes in the Bridger Wilderness area of Wyoming where the water was as clear and flawless as the mountain air itself. The other was on weed-choked, algae-coated Henry's Lake—as "thick" water as ever a trout lived in. And, so help me, it is easy. Just as he claimed years ago, Ted can catch trout in a

lake as long as there are any left. And now, after watching him in action, even I can do a pretty fair job on a lake.

The technique is exactly as he first outlined except that now he has added to it the great advantage of a sinking fly line: a long cast is made, the line and fly given time to sink, and the retrieve is slow. The rod is pointed almost directly at the fish when the retrieve is made so that there is a direct pull from hand to fly. This way, when a fish strikes, he hooks himself. The fly should look natural, like a nymph or shrimp.

For those who lack the perseverance to learn this slow-motion (until the trout is hooked) technique, larger and more conspicuous fly patterns are in order. These are known as the attractor-type flies, which are better adapted to large water than small. In a stream, the currents tell a fisherman almost the exact position of a feeding fish and he can put a fly to him accordingly. In a lake, he may have to attract a trout from a considerable distance.

For this type fishing, large flies—as big as No.

6s—in bright patterns, such as steelhead or salmon flies, work best. A sinking line again is a help. Also, on the retrieve the rod is pointed almost directly at the fly. The line is carried through the middle finger of the right hand holding the rod, then is retrieved in short, sharp jerks by the left hand. The slack so retrieved is allowed to fall loosely at the feet or on the bottom of the boat, as the case may be.

When trout subsist on a strictly meat diet, as is the case in many large lakes, the fly fisherman really has his troubles. Often the school fish on which the trout live, such as the little redfish, remain deep; then the trout are out of the fly fisherman's hands and in the province of the deep troller, for wherever the small fish are, there will be the feeding trout.

Occasionally, however, the school fish will work into the shallows and then a fly-rod man can get in on the fun. This is more a matter of chance than anything else with the common food fish—such as smelt, redfish, ciscoes and the like—but one little school fish called a sawbelly doesn't necessarily remain deep. I knew one man who proved that they didn't limit such lake fishing to the troller. The sawbelly is a small, shiny form of herring, and this inventive fisherman fashioned a replica of a sawbelly out of balsa wood, mounted it on a bass-bug hook, painted it silver, and caught more big trout than anyone on the lake. Of course to use such a lure, or a bucktail or streamer, successfully under such special conditions, the fisherman must study his lake and the habits of the food fish thoroughly so that he will know where and when the big trout will be feeding in shallow water.

A better opportunity for the fly fisherman lies in lakes where there is no single item of ideal food, such as the sawbelly, smelt, or little redfish. There the trout may still feed extensively on minnows, but most native minnows live singularly and in shallow water, and in such conditions the fly fisherman can work the shore line at random with a bucktail or spinner and pick up good fish.

Spoon

Maybe it's because I don't know any better, and maybe I have a lot to learn, but I've never taken any stock in the statement: "Brother, in this lake you gotta use bait." I have yet to see the conditions where a good man with artificials couldn't hold his own or do better than the best man with bait. That's why I can never support any argument demanding that bait fishermen be outlawed from a certain stretch of water. If bait fishermen are outlawed, then certain forms of artificial-lure fishing such as spinning, bait casting, and trolling should be outlawed as well. Limiting certain small areas to fly fishing only is fine, because a trout is essentially a fly-rod fish, but outlawing bait and allowing the indiscriminate use of all artificials is ridiculous.

I like to find trout waters where the fish cannot be taken on artificials. The last such place I found was a western reservoir about eight miles long. The favorite outfit on the lake was an ungainly looking rig consisting of a single salmon egg trolled behind two huge three-inch attractor spinners. The first time I tried the lake, after being told I might as well take my gadgets home, I selected a long arm of land that extended a third of a mile into the lake and dropped off rather steeply at the end. I assumed that any cruising trout might strike this spit of land and be forced to detour around its tip to continue on its way. This may have been the case, or I may have just accidentally happened on a natural feeding ground. The water was calm when I arrived early in the morning and there was no sign of moving fish. I tried a fly for a few minutes without confidence and without results. Then, because I was anxious to prove a point, I shifted to a casting rod and spoon and began dredging for them. Those bait-eating rainbows went wild! In an hour and a half I landed three trout which would have made my ten-pound limit, kept one four-pounder, and carelessly lost a spoon in a really beautiful fish. The accepted bait-eating myth had kept this lake virgin territory for the artificial-lure fisherman.

The spoon-casting technique is quite simple. The outfit and the lure are the same as described for stream fishing in the chapter on "Bait Casting." While the smallest standard red-and-white spoon is best for all-round stream fishing, I prefer the medium or large sizes for lake fishing, at least where the trout run from sixteen to twenty inches and maybe bigger. The larger spoon will also give added distance, and I like a long cast in a lake. For one thing, especially on a calm day, a spoon hits the water with a very startling splash, and it is better to drop it well beyond the supposed location of the trout. Also, naturally, a long cast covers a lot of ground.

There is a variety of retrieves that can be employed, but after considerable experimenting I have pared my fishing down to one basic type, and vary it only by depth. This retrieve consists of a sharp spurt and a tumble, brought about by raising the rod tip sharply on a taut line then lowering it and reeling slowly. This procedure is repeated regularly until the spoon is retrieved. The strike generally comes while the spoon is tumbling. Don't worry about missing a strike because of a slight amount of slack while the spoon is tumbling. A trout leaves no doubt when he hits a spoon. He hits to kill.

Other heavy lures, such as devons, small bass plugs, flatfish, and the like, can also be used on a casting rod. I personally have a single-track mind when it comes to this type of fishing and stick to the casting spoon. However, there's no doubt that a spinning outfit with a deep-running devon minnow about two inches long would be effective for lake casting.

Trolling

There are different forms of trolling (i.e., the practice of drawing a lure through the water by means of the motion of a boat either paddled, rowed, or power driven). Some men use flies on a fly rod and merely consider that they are engaging in an extended form of fly fishing. Trolling with a single streamer fly, such as a Gray Ghost, is a common practice in spring in the deep ponds of Maine. When the trout are near the surface and such methods are in order, this use of light tackle is the sportiest of the various forms of trolling. The outfit is identical with that used for fly casting, and the fly is merely allowed to float shallow forty or fifty feet astern of a slowly moving boat.

Other trollers with spinning gear fish somewhat deeper employing light-action trolling spoons, or a minnow behind an Indiana or airplane spinner. Still others go in for deep-water work, sometimes with a wire line and rods and reels similar to those used in salt water. This can hardly be considered light-tackle fishing, but such men are going after trout that could not very well be taken by other means. It requires no skill in hooking or playing a fish but considerable knowledge of the habits of trout when deep.

The trolling method and tackle used depend not so much on the sporting inclinations of the fisherman as upon the demands of the lake: the current depth of the trout. Immediately following ice-out, trout may prefer surface waters because they are warmer, but in midsummer the surface temperatures rise too high in certain lakes and the trout are driven deep. If the water rises to seventy degrees for instance, they won't remain in it for any length of time. They will more likely be at a level where the temperature is around sixty to sixty-five.

Trolling is the best possible way for a beginner at trout fishing to get action. If he teams up with someone who knows the correct rig and location for trolling on any particular lake, his chances of success will be as good as anyone's. For instance, a man who had never before caught a trout could be trolled around Pend Oreille Lake by an experienced hand, and with a stout rod and a salt-water capacity spinning reel he would be in an equal position with others for taking a record rainbow.

Reading a Lake

The broken surface of a stream tells the trout fisherman the nature of the water beneath and the likely locations of feeding fish, but not so the flat surface of a lake. In ponds and small lakes where conditions are suitable throughout, a trout might be anywhere at any time. In a clear mountain lake it is possible to watch a trout cruise around, here and there, shallow and deep, with no apparent purpose other than a random search for food. When conditions are not everywhere suitable, as in the warm summer weather on some of the little raft-sized ponds of New England, a knowledge of the underwater springs is helpful.

Larger lakes have currents around which trout live and feed, but they are imperceptible to the observer. Due to these currents, and probably other factors, there are temperature differences about the lake which attract or repel trout. Some of the bottom may be muddy, other parts rocky. Certain areas produce more trout food than

One of the most promising spots to find feeding trout is where the water accelerates at the natural outlet of a lake.

others. All these factors and others influence the concentration of fish in any one spot. But no man can look at a lake for the first time and pick out the hot spots.

There are a few very general rules that can be followed in attempting to read a new lake. The area around an inlet provides good fishing. If a clear lake can be observed from a high neighboring point, it is sometimes possible to pick out by the tint of the water the rocky shoals extending into the lake or any offshore reefs, which are always good for trolling. If an arm of land protrudes far out into a lake and drops off into fairly deep water at the end, this is generally a good place to fish. Cruising trout must go around such a point of land, and there may also be a current around it. And as a rule a trout shows a definite preference for a clean bottom rather than one of soft mud, but he will be wherever his food of the moment may be, regardless of the nature of the bottom.

Coves, especially if they contain weed beds for insects, are good bets for fly fishing. This is particularly the case in the mornings and evenings. Trout often retire from shoal water during the bright part of the day and work in the shallows between sunset and sunrise. If a breeze is blowing, the trout will likely be to the leeward of a weed bed when the insects are hatching. In the morning and evening calm the fly fisherman has an advantage in that he can spot rising trout for some distance.

All these general rules for reading a lake are contingent on water temperatures. In a lake, as elsewhere, temperature forever governs a trout's activities. In a high mountain lake, up around ten thousand feet, the heat of the day will be the best time for fly fishing, even in midsummer. At lower altitudes the trout may come up within reach of a fly in hot weather only after the sun is down. And at sea level in summer the trout will remain down at trolling depths.

Trying to read any lake at first glance is a haphazard business for any fisherman. Sometimes the contour of the shore will be a key to the character of the bottom, and the shape of an island will indicate whether or not a rocky reef continues from it. A clear pond may indicate the nature of its entire bottom by the shades of blue or green in the water; and if a strike is had over a spot of dark green, for instance, then similar spots around the pond will be the places to fish.

This uncertainty of the location of trout in still waters is one of the reasons that makes trolling the most popular, if least inspiring, method of lake fishing. The troller can cover so much ground with so little effort. He can try the margins of the weed beds, then a rocky shore, then an offshore reef. If these don't produce, he can try over deep water. With two or three lines over at different depths, he can soon explore all possibilities and levels until he locates the trout.

The best possible advice is to try to learn one lake well, and where this isn't in order, take a tip from the local fishermen who have spent years at it. I have found that most of these successful fishermen are more than willing to tell what they know. This may be altruism, or it may be a matter of pride in exhibiting their superior knowledge. But without even asking questions, the newcomer can keep an eye peeled for the fellow who is getting results, then follow his methods.

So much for lake fishing. Most of us characteristically associate trout with broken water and clear, tumbling streams. When he makes his home among the currents and eddies he has his greatest appeal, for there he is unique among the game fish of the world. But a trout doesn't lose his charm when he takes to living in still waters. He presents new problems, often more difficult to solve, and he adds variety to his already colorful personality. Often in a lake a trout may be even more perplexing than in a stream, and therefore even more fascinating.

Chapter 20

LAKE-TROUT FISHING

To say that lake-trout fishing is different from lake fishing for trout would confuse some people, but not a fisherman. A fisherman knows that the lake trout is something special, quite unlike other members of the trout tribe. He knows the lake trout as the largest fresh-water game fish in America, a rather cumbersome giant who lives not in streams with his brother trout but in the cool, dark depths of northern lakes. He may know him by any of a variety of names, such as togue, Mackinaw, Great Lakes trout, lounge, salmon trout, or gray trout, but he could never possibly confuse this trout with other species. Where most of us know him his habits are just about as unlike those of the brook, brown, and rainbow trout as are those of a tuna. Yet he is a trout, a not too distant relative of the dainty little eastern brook trout.

This is primarily an arctic fish, and it is because he can retire to the cold depths that his range extends into our northern tier of states, and this, of course, is where most of our lake-trout fishing is done. In northern Canada and the Arctic, where the water remains cold throughout a lake, he goes only as deep as does his food source. There, where he is more at home, he is more typically troutlike in his habits.

But even in the southern part of his range, enthusiastic lake-trout fishermen prefer this sport to all other forms of angling. This is the deep-sea fishing of fresh water. It requires keen perception and imagination to envision the lake bottom where the fishing is to be done, and success demands considerable knowledge of any one lake and of the habits of the fish. The reward lies in the fascination of solving these dark mysteries of deep water and also in the size of the huge trout, but usually not in the thrill of a light-tackle battle. The lake trout is not spectacular, although a large one will exhibit an amazing amount of power and endurance when not hampered by a load of heavy trolling gear.

Except in the north country, the lake trout rarely lives in lakes with a maximum depth of less than 100 feet and prefers large lakes with a depth of at least 200 feet. He must have very cold water. In midsummer, when most sportsmen have an opportunity to fish for him, this fish is seldom found in less than 60 feet of water and commonly retires to depths 100 to 200 feet below the surface. Commercial fishermen in Lake Superior have taken this fish 750 feet down, although they are not common at a depth over 350 feet. Twice a year they venture onto the shoals, once in the spring and again in the fall.

According to all the books, this fish habitually spawns in still lake waters, so does not participate in an annual spawning run up an inlet stream. In my experience in the North I have found lakers more prevalent in rivers above lakes in the autumn than at any other time, and they are heavy with roe. I suspect that they have a good reason for being there. Nevertheless, it is true that the lake trout—unlike any other species of trout—can live and spawn within a lake and without access to moving water. In lakes their spawning migration is a comparatively short one: from deep water to a nearby shoal of gravel or rough-surfaced rock. Spawning may take place near shore or on an island or, as is often the case in Superior or Great Slave Lake, on a reef many miles offshore. The depth of spawning varies from as little as six feet to as much as one hundred. This operation takes place in the fall, generally in late October or early November, then for the winter the trout return to deeper water. Immediately following ice-out, lake trout can be taken on gravelly shoals in from twenty to sixty feet of water. The biggest fish will remain deep, as these giants venture into shallow water only to spawn, and the top limit for spring shallow-water fishing in the southern part of the range is usually twelve to fifteen pounds.

The farther north a person goes, the shallower the water in which the lake trout lives. Most fishing for lakers is done along the southern limit of their range where the water is so warm that they must remain at extreme depths. Only as far north as the northern shore of Lake Superior do small lakers remain in water shallow enough that they can be taken by casting any time during the summer. As far north as northern Saskatchewan he is an exciting fish. There it isn't unreasonable to expect a thirty-pounder in shallow water.

Trolling

Deep trolling is by far the most widely employed method of taking lake trout. The outfit used is anything but light because the most practical way of trolling the lure sufficiently deep is by means of a metal line. It is possible to use a silk, nylon, or linen line by adding enough weight in the form of sinkers near the lure, but this is not so satisfactory. The light line tends to plane upward when being trolled and it requires too much weight to overcome this action, sometimes as much as a pound. Also the inverted belly in the line so formed cushions a strike and makes it difficult to hook the fish.

Metal lines are of three basic types. One is twisted of many fine wires, laid in the fashion of wire rope or cuttyhunk line. Such twisted lines are commonly of copper and occasionally of a noncorrosive alloy. A twisted metal line is strong and pliable. Another is a lead-core fabric-covered line. The third is a single-filament line, and the best material for the purpose is an alloy known as monel metal. This single-strand monel line has become a great favorite with deep trollers.

The weight of the line is chosen not according

Waterbury Lake in Saskatchewan has some huge lake trout, and guides who know where they are.

to the size fish one expects to catch, but according to the weight necessary to carry it down to the desired depth. Monel lines, for instance, are made as light as three-pound test and are sufficiently pliable to cast on a bait-casting rod, but such a line would not have the weight to sink deep enough for summer trolling. Lake-trout trollers sometimes select lines of fifty-pound tensile strength. No such strain would ever be applied to the line in fighting a fish, of course, but a line of this weight will troll down where the fish live, with little or no additional weight. The lead-core line will penetrate to the greatest depths.

The lake trout is essentially a bottom fish. Even when in shallow water, he stays close to the bottom, leaving it only to pursue ciscoes or whatever else may be his food. Therefore, it is essential in trolling to take the lure down where he can see it. Also, this fish demands very cold water and won't be found in temperatures over 50 degrees. When he is on the reefs just after ice-out, or in late autumn, the water temperature will be 45 degrees or less. In summer the troller must get his lure down to a depth with this temperature. No set rule can be given as to how much line is necessary to accomplish this, as the trout frequent different depths in different localities and seasons. Sometimes 150 feet will suffice, but Great Lakes trollers occasionally use 2,000 feet of line. If the line goes down at a 45-degree angle off the stern of the boat, 200 feet of line overboard should be ample for most waters. The best place to troll is near the bottom along a reef.

Some fishermen troll with bait, such as a smelt, herring, chub, or whitefish. This bait can be hooked in such a manner that it will rotate, or it can be rigged in an English-type spinning harness which has alternate and opposite fins at the head in the form of a propeller. Or the minnow can be trolled directly behind a June-bug or double Indiana spinner for an attractor; or—and this is the strangest-looking contraption ever seen roaming a lake bottom—it can be rigged behind one of those gangling assortments of spinning blades and red beads like the Davis spinner. Large hooks, size 4/0 and 5/0, are standard.

Most trollers prefer spoons to bait—and of course a trolling spoon should never be combined with bait or its action would be impaired.

The most popular summer lake-trout trolling spoons are probably the Jarvinen and the K & B, although many patterns are good. Some of the Pacific salmon spoons, such as the McMahon and the Andy Reeker, can be used but are designed for faster trolling than is most effective on lakers. Three miles per hour or slower is the usual lake-trout speed. An excellent lake-trout spoon, but one which to my knowledge is used only in the Finger Lakes region of New York, is the Keuka Wobbler. This spoon is made in three basic designs and is of extremely light construction so that it will have action at the very slowest speeds. This can be very important. If a person is fairly certain that he is working the correct location and depth of water, it will pay him to troll slowly and thoroughly.

For spring trolling in shallower water, in addition to these spoons, spinners such as the Prescott, Michigan, and Bear Valley are very good. My favorite spinner, and one which I have never seen others use, is the largest Colorado, the size 4, trolled without bait of course. It makes a big fuss at slow speeds; in fact, it spins so freely and has such a drag that it is not practicable to use it at other than slow speeds. Its resistance also tends to make it climb, but in the spring when the lakers are in shoal water this is no great problem. And the trout like it.

The best method of preventing a spoon or other spinning lure from twisting a line is a triangle rig. This consists of a piano-wire triangle with an eye twisted in each corner of the triangle. The trolling line is attached to one eye, the leader wire to another, and a line to a dipsey sinker to the third, the leader and sinker line each being about six feet long. This not only prevents the line from twisting, but can be used as a sounding device to keep the spoon the desired distance from the bottom. In other words, the dipsey sinker is hung on a dropper line just long enough that when it drags bottom the spoon will be trolling a few feet above. This dropper line should be the weakest link in the outfit in case the sinker becomes fouled on the bottom. Some fishermen prefer a keel-shaped aluminum triangle with a hole bored in each corner and rigged in the same manner. Of course, swivels must be placed between the triangle gear and the lure for spinning freedom.

There is sufficient water resistance to a trolling outfit that with sharp hooks the laker will

Harvey Dryden reads these scales at 26 pounds—enough, except that last year a Saskatchewan commercial fisherman caught a lake trout nearby which weighed well over a hundred pounds, more than four times the size of the big one pictured here! It puts a strain on the imagination.

usually hook himself. Trolling tackle is strong enough, however, to come back hard on the rod a couple of times for good luck in case the hook is in the bony part of the mouth.

Still-Fishing

Still-fishing for lakers requires a more intimate knowledge of the habits of these fish than does any other form of lake-trout fishing. The still-fisherman has to be certain that he has selected a trout feeding spot because he covers no ground once he starts fishing. He must do all his exploring before he wets a line, whereas the troller explores as he fishes. Still-fishing has one very pronounced advantage over trolling, and that is the fisherman can use light tackle. For in-

stance, in our Adirondack fishing we used regular bass casting rods, silk line, and a one-ounce sinker to take the bait down the necessary seventy-five feet. A lake trout that wakes up to his plight in time can give a man a fit on such an outfit.

Great Lakes commercial fishermen who use bait have a dainty little rig to overcome the limited range of still-fishing. About every sixteen feet along a heavy trawl line is attached a four-foot light line with hook. Four hundred hooks may be on one box of line, and as many as eight boxes of line may be used. In other words, a line containing over three thousand hooks baited with fish known as bloaters is stretched for miles along the bottom. This is still-fishing in the grand manner.

Ice Fishing

Ice fishing is fun. Where the trout frequent shallow water, the outfit I like best is a portable shanty over a hole in the ice. The dark interior of the shanty makes it possible to look down into clear water a surprising distance. It affords a peephole through the curtain that separates the above-water world from the under-water. There is not so much activity on the lake floor in the winter as in the summer, but certain fish, such as pickerel, perch, walleyes, smelt, ling, and lakers, are on the prod for food. The lake trout will be found on a gravelly or sandy bottom sometimes in forty feet or less of water, and he moves about the lake floor in search of food like a hound on the trail. In a very clear lake his actions can be seen from the ice-fishing shanty and it's exciting business to tempt one over to the bait.

The choice bait is a sucker or chub minnow four to six inches long. It should be hooked lightly through the back so that it will remain alive and active. The outfit is the simplest one possible, merely a hand line. The minnow is generally jigged up and down slightly to attract the laker's attention. Where chumming is permitted, the fish soon learn to frequent a spot where free chow is being served.

Tip-ups can also be used for lakers. Where the water is clear and the trout are in sufficiently shallow water, I prefer the shanty because it is as much fun watching the fish as catching them; but where this isn't true, the tip-up is more practicable. By means of a string of tip-ups at various depths, the fisherman covers much more ground and so stands a better chance of success.

The most popular method of ice fishing is that practiced on Lake Superior. It is known as bobbing. The fisherman works over water from seventy-five to one hundred feet deep and jigs with a heavy, tar-treated hand line. A flat, eight-ounce sinker is used to take the bait to the bottom, and the bait, or "bobber," consists of flat pieces of herring which, when the outfit is jigged up and down, apparently dance around in an enticing manner. The bobbing season is February and March.

Casting

This is where a lake trout comes into his own to my way of thinking. The casting season is short in the States except, of course, in Alaska. It is best for the first two weeks following ice-out, and the particular conditions of any one body of water may concentrate them. For instance, they may pursue smelt to the mouths of their spawning streams and even make forays in after them. If the bottom off such an inlet stream is clean, this is often a good spot in early spring. Otherwise, look for a reef with deep water on one side. A point projecting toward an island generally indicates a reef in between. In the lakes of northern Canada, this is an ideal place for casting at any time of year. I've never been down there to watch them operate, but I have as good an imagination as any fisherman. My guess is that they lie along the edge of such a reef waiting for the school fish on which they feed. The wandering smelt, tullibees, whitefish, or whatever are forced up and over such a reef, which gives the lake trout an ideal chance to ambush them.

Casting is practical in depths over a hundred feet. It is not only practical, but many fishermen are discovering that it is more productive than trolling. A troller must make wide sweeps to return over a good hole, but the caster can put a spoon down where they live time and again.

The procedure is to make a cast (it doesn't have to be a long one; many fishermen simply drop the spoon over the side of the boat), give the reel free rein and allow the spoon to come to rest on the bottom. Always remember that a lake trout is a bottom fish. Although you may hook one near the surface, such a fish has followed or pursued your lure from the bottom. Therefore, the caster has another advantage over the troller; he can put his spoon on the bottom without question. Once it has touched, the retrieve is made. If a moderate retrieve doesn't bring anything, the spoon should be reeled in as fast as possible. A lake trout may look slow, but he can catch it. He may catch it near the bottom, halfway up, or actually where he boils the surface near the boat, but if he really wants it he'll get it.

A variation on this system, useful when the trout are not coming, is to jig the spoon a few times near the bottom by raising the rod tip to give the spoon a spurt, then dipping it to allow it to tumble. Quite often when the rod tip is raised to give it another spurt, there's a laker on the other end. If not, after a few such jigging

In casting for lakers always per ... *en a sudden, rapid retrieve directly to the surface will often bring a strik* ...

motions to attract the ... the bottom in a hurry, and a sinker of
be near, start the spoc ... not only would tend to destroy its ac-
fast as the reel handl ... it it succeeds in tangling the line and
may not have wante ... on about every other cast.
but if he thinks it ... is light tackle gives a lake trout every op-
then he knows it's ... unity to show his stuff. In spite of this, some

There are seve ... them come up like a sack of sand. Then along
I have given m ... ll come one with such power, determination,
waters that I d ... nd stamina that your arms ache from the strain
stout bait-cast ... long before he shows any sign of weakening.
to jig the sp ... And as big as that one may be—if you land him
want to give ... —there's always another maybe twice his size
enough to hand ... waiting for your spoon on the next cast. A Cana-
bait-casting reel, a shon ... dian lake in the north country is an alluring
important item, a pike-size re ... r- place for this reason. It is a grab bag with lake
devle. No additional weight is ever ... his trout as the prize, and there seems to be no limit
casting spoon has sufficient weight within itself to the size of the prize.

Chapter 21

STEELHEAD AND SEA-TROUT FISHING

Steelhead fishing is the ultimate in trout fishing, the graduate school for the fly caster. A steelhead is big, fast, and strong, and he jumps as if he had a bee on his tail. He has the dash and cunning of the trout, the power and vitality of the salmon. He'll take a fly readily—and take the fisherman's tackle along with it. He's a fireball; he's lightning; he's a chain reaction. In other words, he's good.

The better steelhead rivers of the West Coast are listed in Chapter 24, "Where to Go." In addition to those named, there are a few other large rivers which are as good, and scores of smaller streams have steelhead runs. For instance, there are a few small streams well down the California coast, almost as far as Los Angeles, which swell in winter and have runs in January and February. I enjoy fishing small streams and tributaries the size of an ordinary trout stream, as the large size of the steelhead is magnified by the comparatively limited surroundings, but these small waters present a difficulty in timing: the trout have less distance to travel to the spawning grounds and consequently do not spend so much time in fresh water. This is a serious problem in fishing for steelhead in southeastern Alaska. The big rivers are so milky with glacial silt that they don't afford any fly fishing, and the small streams must be hit at just the right moment to strike the fresh-run fish. In the big rivers to the westward on the Alaskan Peninsula there is good steelhead fishing the year round.

On some rivers in California, Oregon, or Washington, this time element is important. For the area in general, it is not. Somewhere in the Northwest steelhead can be found in fresh water

no matter what the month. In specific locations, however, only certain seasons are productive.

There are two fairly distinct steelhead runs each year. The first, the summer run, is composed of smaller fish than those in the winter run. Among these are some precocious trout known as "half-pounders," although they actually weigh two pounds and more. These immature fish often precede the big ones into fresh water and are an indication that things are about to happen. Most summer-run fish fall between two pounds and about eight pounds. They are an ideal fly-rod size. They enter the rivers any time from May through November, depending upon the locality. For instance, under normal conditions the summer run might be expected to get underway on the following schedule: Duckabush, May; North Umpqua, July; Klamath, first week in August; Rogue, mid-August; Smith, early November. Many fishermen in Washington, where there are other good summer-run streams such as the Dosewallips, Skykomish, and Quinault, consider the last week in July an ideal time to fish for summer steelhead, but farther south the preference is later in the season. Some of these summer-run trout may remain in fresh water for nine or ten months before spawning, so they are available to the fisherman for a long period. They are at their very best when fresh run, and anyone planning a steelhead trip should make local inquiries in advance as to the most likely time to strike the fresh-run fish in the particular locality he chooses.

Summer steelhead are not so abundant nor so widespread as the winter-run fish. They pass by

Fishing for sea-run trout provides the opportunity for catching large, acrobatic fish together with the pleasure of fishing moving water.

some rivers altogether. However, these fish rise to a fly better than the winter fish. Because of the condition of the rivers, they afford the surest sport for the man with the long rod. In any of the five months from July through November somewhere in the Northwest there is bound to be good fly fishing. In general, the choice time for steelhead fly fishing is late summer and early fall.

The later in the year, the larger the fish that enter the rivers. The winter-run steelhead are the heaviest of all. These come into the rivers between December and April and spawn soon after they arrive. The run of the largest fish seems to be that in the Eel in late December. There is also good winter fishing on Washington's Olympic Peninsula where there are a lot of fresh-run fish in January and February. If the rains hold off in any locality until the winter run

commences, the fly fishing is wicked. I missed it once on the Eel by about twenty-four hours—after driving halfway across America. It had rained hard the night before and the river was already rising fast and discolored. I was so determined to get some fly fishing, though, that I worked my arm weak for four days without a strike; then I broke out the old casting rod, dredged one up with a spoon and went home.

Some fly fishermen do well at any season or stage of the water, but they're better men than I am. A steelhead, like any big trout, rests near the bottom. In clear-water conditions he can see a fly above him and may rise to it. Like an Atlantic salmon, he may even come to a dry fly under the right conditions. But when the water is heavy and cloudy, it is necessary to get down to the bottom and virtually put a fly in his face. Therefore most winter fish are taken on salmon eggs or on an ingenious salmon-egg artificial lure called a cherry bobber which is designed to ride just off the bottom at steelhead mouth level. If bouncing a cluster of eggs or a cherry bobber on the bottom doesn't appeal, as it doesn't to me, winter steelhead can be taken by casting spoons or a variety of deep-running spinning lures. Some fishermen even troll the big pools for them.

Steelhead fishing is unique in only one respect: the quarry is a sea-run fish, like a salmon, the biggest and strongest of the stream trout; otherwise it is not essentially different from other stream fishing for big trout. Any good trout fisherman can take steelhead, although it would be much to his advantage if he had had experience on a large stream, similar to the better steelhead rivers. Naturally, anyone who is familiar with Atlantic salmon knows the answers. He not only knows how to fish a river, but a fresh-run Atlantic salmon and a fresh-run steelhead are similar in appearance, habits, and fighting tactics.

As in all trout fishing, the first consideration is where in a stream the fish will be found. Knowing how to read a stream often makes the difference between success or failure. Many hopeful fishermen waste their time working over barren water. The first thing to learn, then, is how to read a steelhead stream. These migratory fish often lie in different water from native stream trout. Also, it must be remembered that they are on the move. A good run may be barren of fish one day, full of them the next.

A migrating fish will stick close to the main current of a river. The thread of the main current is his direction-finder. It's his compass directing him up to his goal, the spawning beds. He is continually impelled to seek out this main current. It isn't very likely that he will be found in any of the numerous side currents, pockets, and holes so productive of local trout. Nor will he be found in the still water; he must feel the wash of the current over his back. Yet he won't be found up in the white water, as this would be too exhausting. The heavy, smooth flow between the white water and the still water of a big pool is a likely steelhead location. Look for him in the big water: under or alongside a heavy run, alongside a big boulder, under a steep bank where the river bends, and anywhere that there is a mass of moving water. He likes a clean bottom, not mud, and wherever the gravel can just be seen under a riffle is a likely place to cast a fly.

As with the Atlantic salmon, steelhead of succeeding generations exhibit a strong preference for certain pools and certain "lies" in those pools —unless, of course, the pool is changed in the meantime by very high water. Also, like the salmon, such a lie is often near the tail of a pool where the slow water is concentrating and picking up speed again. Wherever a big pool does empty through a main shoot, the slick water just before it breaks off into rapids is a good place.

Also, the steelhead likes deep water as a rule. He will choose a deep run, and, to repeat, he will lie close to the bottom under the run to take advantage of the slower water there. He likes water six to ten feet deep, but of course in smaller streams where there is no such depth, he will take the best at hand.

An ideal place to look for steelhead is a long sweeping curve in the stream where the current cuts deep and smooth along the outside of the bend. The current is best fished from the inside of the U-shaped curve where there is generally a sloping gravel bar. The fisherman can wade out on the gravel to a point where he can fish the main current comfortably and will work downstream six or eight feet at a time between casts until he has covered the likely water. In a sizable river, this will often demand a long cast. This is where the distance-taper fly lines are most helpful to the trout fisherman.

When steelhead are seen to leap clear of the water and splash back in, as if playing, it's time to get a fly in the water in a hurry. This is said to be a sign that they are getting ready to run upstream another lap, but whatever is the cause of the activity, it's a pretty good indication that they are ready and willing to strike.

The accepted cast for steelhead is directly across current or quartering slightly down; then, as the current sweeps the fly around in an arc, the rod tip is lifted up and down to give the fly a rhythmic motion. Many experienced steelhead fishermen suggest that the fish be allowed to strike directly against the reel. He will hit hard enough to hook himself, and if he strikes against a line held solidly he will break something. Therefore they advise against stripping in for the next cast until after the fly has swung through the main current.

When a steelhead strikes, the rod should be held high and the fish allowed to run free. You should always play him against the reel, never strip him in. If a fish should strike while the fisherman is stripping line and has coils of slack in his left hand, his first job is to get this slack on the reel. From then on any line gained should be picked up on the reel, not by stripping.

Where conditions permit, it's a smart move to head for the beach the moment the fish is hooked. It is far easier to follow a running fish and retrieve line when the fisherman's feet are on dry land than when he is skidding and cavorting over slippery rocks. And of course the fish must be followed wherever possible. Even when played out he'll be too heavy to bring back upstream unless he can be led into a backwater. Land him by beaching him on a gravel or sand bar. If none is available he will have to be played to a standstill so that he can be picked up by the gills.

Although any qualified Atlantic salmon fisherman is ready to tackle steelhead, he may be surprised at the comparative lightness of the fly-rod equipment used by the better steelhead fishermen. Salmon fishermen in eastern Canada have long been plagued by a hangover from British methods in which ungainly rods, many of them giant two-handed affairs, are the custom. American fishermen have never gone in for this sort of thing. A steelhead rod of good Tonkin cane will weight from 5¾ to 6½ ounces and be 9 to 9½ feet in length. The reel should have large capacity, with a drum 3 or 3½ inches in diameter, and should have a smooth click or drag. It should be large enough to hold the usual thirty yards of fly line plus one hundred yards of monofilament backing. Fifteen-pound-test braided nylon casting line can be used for backing if preferred to monofilament. A double-tapered line, such as DT7F will do well, but since a long cast is often profitable in steelhead fishing this is one place where a distance-taper line can prove a definite advantage. A normal rod will require a WF8S taper, a stiff one a WF10S taper. On a big river, and certainly in the heavy water of the winter run, a sinking fly line in a shooting head will be a help.

The leader depends on conditions. In heavy water it is possible to get by with one 7½ feet in length. A 9-foot leader tapered down to anything from 5/5 to 1X is the standard. In very bright conditions it might be necessary to extend the leader to 12 feet, but it is rather foolish to taper it smaller than 1X.

The selection of flies is important, as it is with all trout fishing. Steelhead flies, like Atlantic salmon flies, are brightly colored. They don't represent any particular stream insect, but are colorful and attractive. Since steelhead lie deep under a current, the fly should sink readily. Therefore, the fly should be sparsely dressed on a heavy-wire hook. Some fishermen use a double hook on flies size 8 and smaller to give them added weight.

As in fishing any new locality, it's a smart plan to buy some flies on the spot. The local boys will know what pattern and size fly is effective at that particular time. In general wherever steelhead run, though, there are a few patterns that are outstanding. It's wise to go prepared with a stock of these on hand. Some of the standard patterns that seem to be universally acceptable to these fish are the Thor, Carson, Golden Demon, Silver Demon, Humboldt Railbird, Alaska Mary Ann, Polar Shrimp, Cardinal, and, of course, the ever-effective Royal Coachman. For normal summer fly-fishing conditions, sizes 4 and 6 are popular. For winter fishing and cloudy water a No. 2 fly may be in order. Where there are large trout that because of clear-water conditions demand a small fly—sizes 6 and 8 and smaller—a good idea is to tie such a fly on a short-shank No. 2 or 4 hook. This larger size will have the bight necessary to hook and hold a big fish, and the short shank provides less leverage by which the hook can be worked out.

To the late C. Jim Pray, master flytier of Eureka, California, goes the credit of introducing the optic steelhead fly. This innovation proved its worth immediately and conclusively. The optic head is so large that it makes the fly appear quite overbalanced, and it is heavy enough to sink the fly rapidly. This outsized head is painted with conspicuous minnow-like eyes. Such flies, like the Red Optic, Thor Optic, and the like, are the sole choice of some steelhead fly fishermen. Then Jim Pray produced another surprise for the steelhead. It is a metal-bodied fly, the body finished in gold or silver or enameled in the color called for in the particular pattern. The advantage is obvious: the metal body will take the fly down to the big fellows right away. Just like its creator's optic series, this type fly has brought the smile of success to many a hopeful steelhead fisherman.

In addition to the specific steelhead patterns, a number of Atlantic salmon flies are successful on these sea-run trout. This is hardly surprising; the standard patterns for each are attractor-type flies. Salmon patterns such as the reliable Jock Scott, Dusty Miller, Thunder and Lightning, Black Dose, Fiery Brown, and Silver Doctor are good medicine for steelhead.

A few steelhead are taken on a dry fly. The best type fly for this fishing is a palmer-tied hackle. The palmer has a lot of floating power and will support a fairly large hook even on broken water. Typical examples are the Brown Hackle Bivisible, Palmer Gray Hackle, and Pink Lady. This is a very specialized form of steelhead fishing, enjoyed by a few perfectionists only, but certainly there are few thrills in fishing equal to the breath-taking rise of one of these silver giants to a pert dry fly bobbing high on the crest of a run.

A five-pound sea trout (sea-run eastern brook trout) taken from Fourteen Mile Creek on the south shore of Hudson Bay, Manitoba, by this young angler. As can be seen by the expression of the Cree in the background, this is remote country seldom visited by outsiders carrying such gadgets as cameras.

Sea-Trout Fishing

There are sea-run trout the world over, such as the sea-run rainbow, or steelhead, just discussed. The sea trout referred to here, however, is that very colorful and acrobatic game fish of eastern Canada, the sea-run eastern brook trout. This is as fine a fish as the fly-rod fisherman could ever meet. However, he suffers the humility of being found in rivers which also contain the mighty Atlantic salmon; therefore, he receives little publicity and he will be treated only briefly here. Fishermen who travel to the salmon streams of the Maritime Provinces and Newfoundland are looking for salmon. The sea trout must remain a side issue. In smaller streams not frequented by salmon and in the Hudson Bay country beyond the range of the salmon, the sea trout comes into his own. But these waters are not only not frequented by salmon; they are not frequented by sportsmen.

June is the choice month for sea-trout fishing in the salmon rivers of the Maritime Provinces, although sea trout are on hand in sufficient numbers throughout the summer. In the estuaries near salt water, they can be taken almost any time of year. June, nevertheless, is usually the time of the biggest runs and the most action.

Sea trout are fished with flies and flies only. Canadians frown on the use of bait, spoons, spinning lures, or other dredging gear on their salmon rivers. Both trout and salmon will take a fly readily and there's no excuse for resorting to other means. As to the choice of flies, standard brook-trout patterns work well; it would be difficult to beat the Royal Coachman, Silver Doctor, Parmachene Belle, Black Gnat, Montreal and Yellow Sally. Bright flies are the choice. In addition to these trout patterns, the sea trout will often strike standard salmon patterns, such as the Fiery Brown, Black Dose, Jock Scott, Thunder and Lightning, and Dusty Miller. The only possible drawback to the salmon flies is their size. The trout do best on sizes 10 and 8.

These trout of the salmon rivers do not run large. They are usually between twelve and twenty inches; and, although they have a lot of power and speed for their size, they are no match for heavy salmon tackle. If a person were going to make the most of the sea trout, he would go to a small stream where there were no

Sea-run trout commonly lie near the main thread of a stream's current.

salmon, such as the coastal streams of Hudson Bay (where I have caught sea trout weighing over five pounds), use a light fly rod, and let them show their stuff. In these small streams they run later in the year, but are plentiful by the end of August. They are fished for much in the same manner as nonmigratory brook trout. And, taking a rather limited view of things, I'll say this about the sea trout: he is certainly one of the best-tasting fish around.

Chapter 22

MOON, WIND, AND STARS

When a person gets back away from the highways in the coastal plain area of the Carolinas, he finds himself in a different world. The people live at a relaxed and comfortable pace. Since they don't make a mad race out of their existence, as some folks are inclined to do these days, they have more time to contemplate life and the nature of things about them. As a New York taxicab driver is a master at crowding through traffic, so these men who live close to the earth become authorities on the ways of the woods and the wild creatures who live in them.

Such a man is Jeff Corbett of the Black River in North Carolina. It's a privilege to hunt or fish with him. One day while sitting among some post oaks on a turkey ridge we got to talking about fishing for robins and mud chubs and rockfish. I asked Jeff when was the best time to fish. He was surprised I didn't know. Everyone should know that.

"South moon," Jeff said, "is the time to catch 'em. South moon in the month of May. That's the time."

I asked him to explain south moon to me, that I had never heard the expression. Jeff fingered his willow-wood turkey call for a moment, then looked up through the treetops.

"When the moon gets directly overhead, neither rising nor setting," he explained pointing up in the sky, "that's what's known as south moon; and, night or day, that's when the fish will bite. Sometimes if you'll sit quiet and listen just as the moon arrives overhead, you'll hear an old owl down in the swamp give a lone hoot, and that's the time to start fishing. About twenty minutes later he'll hoot again; then it's all over."

I have never seen south moon worked into a fishing chart, although almost everything else has been at some time or other. A few fishing charts are constructed around the phases of the moon: some days are good, some bad, according to the state of the moon. A few fishermen read their luck in the stars, just as the astrologer makes his predictions in a horoscope. Still other fishing charts are based on some mysterious formula known only to its creator.

Then there's the old fishing adage that "fish bite best when the wind is in the west, least when it is in the east." Others swear by the tides, some insisting that the rising tide is the time to fish, and a few say that fish bite on the falling tide. Tide enthusiasts have worked out charts for the tide over the entire country where, although the tide is not evident to the human eye, it may be felt by fish. One of the most recent schools goes fishing according to the state of the barometer on the theory that the activity of fish is subject to subtle changes in atmospheric pressure.

All these theories are good. All are good even though no two of them agree. They are good if the fisherman believes implicitly in the one he accepts. He must believe, and then he has confidence and enthusiasm, which is a combination hard to beat.

I don't use any such system simply because it would be too disappointing on the one day I might be able to go fishing to look at a chart or barometer and discover that I might as well stay home. If I did use one I would pick the kind that indicated at least two good fishing periods a day, and preferably more. Then you can't miss. Every day has its little bright spots, and everybody is happy.

No, I believe in going fishing whenever I can,

and hope for the best. Any and every day that I am privileged to go fishing is a good day, and no one can tell me different.

Effect of Moonlight

Several theories have been advanced regarding the effect of moonlight itself, not the position of the moon, on fishing success. Two of these attempt to explain the effect of moonlight at night on fishing in daylight. These theories are equal and opposite, and therefore effectively counteract one another. One says that trout feed extensively by the light of the moon and therefore feed but little during the corresponding daylight. The other theory was advanced as long ago as 1698 when a John Worlidge in his *The Mystery of Husbandry Discovered* stated: "After a clear moon-shiny night . . . is a very good time for Angling: for it is the nature of most Fish to be fearful to stir in the bright nights." The fisherman can take his choice.

Another theory relates to the effect of moonlight on night fishing. This states that trout can see better by moonlight and therefore are not so easily deceived by the fisherman. Most good fishermen with whom I have talked seem to agree with this theory in effect; that is, that night fishing is better on the dark of the moon than by bright moonlight.

Two different surveys have been conducted by biologists in an attempt to arrive at a definite and scientific conclusion regarding the effect of moonlight on fishing success. One was conducted on Paul Lake, British Columbia, and the other on Fish Lake, Utah. The biologists conducted creel surveys and attempted to correlate the fishermen's results with the existing moonlight. Neither survey resulted in any definite conclusions, but both indicated that moonlight tended to reduce the fishermen's success. The British Columbia survey concluded conservatively that "the evidence suggests that bright moonlight nights may be responsible for a reduction in the catch at certain times." The Utah survey could determine no significant difference in the results of trolling—but trolling, since it does not depend on the craft or cunning of the fisherman, is likely not to show the effects of the wariness of the trout. Fly-fishing results, on the other hand, were apparently adversely affected by bright moonlight.

Night Fishing

From the above it would seem that the night fisherman might expect better results on a dark night than on one with a bright moon. The poor soul who tries to take trout by stumbling and slipping around in the dark of night comes to realize that night stream fishing is bad enough by moonlight, but on a black night it's murderous.

Some western states don't permit fishing for trout at night. This is a kind law. I am sure that the man who put through such legislation did so out of pity for the fisherman. Certainly such laws have saved a lot of tackle and tempers.

Other than this touching feeling of parental care for fishermen, I have never quite understood why night fishing is not permitted in some sections. Certainly the fishing is not enough better at night to warrant such a restriction. Possibly the idea is that by keeping all people off the streams at night, the poachers, too, will stay away, for a poacher can literally perform his blackest deeds at night with dynamite, jacklight, and gig. But the assumption that a crook will stay away because honest men do is rather naïve. If no other fishermen are around, these slippery characters can fill a gunny sack with trout unmolested.

I'm all for permitting night fishing. Maybe it's because occasionally I like to get out and try it myself. I never seem to catch much, and I invariably ruin some tackle, but the mystery and excitement of working in the darkness make up for it. There have been times when I have had strikes that sounded like a dog jumping in the water, with the results that I come back on the rod as if I'd been shot and, of course, hang my fly in the top of the tallest tree. Some day, though, I intend to hook one of those monsters that slosh around at night.

The night vision of trout is difficult to explain, but we know that it exists. It is certain that trout feed extensively in the darkness. Often in the still of the night they can be heard splashing around as if they were playing water polo. It's also certain that either they cannot see so well at night or are far less cautious because I have had trout splash and rise right around my boot tops. Trout just don't act that way in the daylight.

It is likely that their eyes have a broader range of vision than ours and certain insects reflect a ray of light visible to trout but not to us. Possibly they manage to take advantage of the light from the sky. By resting deep in the water, they can see anything which passes overhead silhouetted against the sky. There is always light at night, even on the blackest night, and what light there is comes from above. Lookouts on blacked-out ships at war might have had difficulty seeing anything against the black water near at hand, but a ship or other object on the horizon could always be spotted, even miles away. Only fog, not darkness alone, could blank out the horizon.

Working on this theory, many fishermen use a surface lure for night fishing. For big trout they use bass bugs, or even a small bass plug on a casting rod. For normal fishing, a large palmer-tied dry fly dragged on the surface or a large wet fly fished near the top may be a good choice. The natural inclination is to use a light-colored fly at night. It seems at first thought that a white fly would be more evident at night than a dark one, but such does not seem to be the case. A black fly apparently is the best selection. If a trout does actually see his food by silhouette against the faint light of the night sky, this would account for the effectiveness of the black fly. Regardless of the color or pattern of a fly, it should be fished slowly. I like to use a bucktail at night and fish it as slowly as if it were bait.

On very heavily fished streams, the trout may become more nocturnal than usual. Ducks in some sections where the shooting is heavy have become almost strictly nocturnal, and such seems also to be the case with civilized trout. Also, in the heat of summer when the streams are low and warm, then certainly trout are most active during the hours when the sun is set. The many fishermen who are limited to this time of year for the most of their trout fishing due to vacation schedules should try a little night fishing. It will be exciting and possibly productive.

Rain

I don't like to fish in the rain, or sit in the rain, or walk in the rain. Some people do, but I don't. It's all right for a few minutes maybe, but when that first cold drop of very wet water starts to worm its way down my neck, there's no whistling in the rain or singing in the rain for me. Many's the time I would have just packed up and gone home—if the fish hadn't been hitting. But a fellow can't stop fishing when they're hitting just because of a little rain. Anyone knows that.

Of all the elements, rain is obviously the most important to the fisherman. There's something about a midsummer shower that brings fish out of their holes, the way a ferret brings rats out of a corncrib. One minute it's a hot, sticky, dead day, with nothing stirring except a few fishermen, like myself, who don't know any better anyway; then suddenly the skies let loose and ten thousand tiny geysers spring up on the still water surface. Obeying the powerful law of self-preservation, the fisherman begins to reel like mad in order to head for cover and, of course, he gets a strike. That does it. First thing he knows he's soaked to the skin and it doesn't make any difference anyway.

There's no mystery to it. The heat of day in midsummer is drowsing time. When the sun has set and the evening mists begin to rise, then a trout stretches his fins and gives a thought to satisfying that craving in his stomach. And even if not very hungry, it might be fun to scatter a school of minnows; they scare so easily.

The darkening of the sky, like the coming of evening, puts pep in a trout during a shower. It's the sudden relief from the glare and heat and the summer sun. It's the hint of gloom in which a trout is so at home. And, after the rain gets underway, surface water draining into a stream brings with it an assortment of food: ants, grasshoppers, beetles, crickets, and the like. If the rain continues long enough earthworms are drowned out of their burrows and washed into the stream. The rising water of the stream itself covers new ground and picks up more food. Consequently, trout are very prone to feed on rising water. And if the rain water brings with it a little silt, the water turns milky, sometimes just enough to deceive a trout too discerning to strike otherwise. Then's the time to fish slow and deep. When a stream becomes very high and muddy, practically no caution is necessary. The trout are deep and a fisherman can stand directly over one without being seen through the discolored water. An inexperienced fisherman might catch the wisest old trout in the stream under these conditions.

Such a rise in stream level often puts migratory fish on the move. A run might be delayed for weeks by low water. The trout lie off the river mouth and wait for a "spate" to come down. Even nonmigratory trout are often sent roaming by a rise in the stream level since it alters their normal feeding stations.

A rain is an annoying time to fish a dry fly. Yet if the skies become sufficiently dark, an evening hatch is occasionally brought on prematurely, and a man who likes to see a trout take a floating fly can't pass up such an opportunity. I don't like to use oil on my dry flies. I don't want them gummed up in any possible way. But in a rain it's something else again. A fly can't very well be whipped dry in the wet air, so a good fish rising at such a time can be a problem. Whenever this happens I would give my shirt for some fly oil, but since I'm not in the habit of carrying it I never have it when it's really needed.

A heavy rainstorm is really the time for a bait fisherman to go to work anyway. With cloudy water his terminal tackle does not have to be too refined. Also, the fish's visibility is impaired to the point where he won't see a lure unless it's right in front of his face, but he will surely locate a piece of bait leisurely drifting around his pool. This is the ideal moment for the worm fisherman.

A moderate rain, however, just enough to wash insects into the water and turn the stream only slightly milky, is a fine time for wet-fly fishing. The trout are feeding on a miscellaneous assortment of things and are not too selective as to pattern. A cast made up of two or three buggy-looking and rather bright flies, fished slowly, will certainly bring results.

These formerly barren lakes in the Bighorn Crags of Idaho's Sawtooths are flourishing today with golden trout imported from their native California. Like all golden trout lakes, they are nestled among high peaks, shining like jewels in a crown.

Chapter 23

THE HEAVILY FISHED STREAM

Many of my undergraduate trout-fishing days were spent on the New York City watershed system. It was a tough school. At that time the streams which connected the various reservoirs were not stuffed at intervals with ten-inch hatchery trout and they were as heavily fished as any trout water in America; still, there were more than enough trout of all sizes to go around—*if* you could catch them. The larger ones were wise in the ways of lures and leaders. However, there were a few fishermen—noticeably few—who were consistently successful. It was from those men that I learned, and that's good advice for any young fisherman. It is possible to learn much of what there is to know about this game from the trout themselves, if you see them under enough conditions and if you live long enough, but the short cut is to learn from successful fishermen. When a person arrives at the point when he thinks he has nothing to gain from the other fellow—when he thinks he knows all the answers—he's finished. He'll soon be eating codfish.

I didn't learn by asking questions. Unfortunately some of the best talkers have the least to say. But I did keep my eyes open. As time went along I could see which fishermen were consistent, such as a pair of brothers named Mike and Tom Mahoney, and which were merely hopefuls. If one of the good fishermen wanted to talk, I was all ears; otherwise I watched.

We've all known the occasional "Mahoney" who can "catch them where they aren't." He can regularly take trout out of heavily fished water where others more commonly fail. It appears to be a mystery, but actually there is a definite an-swer to his success. I know that answer now, even if it took me years to learn it. Although I have given such men considerable thought, the solution came about gradually through my own experience. At first it was accidental; now it's purposeful. On days when I can't seem to find a single trout to play with me at my little game of catch the fly, I think back to the Mahoneys and I commence getting results. It is all quite simple—after you have spent a good part of a lifetime looking for the answer. This is all there is to it.

Almost any man on a stream knows a good pool or a good run or a good eddy when he sees one. He also knows that these are a trout's preferred home. If he is observant, he can actually see trout in such places, and this is proof enough. But there is one thing he does not stop to consider. Since all fishermen know such water, it is pounded unmercifully. The many trout which unquestionably live there are just as aware of fishermen and their offerings as the fishermen are of them. It is quite possible to take trout out of such obvious places because they are concentrated there, but it requires luck or skill—likely a happy combination of both.

When I watched the Mahoneys in my younger days, I was looking for something too devious: the length of a leader, a type of fly, or the way he twitched it. The answer is easier than that. What I saw, but which didn't register, was that as each went his way up or down the stream he would drop his fly or worm in outlandish places. He missed nothing.

The answer is to fish the good holes, yes, but not to waste time on these educated trout. The system is literally to look for trout "where they

On heavily fished streams in the East try the unusual spot and the unusual method, such as fishing a wet fly, nymph, or small spinner upstream as a dry fly is normally used.

aren't," and when you find one in the odd place, to mark it well. This is sort of a combination of hunting and fishing, and the man who is good at it is a worse hazard to a stream than a whole family of otters.

I use two methods. The first sounds stupid. I fish water so convenient and obvious that most fishermen would label it worthless without a try. For instance, in the East most small towns have a mill dam, with the town or small city built around the mill. Youngsters with no transportation may fish the pool below the dam occasionally, but men with automobiles have sense enough to get out of town at least. Consequently, I try the opposite. It doesn't always work, of course, but I have found many a fine and unsuspecting trout right under the shadow of a mill, or practically in someone's back yard, or under the back porch of the general store.

A variation of the same system, except in the country, is to fish deliberately in a farmyard. One such place I know is actually a cattle crossing. The stream separates the pasture from the barn and the dairy herd is driven across it twice a day at milking time. I must have been desperate to try such a spot in the first place, but it produced. One reason trout hang around just below the crossing is probably that the cows stir up a lot of nymphs and larvae at each crossing, but the main reason that I can get them there is that no one else ever tries it. The trout are unaware.

In the West it is often possible to walk farther from the road than the other fellow. I'll gladly hike for two or three hours in order to find a spot where the stream and the trout are unmolested, and to enjoy the solitude and the passing wildlife that go with such fishing. On heavily fished eastern streams, however, it is unlikely that you or I can find a spot any farther from the road than can the next ten fellows. It's natural to try, nevertheless; therefore, the hole directly below the bridge may be less often annoyed than the one a quarter-mile around the bend.

That's one system, as foolish as it sounds. The

Working the difficult spots such as under those overhanging branches often pays off.

other method, the one the Mahoneys undoubtedly employed, is more subtle. It cannot be set down by positive rules because it varies from stream to stream and from mile to mile on any one stream, but in general it can be stated as follows: the particular water which is productive is for one reason or another passed up by other fishermen. Every stream, no matter how heavily fished or how well you think you know it, has its share of such water. Some of these hidden holes are discovered quite by accident; others just as deliberately. I could name a hundred such places.

An unusual spot I happened on quite by accident one day was a large spring hole out in a meadow. The overflow from the spring was hardly more than a soggy spot where it entered the main stream, so no one would ever follow it up. Then one day when I was cutting cross-country on my way home, I chanced on the deep spring hole. The main stream was populated by rainbows and browns only, but the trout in this hole were all brookies. They must have been there from time immemorial. It turned out to be

my private hatchery, although I never overdid it. Only on days when I was completely defeated on the main stream would I go there and get a plump twelve- or fourteen-inch native. Other times I would merely crawl up to the hole on my belly just for the pleasure of looking at them. What a spot!

And I made another use of it. In warm weather I would fish the near bank of the main stream just below the point where the big spring seeped in. There were always trout collected there.

It's an exciting and happy experience to find such a place, but it is just as unusual. Not so unusual—if you employ a little initiative, imagination, and energy—is to find equally rewarding spots on your favorite streams, no matter how well acquainted with them you think you are. For instance, most streams are deepest in the main channel, shallow along the edges. We look for trout in the deeper water, of course. However, there are often small pockets and holes right under the bank which hold good trout and which are rarely fished. Big trout—old lunkers—

usually live in the expanse of a big pool, but this is not necessarily a set rule. A big fellow has to work for his living and he doesn't like too much competition. He's not as fast as the six-inch fly-snatchers which also live in a big pool, but there's not much he can do about it. He can dominate a smaller hole, however. If a six-incher wanders in, he will wind up as fodder or have a few scales scared off him. The big trout keeps such a hole and its food, to be eaten at his leisure, strictly to himself. So watch for these pockets. They must be deep—unless it is early spring when the rainbows are on the move or fall when the browns are getting ready to spawn, when they may be found temporarily in almost any pocket—and it must have a current to bring in sufficient food. But it does not have to be large in surface area to hold a big trout.

And if you take a big trout from such a hole, or a fair one from a smaller hole, remember it. Before long another like him will take over his old stand. When you get enough hidden places located on any one stream, you have it made.

Another place to look for unsuspecting trout is in spots which are difficult to cast to: under overhanging branches, under a bridge, in a deep section bordered by a solid wall of trees which interfere with a backcast, and even in such a strange place, perhaps, as where a pasture fence cuts a stream and would be an obstacle to a normal cast. Many fishermen seem to be more concerned with the danger of losing a fly or lure than with catching fish. Don't be. If you take a lot of trout, you also leave a lot of flies and lures behind, either in the trees or on the bottom. And remember this also: you must hook a fish if you are ever to land him. Try the odd spot even if it does appear impossible.

Most people fish downstream. The dry-fly fisherman works upstream, but since his fly must float back naturally with the current, there are many spots within his reach which he never touches from below: eddies, backwaters, the reluctant water against the bank inside a fast run, the little slick spots immediately behind rocks, logs, and other obstructions. Even much of the water which the dry-fly fisherman does hit is never noticed nor investigated by the downstream fisherman. It may be behind a protruding clump of brush or a rock, or intervening deep water may make it out of reach from above. In waters normally fished by downstream fishermen,

the trout, especially in heavily fished streams today, are well-acquainted with his lures. There have been other fishermen there before him, fishing in the same manner. Therefore, the man who reverses his tactics—the wet-fly or spinning-tackle fisherman who works upstream for a change, and similarly, the dry-fly fisherman who occasionally works downstream into new pockets—will be rewarded. He may show some old trout new tricks.

And one of the best bits of advice anyone can give is the first lesson I learned from the Mahoneys. If anyone tells you a stream is fished out, don't you believe them. Warm water or pollution can kill all the trout in a stream, but not fishermen. Reasonably good habitat has an amazing number of trout in it, no matter how heavily fished. Biologists making stream surveys with electrical shocking equipment have learned this in recent years, and the Mahoneys taught me the same thing long ago.

So stick with it. And don't stick with it for the first two weeks of the season only. The streams are so jammed then that smart trout have their heads in muskrat holes. Come back to the same stream a month later and you'll have ample room for a backcast. By August or September you may have the entire stream to yourself. When the rumble of the hatchery truck has died away and the disbelievers have taken up golf, a stream comes into its own. The trout, no longer fearful of being trampled to death, will have returned to a normal pattern of behavior.

And follow the line of thought I have given in the suggestions here. Don't fish where and as the others do. Be contrary. Take the least traveled path. Cross the stream and fish the opposite side even if you have to get wet in the process. You'll dry off in time. Experiment and explore, and as you explore, be thorough. Try the unusual, not the usual, such as fishing the small branch rather than the main one where a stream is divided by an island. In time you will locate a number of trout pockets which are not obvious and not fished. That way, by going down the line from one to another, you can employ what I like to call the Mahoney Method. Then you may become the mysterious fisherman with the heavy creel, the one who makes the other fellows talk and scratch their heads in bewilderment.

Chapter 24

WHERE TO GO

How many can identify the variety of trout referred to in the following statement, written by our leading authorities on game fish at the beginning of this century: "This interesting trout is one of the *best known* species in the West."? Other than taking the liberty of italicizing the words "best known" for emphasis, I have quoted this exactly from the classic work, *American Food and Game Fishes,* written in 1902 by the noted scientist-sportsmen, David Starr Jordan and Barton Warren Evermann, who go on to say that it had been their pleasure to fish for this trout in many waters, mentioning "with particular satisfaction" such places as the Pend Oreille River, Pend Oreille Lake, the Redfish Lakes, and the upper Salmon River high in the Sawtooths.

Pend Oreille Lake is world famous today for its huge rainbow trout. Was it a rainbow they were speaking of? Or, more likely, one of the many varieties of cutthroat found far and wide throughout the West at that time? Strangely, it was neither one. The native trout of Pend Oreille, which was once so popular and of which these gentlemen spoke so highly, was a species which most western trout fishermen have never seen. It is hardly one of the "best known."

This "interesting" trout—as interesting today as it was in Jordan and Evermann's day—is the Dolly Varden. Another name by which he was commonly called, and which will ring a bell with many Westerners, was bull trout. Like the name Dolly Varden, the name bull trout carried its own compliment, although in a different fashion. Certainly an old Dolly was a bull among trout. He hit viciously, then he tore things up in a furious battle: a thrashing, rolling, lunging fight, as though he were in a blind rage. But all the Dollies of the western states weren't bulls. Those in the deep holes of the big rivers, some

of which actually weighed as much as twenty-five pounds (think of it!), certainly were, but the Dolly Varden was also the sparkling little mountain trout of many high-country creeks and lakes, a colorful and delicate fly-rod fish. His range was great, not only from valley to mountaintop, but over-all. It was about the same as the original rainbow range (the West Coast watershed from California up through western Canada into Alaska) except that it extended considerably farther inland—into Wyoming and Montana—and also much farther north. I have seen them in streams on the north side of the Seward Peninsula, which empty into the Arctic Sea, but here he is gradually replaced by his first cousin, the arctic char. The range of the arctic char, in turn, extends around the northern perimeter of the continent until his place is taken by the eastern brook trout, the second cousin of the Dolly Varden.

This was the first chapter in the history of this trout. He was distributed over a wide area and he was appreciated by fishermen throughout, a fact attested to by his names if nothing else. Then comes the sad part. Jordan and Evermann referred to him as an "interesting" trout. They didn't know how interesting his story would prove to be. They could hardly visualize, for instance, that our government would actually put a bounty on so fine a fish or that by now he would be all but unknown in some western waters where they had enjoyed him so well.

The stigma of the bounty—as ill-advised and as short-lived as it was—undoubtedly was the cause of his decline, but he would hardly disappear of his own accord merely because he was once branded as vermin. If anything, such action usually seems to make the victim more persistent. It worked in a different fashion. He disappeared as a direct result of hatcheries and their indiscriminate and persistent stocking of other competitive species.

Hatcheries

We Americans are hatchery happy. For the past three-quarters of a century—ever since it was discovered that the eyed eggs of trout could be transported great distances if held at low temperature—we've been hauling eggs, fry, and mature trout back and forth across the country: up mountains, down valleys, over divides: everywhere that a truck could drive, a horse could pack, or a man could walk. Brown trout were brought from Europe, brook trout were carted from the East Coast and planted all through the West, rainbows were taken from the West Coast and planted all through the East. Even today, if we don't get the facts and figures that so many thousand legal trout were planted in a certain river, we are so hatchery conscious that we consider that river hardly worth fishing.

Once even the fry of cutthroat were hatchery distributed. Thousands of eggs were taken from Yellowstone Lake, hatched, and planted in the West. A little later the brown trout was all the rage. Now we seem to have settled on the rainbow as the utility fish. Apparently he conforms best with the modern hatchery's mass production methods, to the point that some of our rivers are crowded with them at times.

But in this enormous and long-lived hatchery operation, not one single, solitary Dolly Varden trout has ever been hatched and planted anywhere at any time. Is it any wonder that today the bull trout is not exactly common?

In the East the native brook trout also succumbed to our hatchery operations to a large extent, although not as drastically as has the Dolly Varden in the West. The State of Maine has done a fine job in resisting this trend. The beautiful Montana grayling, which was originally the only game fish available in much of the upper Missouri River watershed, has been crowded out. And the cutthroat, once the only trout in all the West outside the Pacific drainage, has disappeared from most of his native waters.

The end result of our trout-planting operations is by a wide margin on the plus side. We now have hundreds of miles of fine trout streams and endless acres of trout lakes which were originally barren of game fish. Most of this stocking was accomplished, rather haphazardly, years ago when enthusiasm ran high. It must have been a· rewarding experience. A man could dump a bucket of fry into a barren lake and watch his meager planting produce a bountiful harvest of trout in a few years' time.

In those days a hatchery was exactly what the name implied. It was simply a place to hatch trout. It was located at a spot where wild spawners could be trapped, stripped, and their eggs fertilized and hatched more efficiently than by nature; then the fry so obtained were spread far and wide.

We still have the occasional opportunity to populate such new waters with trout. When reservoirs are built of sufficient depth to settle and cool the water in an otherwise troutless area, the water below the dam becomes a suitable trout habitat. When these dams are built fairly well south—such as Norfolk and Bull Shoals Dams on the White River in Arkansas and Table Rock Dam in Missouri—trout grow much faster than they normally do in their natural surroundings farther north. This is due to a longer growing season, of course.

The hatchery today is far more than the name implies. It not only hatches fish, it rears them to catching-eating size. And it doesn't waste time trapping wild fish for eggs. It raises and strips its own breeders. Consequently, the trout which are stocked today are big enough to catch and take home when they leave the hatchery, and they come from a long line of trout which has spent generations within hatchery tanks.

Such hatcheries do a great service. When the fisherman traffic is very heavy at any given time, their help is necessary if there are to be enough trout to go around. And on many waters, stocking is not merely helpful, it is essential. These are of two types: one, lakes and ponds which have no natural reproduction of their own; two, sections of rivers which will not hold many if any trout from year to year due to excessive heat, stagnation, or even pollution. Such waters which are not naturally suitable trout habitat can provide good fishing as a result solely of hatchery operations.

However, the fisherman should not be carried away by the sight of the hatchery truck. As vast and important as our hatchery operations are, they can add but a little frosting to the cake. Other than in these special cases, our sport comes from wild trout which hatch, live, and spawn in the stream itself. Such trout are not only better game fish, but they—not hatcheries —populate our waters. And excessive planting of mature trout where not needed can actually be a detriment to the fisherman since the constant stocking eventually crowds out the desirable wild fish, and since mature stocked trout rarely survive. They are either caught soon or washed downstream to die of starvation, exhaustion, or suffocation. Contrary to the old adage, it is possible to overdo a good thing.

If a trout is given a good environment, he needs no hatchery. He creates his own. As an example, I'll use Yellowstone Park, which I consider the finest trout-fishing area for its size in America. Surveys show that fishermen take as many as one hundred tons of trout in a season out of Yellowstone Lake alone, and the lake is only the beginning. Certainly more are taken from the many fine streams in the park than from the lake; still, with this enormous poundage removed each year, these waters seem to me to be little different from when I first fished there as a kid. And—this is the point—the only hatchery which ever existed there was for the purpose of taking trout *out* of the park, not putting them in. Large-scale planting of mature trout, as is practiced in many areas today, would destroy the outstanding fishing, not improve it.

The hatchery cost of providing the trout which Yellowstone Park waters produce for themselves would be at least a billion dollars. Not the entire output of all the hatcheries in America for several years combined would come even close to matching the natural reproduction of this one area.

In one instance I know of, a hatchery even had a destructive effect. A small New England stream aptly named Trout River was richly populated with big, hard-to-please browns. The state happened to discover it and immediately stocked eight-inch rainbows together with a parasite which wiped out the thriving local population. Then the damage was compounded by unlimited dredging of the streambed for gravel.

Here and there across the country, such things as pollution, stagnation, channeling of streams for the convenience of highways, burying streams behind dams, diversion of water for other purposes, and other dangerous practices threaten trout waters. One western state, for instance, openly admits that recreation, made up principally of trout fishermen, is the state's third largest industry. As a revenue producer it is outpaced by only agriculture and mining; yet, in water usage, recreation is placed seventeenth on the priority list. Whoever wants to divert trout-stream water for any other purpose is welcome to do so by this standard.

As the Yellowstone Park example shows, the value of hatcheries is infinitesimal compared with a good environment. The answer, then, is to use some of the fisherman's dollar to improve environment, or, short of that, at least to prevent any further destruction of good trout waters.

We have waterfowl shooting today due solely to the foresight of a handful of men who inaugurated the system of duck preserves throughout the country, the purchase of wetlands to insure the future of ducks and duck shooting. No one can dispute the necessity for the preserve system nor its great rewards. Trout fishermen outnumber duck hunters, yet they have been given no such guarantee about the future of their sport. We have our national parks and we have a few wilderness areas, but that is all. The reason? The reason is this misconception of the role of the hatchery. Contrary to the opinion of the uninformed or the arguments of the prejudiced, hatcheries simply cannot supply all the trout fishermen can catch. Our hatcheries do an excellent job in putting the polish on the apple, in adding that little extra something that makes the difference between fair fishing and good fishing on the occasions when there are too many fishermen for a stream, and they do an equally fine job in maintaining fishing in places where the environment is not natural or where it has been all but destroyed already. Otherwise our trout-fishing dollars would be more wisely spent by improving stream environment, many methods for which are well known to biologists; by setting up guarantees for the preservation of good waters; and certainly by fighting any further destruction of trout waters.

And, where hatcheries are concerned, I personally would like to see the emphasis put on quality rather than volume. Lack of discernment is not the fault of the individual hatchery operators nor of the state and federal biologists with whom they are associated. It is the fault of the economic priorities set for them. These are: volume produced per dollar spent, and "return." The latter term translated means the percentage of stocked fish which are eventually caught and killed. This is supposed to indicate the economic worth of any particular trout planting. If half the stocked trout reach the frying pan, for instance, this is considered excellent because there is only a 50 per cent loss, that 50 per cent being the other half of the planting not "returned."

However, there is an implied danger in these criteria of return and volume produced which may outweigh either consideration. Once a trout has been degenerated to the extent that he provides a high "return," he will have been deprived of his most essential qualities as a game fish. It would be a sad day indeed if trout were ever made so pathetically unaware that a 50 per cent catch were a certainty. It would be preferable to hand out one such "trout" to each customer at the hatchery door than to contaminate our streams with them. Then there would be no loss—a 100 per cent return from the hatchery to public—and the incomparable rewards afforded by our sport of trout fishing would not be threatened by any attempts to make a sucker of a trout.

We can't help what already has occurred, but any further decline of grayling, cutthroat, Dolly Varden, and brook trout can and should be avoided. None of these is a match for a rainbow, admittedly. The rainbow in his many roles, including that of steelhead, is the world's finest game fish. But there is something to be said for the others, too. Each has his distinctive qualities and each is a fine game fish.

Fortunately for us, Canada never went in for the craze of shuttling fish back and forth all over the country. Saskatchewan has introduced browns and rainbows, but only in prairie reservoirs far from natural trout waters. Of course they are far too wise to imperil their great grayling waters of the north by introducing trout. And Alaska has had little need for hatcheries as yet; so, north of the Canadian border, we still have rainbows, cutthroat, and grayling in the Pacific drainage, grayling and arctic char in the Arctic drainage, and brook trout in the Atlantic drainage, just the way the good Lord planned it.

South of the Canadian border, the subject of the distribution of trout is difficult to define since the diffusion of species has been so thorough. However, I will attempt to do so, naming certain spots which I consider outstanding for each variety.

Eastern Brook Trout

In the West, where introduced, the best brook-trout fishing I have seen recently has been in a rich, spring-fed, weed-choked lake located near the Continental Divide at the head of the Snake River. Often the alien—the brook trout in this case—takes over, but not so here in Henry's Lake. The native cutthroat are also flourishing.

In the East, which is the native range of the brook trout, it is now either a matter of small trout in small headwater brooks and ponds or a matter of going to the State of Maine. There is little in between. Maine still has fine squaretail fishing, especially in the following places: Portage area (Aroostook County); upper St. John and Big Black rivers (northwest boundary of state); Allagash watershed (tributary to St. John); Moose River area, including fifteen small ponds (near Jackman); Cold Stream area (small ponds and streams in Somerset County south of Moose River); and Kennebago Lake area, near Oquossoc (northwest of Rangeley Lake). Specifically, seven highly recommended Maine squaretail lakes, from north to south, are: Musquacook Lake, Long Lake, Allagash Lake, Nesowadnehunk Lake, Moosehead Lake (shoals and inlets), Pierce Pond, and Kennebago Lake.

And for the biggest brookies, those who have the opportunity will get off the beaten track in Canada. Quebec has some excellent waters in the Laurentians and farther north. Ontario has such rivers as the Nipigon, Sutton, and Albany, all of which I have fished and all of which have produced trout weighing four pounds and up for me. Still, the best by far in my experience has been Gods River in Manitoba. I took several brookies there better than six pounds—which is quite an eastern brook trout—and one which topped seven pounds. I was fortunate to be one of the first to give Gods River a good going over, which had much to do with the size of the fish just mentioned, but a bit farther north in Manitoba there are unquestionably equally good waters which are untouched as yet.

Dolly Varden Trout

As indicated earlier in this chapter, the Dolly Varden fishing south of the Canadian border—the thrill and suspense that the mere thought of an old bull trout provoked—is pretty much a thing of the past. Fishermen still come up with one here and there, but they are uncommon enough that no one really expects to see one any more. The magic of the big hole and its big bull trout is gone.

Most of the Dolly Vardens still come from Pend Oreille Lake. Trollers come up with some good ones, but they catch them incidentally while fishing for the introduced Kamloops rainbows.

Anywhere a man fishes near salt water in Alaska, he should find some Dollies. They are at their best near the mouths of rivers and streams where they wander in and out of salt water, are bright silver and full of spunk. But in Alaska he is common; therefore, not appreciated. And he keeps company with either salmon, which are stronger, or rainbows, which are harder to come by. Consequently, the Alaskan Dolly Varden doesn't seem to be the same fish as the old bull trout of the West, which was both the big fish and the special fish in each pool.

Lake Trout

Anyone who takes his lake trout seriously, who wants them big and active, should go north. They are at their best in both size and numbers in northern Canada.

Practically all the thousands of lakes in that portion of Canada known as the Pre-Cambrian shield afford lake-trout fishing. There are hundreds of fine ones across northern Manitoba and Saskatchewan. Gods Lake and Island Lake in Manitoba are good examples; and, as good as they are, the best I have ever seen have been those in northern Saskatchewan from Lac La Ronge on north. They'll eat out of your hand there. For the adventurer, huge ones come from Great Slave and Great Bear lakes.

Sea Trout

There are no sea trout (seagoing eastern brook trout) in the United States other than a limited number in Maine. Today this is a Canadian trout. He is present in all the salmon rivers of the Maritime Provinces and is also found in smaller coastal streams not inhabited by salmon and salmon fishermen.

The best sea-trout fishing to my knowledge is farther north. This is in small, meandering streams on the south shore of Hudson Bay. There are no salmon in Hudson Bay, only sea trout. Most of the sea-trout streams I have fished are small enough to be covered conveniently from one bank and are wadeable with hip boots at the riffs. And the trout are considerably larger than any of the Maritime Provinces, are as bright as salmon, and are plentiful. It is what I would call abundant fly fishing (although flies are hardly essential; an Indian I was fishing with one day hauled some out with a chalk line and a spoon hurled in David's-sling fashion).

These sea-trout streams are numerous and untouched, other than by an occasional Cree, seal, or otter. The only ones I call by name are a couple east of the old Hudson's Bay trading post of York Factory: French Creek, and Fourteen Mile Creek.

Arctic Char

This colorful giant is becoming somewhat more available today, but he still lives a long, long way from the nearest filling station. He is the most northerly of fish, living in the Arctic Sea and migrating into coastal streams. Grayling, lake trout, and occasionally shee fish are found in some of these same frigid streams.

The range of the arctic char on the West Coast starts on the north shore of the Seward Peninsula north of Nome, and he is found from there around the Arctic coast of Alaska and Canada to remote Baffin Island.

In Alaska this big trout can be caught close to Nome in such streams as the Pilgrim River or in numerous Arctic coast streams now accessible by charter plane out of Bettles. In Canada the only place he is available—that is, where plane service and accommodations can be arranged—is at Frobisher Bay on Baffin Island, Northwest Territories. The flight to Frobisher Bay is made all the way from Montreal.

Although I have caught them in the Alaskan waters mentioned, I cannot vouch for Frobisher Bay personally. All I know about it is a crude

The golden in his native California creeks is a miniature breed of trout, but occasionally where transplanted into suitable lakes, such as a few in the Bridger Wilderness Area of the Wind River Mountains of Wyoming, they grow up. An old patch of snow, on which these are photographed, is usually available to the golden-trout fisherman as a handy ice box.

Alastair MacBain puts back a little fellow (Newalen River, Alaska), and this isn't an act. The fun is in catching them, not killing them, and we turned back well over a hundred pounds of big rainbows that morning.

snapshot taken a couple of years ago by a vagrant pilot. What fish! And, that far north, they couldn't have been anything but arctic char. I've been masterminding all manner of plots to get there ever since. Maybe I'll make it one of these days.

Brown Trout

It is almost ridiculous to try to point out any one spot for brown trout in America. Although widely distributed at one time, nowhere to my knowledge is he the sole occupant of any one stream or lake. This is natural since he is an introduced trout and must share with our native trout, whether they in turn were introduced to those particular waters or not. He does especially well in certain places, and I can think of a good many which should be devoted solely to this one fine trout, but this is never the case. Conversely, it seems to be the attitude of fish culturists today that the brown can take care of himself, and, if he can't, that's too bad.

Browns are spread from coast to coast. The best fishing I have experienced with them has been in the Catskills and Adirondacks in the old days and in Montana. It's human nature to buck a good thing, I suppose. Montana has stocked about three million rainbows in the past ten or twelve years, but not one brown. It has been a good fight. She certainly has done her best to overcome her reputation as the finest brown-trout state, but most of her hatchery rainbows have been just money poured down the river; so at the moment it's a stalemate. And, in spite of her gallant efforts to the contrary, I think I would still nominate Montana, with such rivers as the Big Hole and the Madison and such lakes as Wade Lake, as the best brown-trout state in the West. In the East, Pennsylvania or Michigan.

But, to repeat, this is ridiculous. There are browns in almost every trout state, and everywhere there's a brown trout there's likely to be excitement. The neighborhood kid may wrassle a nine-pounder out of a little stream you had scratched off as fished-out.

Rainbow Trout

And if it is difficult to tie down brown trout, it's almost impossible to point in any particular direction for rainbows. They are found in practically all American trout waters.

The biggest rainbows, of course, are the Kamloops variety which grow fat by eating little redfish, the nonmigratory red salmon. The Kamloops was originally a British Columbia specialty, but it was introduced to Pend Oreille Lake, where it has reached the incredible weight of almost forty pounds. However, this is strictly a matter of deep trolling, which to me is about as entertaining as mowing the lawn.

Ted Trueblood had some exciting fly fishing for Kamloops in their native British Columbia waters, and fly fishing for these huge trout *would* interest me. The timing has to be right. According to Ted, they are available to a fly in Little River, British Columbia, in June or early July when the year-old young of the red salmon are descending to sea—and the rainbows gorge themselves on the passing hordes of two-inch fish. These big trout move into the river and can be caught by casting a fly only when the small salmon are passing through.

In the United States we have big rainbows in fast water on occasion, but again the timing must be right. This is the steelhead-like migra-tory run of rainbows out of big lakes, such as the Finger Lakes in New York, or Lake Michigan and Lake Superior into the streams of Minnesota, Wisconsin, and Michigan. Some of the latter streams in Wisconsin and the Upper Peninsula of Michigan are: the Brule, Cranberry, Huron, Mosquito, Silver, Sioux, and others. The trouble with this fishing is that when the run is on, the word gets around. You have to walk sideways to get near the stream.

There is ordinary to good rainbow fishing everywhere in the States, and the unexpected can happen anywhere on a big enough lake or stream. That's about the only rule to follow. A big brown can be taken out of anyone's pasture creek, but rainbows are wanderers and tend to seek large water. Probably the best all-round rainbow fishing is still in the Snake River. Silver Creek has its ups and downs, but when it is up it is ideal for the fly fisherman.

A nice rainbow hooked near the junction of the foreground backwater and the white water of the main current.

Alaska has endless rainbow waters, everywhere from the Alaska Peninsula south, and especially around the Cook Inlet area. The great streams to the westward, the Newalen, Naknek, and Wood River remain good, but another one of the greats, the Russian River of the Kenai is available by highway today with the result that the cream has been scooped off. However, there are many other fine rainbow streams in Alaska which are rarely bothered, such as the smaller ones around Kodiak Island. Karluk is the only one I know personally, but there must be a dozen like it.

And, if anyone wants to dream a little, there are rainbows around the world today far from their native waters of western America, in such exotic places as New Zealand, South Africa, South America—even Sri Lanka. The rainbow is the same great game fish everywhere, but in South America there may be flamingos or black-necked swans flying overhead, and in New Zealand the fisherman will be accompanied up the stream by the musical bellbird and the charming fantail. Also, in a few such faraway places, our transplanted rainbow grows fat and is full of dynamite; then it matters little if the Andes rather than the Rockies are the backdrop. Chapter 27 briefly covers the potential fishing in some of these distant lands.

Cutthroat Trout

This is easy, I am sorry to say. At one time the most abundant and widespread trout in America, the cutthroat is rapidly becoming confined to a few small areas. This, the ancestral rainbow trout, interbreeds with the more dominant rainbow strain when rainbows are introduced and soon loses its identity. The beautiful and appropriately salmon-colored cutthroat of the Middle Fork of the Salmon River are rapidly giving way, as have those of much of Colorado and Wyoming. Only the great barrier formed by Yellowstone Falls—and the wisdom of the National Park Service—has preserved the cutthroat of the upper Yellowstone River and Yellowstone Lake from contamination. When I first fished below the falls as a boy, the Yellowstone River was inhabited solely by "black-spotted natives," as they are locally known. A couple of years ago when I made the last of many pilgrimages in to

Hellroaring Creek, the rainbow had taken over almost completely. There were a few typical cutthroat, many stages of hybrids, and mostly rainbows.

Above the two enormous falls, though, the strain is pure and the fishing is the finest, whether you are a dry-fly man who wants to work the slick river, a troller who prefers the lake, or just someone strayed off a golf course who wants to haul up a trout on Fishing Bridge. And it's all due to the black-spotted native without—as mentioned earlier—one wit of help from any hatchery. We cannot retrieve what we have lost by indiscriminate planting, but I pray that we can continue to preserve this one corner for all future generations of trout fishermen. And, if anyone does introduce other species above Yellowstone Falls, I hope he snags bottom on every cast from here on out; and, from there on, that old Pluto won't even let him catch a carp out of the River Styx.

Aside from Yellowstone, the best cutthroat fishing is found in southeastern Alaska—that is, the panhandle of Alaska with its maze of islands extending southeast from Juneau to Ketchikan. Here among the huge forests of this rainbelt are many fine cutthroat streams, and, as with the Dolly Varden, they are best near the sea where they are silvery and fully charged.

Golden Trout

Nowhere is the golden trout as beautiful or alluring as in his native waters on Mount Whitney and in the other lakes and creeks where the species has been transplanted far up amid the craggy peaks of the High Sierra of California. Enough has been said and written on this that it will not bear repetition.

Something the reader may not know, however, is that in the early days of random fish-shuttling, California let some golden trout get away in the confusion. As a result, I have found larger golden trout in the Bighorn Crags of Idaho and the Bridger Wilderness area of Wyoming than I have ever seen in California. A big one loses his typical parr marks, has a broad blood-red band down his side and, although a striking fish indeed, is not to be compared with the tiny, sparkling golden of the Sierras.

Steelhead Trout

Steelhead are found in the majority of the un-dammed, uncontaminated coastal rivers from the San Francisco Bay area of California north to Bristol Bay in Alaska. California's better streams include the Russian, the Mattole, the Eel, the Mad, the Klamath, and the Smith. A book could be written about Oregon's steelhead fishing alone. A few of her outstanding rivers are the Rogue, the Coquille, the Coos, the Umpqua, and the Siletz. In Washington, tributaries of the lower Columbia, such as the Lewis and Cowlitz, are fine rivers, and they are still getting fish up over the dams to much of the famous steelhead water above. Other good Washington steelhead rivers are the Chehalis, Quinalt, Duckabush, Dosewallips, Dungeness, Skykomish, and Skagit. Farther north, in Canada, two very fine ones on Vancouver island are the Little Qualicum and the Puntledge, and on the British Columbia mainland the Bella Coola and the Skeena are as good as any.

I won't commence to name Alaskan steelhead rivers. My pet is a small one as steelhead rivers go, the Situk, near Yakutat. Its size makes it all the more dramatic. In a pool of the proportions where you might normally expect a twelve-inch trout, a twelve-pounder suddenly blasts things wide open and tries to toss all the water out on the bank. The Situk puts a strain on a fellow's nerves.

The best advice I can give on the "where" of steelhead fishing is to choose one stream and try to learn it or at least a few pools in it. All those mentioned are good steelhead rivers. There are plenty of fish in any one of them at the right time. One of the most dramatic is the Eel River in California during the winter run. This is not only because the Eel River strain of fish aver-ages somewhat larger than others, but because of the surroundings. Everything is big, not just the fish: those redwoods bordering the river, for instance. You can walk around one, feel it, kick it, stand back and look at it, and go away know-ing it's all a lie. There's no such thing, I don't care what they say.

Grayling

Grayling are everywhere in Alaska from the Kenai and the Alaska Range north to the very

An inlet to a lake, large or small, is always a likely spot because of the food carried by the flowing water. In the spring when the rainbows are preparing to spawn and in the autumn when the brookies and browns are commencing to move, an inlet becomes an increasingly productive place to fish.

limit of land, all the way to piddling little tundra streams which seep out of the Arctic barrens and meander into the Arctic Sea. The interior around the Tanana drainage is fine; there are big grayling to the westward, around the Ugashik Lakes; and there is some delightful fishing on the Kenai itself, at Upper Russian Lake, for example. Some of the best Alaskan grayling fishing I've experienced was in a river near Nome, and the only poor fishing was along the Arctic Coast. There the fish were sluggish, which is not surprising. They must have been literally stiff from cold.

In Alaska the grayling somewhat complements the cutthroat. The cutthroat doesn't extend much north of Glacier Bay. He is at his best in the coastal streams south of there. Then the grayling soon takes over, living throughout the vast interior of the body of Alaska.

No one who gets up there needs a guide to grayling. They are everywhere except where a road has made them too accessible.

However, if I were planning to go fishing with grayling as the prime objective, I would not go to Alaska. The fishing in many places there is excellent—no less an adjective will do—but in parts of northern Saskatchewan it is even better. And perhaps the best of all Saskatchewan's many fine grayling waters is the Clearwater River drainage, which river is aptly named. The water is so clear that, with the right light, hundreds of grayling can be seen in a good stretch of water. And they are the most colorful, the strongest, the fastest, the highest jumping, and the largest grayling I have ever seen anywhere.

Chapter 25

HOW TO TAKE BIG TROUT

One way to get a good trout is to go to Kamloops Lake and drag a spoon around the bottom for a couple of weeks (be sure to take a few good books to pass the time), but that's not the type of fishing referred to in this chapter. For one thing, a "big" trout doesn't necessarily weigh ten pounds, and, for another, deep trolling is the only means man has yet conceived to make trout fishing a dull sport.

Occasionally someone catches a big trout because he literally doesn't know any better. To explain this contradiction, imagine someone stumbling on a spot which knowing fishermen have passed by because it gives no outward clue that it harbors a trout. The still-fisherman, the one who sits all day on the bank with his bait in limbo and his mind in neutral, usually gets only one thing, a nap, but even he might come up with a big one. And anyone drowning a worm in high, turgid water may drag out an old monster he normally couldn't have got within a hundred yards of. Such fishermen are one-shots. With considerable good fortune working for them, they get one big trout, and that one must last a lifetime. Fortunately, such a trout has a remarkable ability to continue to grow long after its death.

Consistency is something else. This is a man's reward for all he knows about trout, their habits, their food, and the presentation of a fly, lure, or bait. Such a fisherman is "lucky" time and again. The larger trout in any one stream get that way because they have an edge on their brothers in a trout's most fundamental characteristics: awareness, shyness, and discernment. Everything I have tried to express in this book points to this one chapter. The ability to take such trout with some degree of regularity proves that a man has arrived as a trout fisherman, and this has been my objective. Now, in speaking of big trout in particular, I will be specific, mentioning some rules, some likely places on any stream, and some methods.

Rules

Rule One: Big trout, unless migrating, have ready access to deep water. How deep is relative to the size and nature of the stream. A depth of from four to six feet is sufficient on the average stream. A big trout is conspicuous, which may be one reason he demands the haven of deep water. Another is that a deep hole brings him the quantity of food he needs. Such a hole does not necessarily have to be a stream-wide pool, or a pool at all. The surface area need not be large so long as there is sufficient flow to bring him food and so long as there is depth in relation to the surrounding water. This condition may be met by a comparatively small pocket, such as where a hole has been cut into a bank behind a large tree, or by a slick run.

Rule Two: A large trout lies deep. Unless brought to the surface by a concentration of food, such as a flurry of minnows or a heavy hatch of insects, he will be near the bottom of a stream. I have mentioned this several times, and likely should have started each chapter with the same statement. It cannot be said too often. The success of many spinning lures is due to this one fact: their density, which is necessary to give them casting weight, makes them travel deep almost in spite of many fishermen. They go down where the big fellows live and also where the sunlight reflected from their shiny blades is near a trout's eye level where it will do the most good as an attractor. In clear water a large trout may come up for a tempting fly or lure, but most strikes which occur near the surface are a result of his having followed it from the depths.

Rule Three: A big one, while not actually slow, is deliberate. A rapidly moving lure or fly will most likely escape him. A slow one, which he can see coming and "ambush," is more likely to bring a strike. Where a fisherman has any reason to believe that there might be a big trout, he should be as thorough and deliberate in his actions as the trout is in his feeding habits.

Rule Four: A trout grows big as a result of good eyesight and caution, not the lack of it. Anyone who can cast a good line should do so. Otherwise he should keep out of sight. Even if he thinks he is hidden, he may not be. He should keep low and move slow. Some people can put trout under the banks from a distance of fifty yards, without trying; others can sneak up on a pool and look a big one right in the eye. They are the ones who catch them.

Places

A person must choose his spots with some degree of self-appraisal. A still, glassy, clear pool is a likely place for a big trout for the simple reason that almost every fisherman who approaches it sounds a fire alarm. Even if a man's approach is successful, it requires the ultimate in ability to make a flawless cast on such water.

These are spots where better-than-average trout live on any stream: the pool immediately below a dam, waterfall, cascade, culvert, or other obstruction; the pool formed where a stream has been pinched, such as below a road bridge or railroad trestle; the pool just below a canyon or gorge, and any available eddies, backwaters, or slicks within the canyon; any natural stream-wide pool, such as formed by an abrupt bend of a ledge of rock; the outside of a U-bend in a looping meadow-type stream.

If there is no pool directly below a dam or waterfall, look for a big trout in the first spot below there where he can hold his own. Trout have a tendency to work up tightly against a stream obstruction, and the best one will claim the best hole. The first such hole below the outlet of a culvert from a lake to outlet, even if it has passed through a power house, is as good or better a place than the flow over the dam itself.

Methods

There are a few men who make a specialty of catching big trout. They concentrate on this one objective to the exclusion of all else. Most men who consistently get good ones, however, also get a full measure of enjoyment from a ten-incher. They appreciate all phases of trout fishing. A big one is merely something extra. Through a love of trout and trout fishing they

This is the big moment. Notice the tense hand of Corey Ford, on the left, giving encouragement to Frank Dufresne. This huge rainbow, which Corey hooked at the convergence of Alaska's clear Russian River with the silty Kenai River measured 30¼ inches and weighed 12 pounds 5 ounces.

have acquired an edge on the average fisherman and stand a good chance of getting the good one whenever the opportunity may come along.

Dry Fly: The above statement certainly applies to the dry-fly fisherman. If a man were specializing in big trout, he would not choose the dry fly as a weapon; however, if he plays at it long enough, he will eventually have the opportunity to take his share of big ones by this method, and these are often trout which no one can touch by any other form of fishing.

The first requirement is to find a big one rising. A hatch dense enough to make it worth his while must have brought him to the top. It is rarely possible to bring a big one—over twenty inches—to a floating fly if he isn't already rising. The only way I have accomplished this is by means of a twitched fly on a still pool.

But if a large one is found rising, a good man with a fly rod has an excellent chance of getting a strike at least. This is by no means an impossible way to get a big fish. Of course I have done a lot of trout fishing, but to make this point clear I must add that I have taken several trout over four pounds on a dry, a few over five, and two over six pounds. If a man is fortunate enough to find him rising and if he knows how to float a fly, this actually is the easiest way to get a good one.

Nymph and Wet Fly: This again lies within the province of the dedicated trout fisherman who takes the big ones as they happen to come. Both subjects have been fairly well covered. However, it is well to bear these two things in mind: one, unless a trout builds his way of life around the pursuit of school fish, such as little redfish, smelt, or alewives, his main source of food from birth to death is made up of underwater forms of insect life, and these are represented by nymphs and wet flies; two, the two most consistent takers of big trout I have ever known anywhere have been Jim Webb with nymphs and Ted Trueblood with a wet fly. Of course, Ted's various wet flies often imitate nymphs as well as shrimps and other small trout foods. Anyone who becomes proficient at this form of fishing will never lack for his share of good ones.

Worms: Next to Ted Trueblood and Jim Webb, just mentioned, a man named Mike Mahoney was the next most consistent taker of big trout I

ever watched in action. Mike, again, just naturally liked to fish, and he wasn't looking for big trout only. He certainly caught them, however, and his specialty was worms, but not a worm dangled hopefully from the bank. When Mike fished a worm he was as active as when he fished a fly. He cast it upstream and rolled it into likely pockets. It was wicked.

Spoon: Now we are getting into the realm of specialties. A big, three-inch pike spoon is for big trout and big trout only. On small streams it would not be appropriate; then a smaller model of the same spoon is used. The technique is to have sufficiently good aim to drop the spoon where it will land inconspicuously, not with a splash in the center of the pool. The boiling white water at the head of a pool is a good place to drop it unnoticed, and the current will sweep it down into the pool from which it is retrieved. If the situation is not as simple as this, a spoon can often be bounced off a rock or slammed against a cut bank so that it will merely plop into the water. The other thing to keep in mind in fishing a spoon is to try to figure out ahead of time where in a pool or pocket a big fish might be lying, then to make a cast accordingly. The spoon should appear as though it is trying to escape a trout, not attack him.

Tarpon Flies: Yes, tarpon flies, and don't laugh. One day I noticed quite a commotion in the water at the stream's edge and walked up to see what was going on. It was a big rainbow—one weighing six or seven pounds—trying to maneuver into position to swallow a ten-inch rainbow. The big one swished out of sight into deep water, but the ten-incher was about finished. His scales were half knocked off and he swam crazily in circles on his side until he was swept from sight downstream. That started it.

The flies I use are all designed for tarpon fishing. They are gaudy and they are big. One, for instance, is a white streamer with a red feather at its head which measures five inches from eye to the tip of the last feather. It is enormous, the largest fly tied for any fish, but at that it is only half the length of the trout the big rainbow had knocked silly.

Naturally I use discretion where I try these monstrous flies. It has to be in fairly big, heavy water and I must have reason to believe that it contains large trout. And for the most part I get nothing but casting exercise with them. But I like to take big trout and I like to feel them on a fly rod in preference to anything else, so I continue to sling them around. One thing is certain: I'm never bothered by small trout. The sight of one of these flies leaves them trembling for weeks. In fact, I rarely even get a strike. But when I do, I have a fish! To date, my best on tarpon flies is a five-and-one-half brown, a seven-pound brookie, and a nine-and-one-quarter-pound rainbow. And some day by this method I hope to land a trout so big that I'll have to scale him.

Bullheads: This method, practiced by a few big-trout specialists in the West and by no one in the East to my knowledge, is the surest way to get a big trout. To bullhead fishermen in Colorado, Wyoming, and Montana, a five-pounder is a good one, but they are shooting for ten-pounders. These fellows will tell you that there is a big trout in every deep hole in each of the big valley streams of the West; furthermore, that if you care to stick around awhile, they'll prove it. All a person has to know is how to get them out, and a bullhead is the way.

This bullhead shouldn't be confused with the whiskery, black-faced comedian that goes under the same name, although he has a similar broad, flat head. This is a brown, bottom-loving minnow which exists in all trout streams. Methods of catching him were described in the chapter on bait fishing. The Westerner's method of using the bullhead as bait for big trout is described here.

The best bullhead is a fresh one three or four inches long, but he is not fished alive. A bait hook, such as a sneck or round-bend, with a large bight, in a size 2/0 or 4/0 is used, and the dead bullhead is threaded on. The hook should enter near the tail and come out the mouth in such a way that the point is outside the mouth and gill cover. The tail is lashed to the leader with a few turns of cotton thread so that the bait will lie parallel with the leader throughout its length. It is threaded on backward, with the head down toward the bend of the hook, because a trout always swallows a bullhead head-first. If rigged the other way around, the leader might interfere with the trout's attempt to turn its head down in his mouth and would lessen the chances of setting the hook.

The typical outfit consists of a heavy, single-strand leader, testing around ten pounds. It should be at least 7½ feet long. A limber bait-casting or spinning rod can be used, but a 9-foot fly rod is best. At least a hundred yards of line should be used, for two reasons. In the first place, for best results the bullhead is fished on a long line, and in the second place a big trout doesn't stick around long after he's hooked. Many bullhead fishermen use braided nylon bait-casting line on their fly rods. Such a line, even up to twenty- and twenty-four-pound test, is inconspicuous and it behaves well on the water. However, it must float, and it will serve best if treated lightly with line grease. A long, sunken line will soon become fouled.

Big-trout fishermen sometimes spot their quarry before they fish for him. A thirty-inch trout has trouble making himself scarce in a clear stream and he may be quite evident from a high vantage point. When a big one is located, fishermen sometimes work in pairs, one watch-

Landing a 5½-pound brook trout is an event to make any fisherman happy, but the over-exuberant expression on the character on the right is due to the fact that this particular brookie was taken on a No. 14 dry fly, a big moment in a trout fisherman's life.

ing the trout and his actions and the other handling the rod from upstream.

The bullhead fisherman enters the stream well above—usually seventy-five feet—the spot where he expects to find a trout. The biggest trout will usually be in the deepest part of a big pool, but occasionally he will have a station at the very head. There's no use in walking to the edge of the pool before starting to fish because there is nothing that will make a big trout lose his appetite so quickly as the sight of a fisherman. This is where most men make their mistake. The pool should be fished from a point seventy-five feet up in the rapids above the pool.

From such a position the bullhead is fed downstream gradually, a few feet at a time. Each time the bait is stopped head down in the current, his gills and fins are flared out as though he were alive. Even if the strike does not come at the head of the pool, the fisherman should remain up in the rapids. Instead of walking closer, he continues to pay out line. A big trout may play around a bullhead for considerable distance before striking. Any large trout is suspicious and cautious and is inclined to follow and dart around a bait or lure for some time before hitting. Many a fisherman has had the disappointing experience of seeing a big trout under his lure just about the same time that the trout sees him. Such a fish has usually followed a lure suspiciously for a long distance.

The bullhead fisherman may not get any response until fifty yards of line are out, then the big trout may merely bounce the minnow once or twice before actually taking hold. This is where the bait fisherman has a tremendous advantage over the artificial lure man, because a trout needs to feel an artificial only once to lose interest. If the bullhead fisherman exercises sufficient self-control and gives the trout line until the final vicious strike, he's in for some fun. As soon as he sets the hook, he had better start for dry land because the next thirty minutes may call for some fancy footwork.

This same minnow lives in eastern trout streams and is a staple of big trout. A fisherman employing this same system and a two-inch sculpin on big pools of eastern trout streams would get more than his share of big ones.

Migratory Trout: Migratory trout present a different problem, and by migratory I mean not only steelhead and sea trout which run out of salt water but also rainbows on their spring spawning runs out of the Finger Lakes in New York or out of Lake Superior into the rivers of the Arrowhead country in Minnesota. A trout which lives habitually in running water will select a spot which is often quite obvious to a man who knows how to read a stream. A migrating trout, however, is more interested in getting where he is going than in eating. He has done his eating and now has something more important on his mind. The instinct to eat is still with him and he'll take a well-presented fly, but this is the one period in his life that feeding plays a minor role. When not on the move, his one idea is to rest as completely as possible. A feeding stream trout will be at the head of a pool, but the migrating fish is more inclined to lie in the tail of a pool. The upstream migrating instinct will keep him close to the main current, but he will lie deep on the bottom, not necessarily in a feeding position.

As a final word on this subject of big trout, locating one is part of the battle, and one method of locating an old lunker doesn't occur to most fishermen. If your stream is normal—that is, if it isn't strictly a hatchery-maintenance project—it will have a lot of small trout for every large one. Remember this as you move along it. If you fish an obviously good hole properly without a strike of any kind, don't be discouraged. This is a very likely sign that the hole is occupied by an ornery old-timer who won't tolerate any small trout. This is a spot to try again and again rather than to scratch off the list. If you do finally get a strike there, it will be a good one.

And wherever you do have reason to believe there may be a good one, take your time. One false move will end it. Be methodical in your approach, in the speed with which you handle your fly or lure, and even in setting the hook. A person can't strike a small trout too quickly, but there's time on a big fellow. I know that I have taken flies away from more big trout than I ever caught simply because I saw them coming and my reflexes couldn't stand the strain.

Chapter 26

PLAYING AND LANDING THE FISH

One of the best ways to get the upper hand with a big trout is to prevent him from getting excited, at least until he has used up his first burst of energy. The fisherman's immediate impulse when a big one takes hold is to jump up and rear back on the rod. This is the first mistake. The minute the trout sees the fisherman, he's for getting out of there, like the scared fellow who "didn't set foot on the ground 'ceptin' when it was absolutely necessary."

A trout when he takes a lure has noticed nothing to disturb him. He's in the normal course of feeding. When he feels the barb he knows he's swallowed the wrong thing, but if the tension on the line is not too great and the fisherman remains out of sight, the trout will not realize he has anything to fight but the object stinging him in the mouth. He may just lie there and shake his head from side to side in an attempt to throw it out—and that's a thrill to feel those long, solid head shakes that mean a big trout—or he may take to the air to try to shake it free. But a fly which is set in beyond the barb doesn't shake out. It won't come out until the trout can get enough pressure on the line to tear it out, or at least to tear a hole big enough that the barb will no longer hold. When a fly is snapped off in a trout's mouth, he can't get it out for a number of days, not until it festers and drops out.

So if the fisherman stays out of the picture and gives the trout his head for a while, he can gain a big advantage. This is particularly true with a jumping trout. Jumps take a lot out of a fish, especially when he comes down on his side. In a quiet pool the fisherman can stay back and merely give the fish an occasional prod to annoy him but not give him reason to leave the pool.

He may have the battle won without ever putting any strain on his tackle.

Certainly, if the opportunity permits, it is wise for the fisherman to take advantage of this immediate irritation on the part of the trout and get himself together. The coils of slack held in the hand can be reeled in and the situation surveyed to see how and where the fish should be played. By the time the fish discovers what he is up against, the fisherman should have everything in hand and be ready for the trout's next move. If it's a good trout that may take a long run, the fisherman should get his feet on dry land. Then, when ready, he may even encourage the fish to take off and wear himself down.

A dry-fly fisherman often has an advantage in that he is downstream from the trout, and sometimes if the fisherman is not already in such a position he can work around below the fish. A trout will normally fight against a taut line, and sometimes the fisherman can keep the trout above him where he must fight both the tension of the line and the current of the stream.

Often, the larger the trout, the lighter the tackle necessary to make him strike; and if a fisherman is going to land a big trout on light tackle he must learn to give the fish his head. The biggest mistake a person can make is to try to prevent the trout's taking line. Long runs are what take the starch out of a fish. It's the sulker that's hard to wear down, not the fish that runs and jumps like mad. A trout that will take more than seventy-five feet of line in one run is very unusual; but, when working in water where there are known to be large trout, the fisherman should be ready with a reel with fifty yards of backing. When the trout rests between runs, the

Gods River, Manitoba, is one of the rare places where a camera can first be set on a tripod in anticipation of taking this series of self-timer pictures of hooking, playing, and landing a five-pound eastern brook trout.

fisherman can work up toward him and retrieve line in preparation for the next run.

And it's in fighting big trout that a good reel with a smooth click comes in handy. A normal-sized trout can be landed by stripping line with the left hand, but it's a good practice to fight them all from reel. A big trout must always be fought directly against the reel. When the trout runs, the rod should be held high and the line allowed to flow freely from the reel. There's no music quite like the sing of a good reel responding to the run of a big trout. A fish cannot get a sharp pull against a flexible rod and a smooth-running reel. Even if the rod should be carelessly pointed down toward the fish, the reel will give against the shock of a sudden lunge that might otherwise strain the leader. Between runs when line is being retrieved the reel handle should be held lightly so that if the fish takes off again he won't find anything solid to pull against.

The only time that it is advisable to apply more pressure than that afforded by the click and the friction of the line in the guides is when the trout is heading into rapids where he cannot be followed and from where he cannot be retrieved. In such a case, often a smoother resistance can be obtained by cupping the palm of the hand over the spinning reel handle than by taking hold of the line itself. When no pressure short of parting a leader will stop the fish, a trick which may work is to throw slack. With the sudden relief of resistance, the trout will often stop and sometimes even turn about.

The rod tip should always be dropped to give slack when a trout comes out of the water. There's much less resistance in air than water, and when a trout bursts into the air, his speed and the ease with which he can throw his head about can often part a fine leader. A trout rarely jumps in a smooth, arching leap as he is classically shown in art work. He comes out wrapping himself in knots, with his head and tail almost joining first on one side and then the other. He can apply tremendous leverage against a leader in this manner, and the fisherman must be alert to give him the necessary slack.

A sulker is a tough fish to beat. A rainbow generally puts on an exciting, rushing battle with plenty of acrobatics. Sometimes a brown will fight the same way, but at other times a big brownie will lie deep and just shake his head or try to grind out the fly on the bottom. A big brookie often will fight deep and slowly. The object with a sulker is to stir him up. The best way to play a trout is to make him wear himself out. Trying to wear out a big trout by leading him around is rough on fine terminal tackle.

One stunt that sometimes stirs up a sulker is to tap the rod butt sharply on a taut line. The vibrations are carried down the line and irritate the fish into action. The fisherman who resorts to this should be ready for the consequences. Occasionally a trout is so sullen that even this won't shift him into gear. Several times I have known brownies in the three- and four-pound class to last over an hour. By then the fisherman is ready to try anything, even splashing the water around him with gravel to startle him into running.

A trout is not so inclined to foul the line on submerged brush and weeds as are some fish; nevertheless, it is a good idea to keep him away from snags where possible. Some excellent flyfishing waters are practically choked with weeds, as it is on the weeds that the nymphs grow. If in such a place a trout does get fouled in the weeds, never try to pull him out. The weeds are stronger than a leader. Instead, merely keep a relentless strain on the line, and nine times out of ten the trout will work his own way out.

A trout should be completely played out before any attempt is made to land him, and he should always be led to still water first. Many big ones are lost at the last moment when they could easily have been landed with a few minutes' more patience. One way to finish a trout that is fairly well whipped is to hold his upper jaw out of water. A trout with his mouth open held in this manner against a current will soon drown. Another system which I have heard recommended is to lead the trout into a mud shallow. The mud he stirs up and gets into his gills will supposedly choke him. Never having tried this maneuver, I can't say how effective it may be.

Any good trout I intend to turn back I play for all the tackle is worth to get him in and off the hook before he is too badly beat down.

Large trout are the fisherman's greatest thrill, and I am all in favor of encouraging them in every possible way, even at the expense of a few bite-sized small ones; so I continue to release unneeded big ones along with little fellows. They will be even bigger and wiser next year. But this isn't always easy to do. A big trout will actually kill himself fighting if given the opportunity. One which is badly exhausted should not be turned loose to float belly up. If he is held gently in an upright position he will soon revive himself sufficiently to swim off in a normal position, whereas if he is allowed to float away belly up he might not survive.

When the fisherman is playing a fish for keeps, however, he should wear him down completely before bringing him to net; then, if he happens to muff the job, he hasn't necessarily lost. The net is the most common and best means of landing a trout. The technique is simple. In the first place the trout should not be reeled close to the rod tip. The leader should never enter the top guide. Just enough line should be retrieved that when the arms are spread wide, the rod in one hand pointing in one direction and the net in the other pointing in the opposite direction, the trout can just comfortably be reached with the net. This isn't merely a matter of form; it has a reason. If the trout should make a sudden, last-minute spurt, the rod can be swung back in the direction of the trout immediately and provide twenty feet of leeway. A mere bend of the wrist can ease him into the net or let him have line. A trout snubbed up tight would likely break something before he could be given slack.

The net should be completely submerged and held motionless and the trout led over it; then, at the same time that the net is lifted, the line is slacked gently. When the line is slacked, the trout will turn down headfirst into the rising net and there is no possibility of his flopping out. The line should be slacked gently, but not completely until the trout is definitely in the net. At the beginning of a battle a slack line is of no danger, but by the end of the fight the hook has doubtless worn a hole in the trout's jaw, and slack which would allow it to fall out should be avoided at all costs. Never make a stab at a trout with a net from above; he'll see it coming. No matter how exhausted he may be, he's alert to danger from above, and he's going to get out of the way. This is a perfect way to break a leader

If allowed to run free against the smooth click of a fly reel, a hard-running fish (notice the outstretched line) will soon subdue himself; then he can be brought back in, as the fisherman to the rear is demonstrating. The location of this fast action is Tanalion Point, Lake Clark, Alaska.

or knock a trout off the hook. Instead, come from underneath and move deliberately, not quickly.

There are other means of landing a trout besides a net. I was dry-fly fishing a deep, meandering meadow stream one day and was casting from a kneeling position some twenty feet back from the bank when a fourteen-inch brown took the fly, bore deep for an instant and came out in a very spectacular jump right alongside the near bank. Instinctively, at the top of his leap I tightened the line slightly, changing the trout's course just sufficiently that he dropped back not in the water but on shore. That was a mean trick. It's one way of landing a trout, but it isn't recommended.

Beaching, however, is an excellent way to land a trout. Where conditions are suitable, I prefer this method to a net with a big one. Unless completely whipped, a trout will make one last struggle when he comes too close to a man, as he must when being drawn to a net. In beaching, he may never see the fisherman until it's over. Again, the fish should be close to the exhaustion point; however, although dangerous and not to be recommended, I have seen a fast-running fish turned at the proper moment and stranded before he even started to fight. A little more patience will pay big dividends, and if the fish has turned on his side, he is as good as landed by a man adept at this stunt. At least he

should be played down to the point that he is willing to be led around at a distance.

Choose a spot where the bottom shoals gradually at the water's edge, the more gradual the better. If there's no such place handy but one visible downstream, it's worth going a quarter-mile to take advantage of it. If the trout is done in by then, he can be swung around on a short line onto the beach. Better tactics, however, are not to reel him closer than twenty feet; then, when he can be headed inshore, to back up the beach and strand him on a long line. In this manner he has no reason to be alarmed by the fisherman, and when he feels the bottom under him, it's too late. If he is headed toward land, as he always should be, he may actually flop himself high and dry.

One big advantage of beaching is that the trout is usually landed even if the hook does pull out at the last moment (as hooks in big fish have a tendency to do). If the trout is on his side when he feels bottom, not only will he tend to flop ashore under his own power, but there is little possibility of his righting himself in such shallow water and escaping.

I more often fish without a net than with one simply because it is fun to land trout by other means. The big ones can be beached or picked up by the gills; others can be picked up with the hand with a little experience. Leaving the net home is good training in playing a fish. Without

The safest and surest method of landing a big fish on light tackle is to beach him; then he can be dragged as far back in the boondocks as his size warrants. This is a steelhead from the Situk River in Alaska.

a net the fisherman must learn to play the fish out completely before attempting to land him. When grasped amidships, he will not slip either way. If the hand is warm, he will struggle when it touches him, but if it is cooled off to stream temperature by being immersed in the water for a moment, he won't resist.

Net

In selecting a trout net, see that it has a deep, stout pocket and a mouth wide enough to take a good fish. A net with a round mouth is satisfactory, but I prefer one which is open wider at the far end; that is, shaped much as is the silhouette of a dipsey sinker. The rim and handle of the finest nets are made of laminated wood to give them the greatest possible strength for their weight. A fisherman doesn't want to pack around any more weight than necessary on a hot day. Strength is not necessary in the actual netting of a trout, but a stream fisherman has an annoying habit of sitting down when he least expects to, and sometimes the net takes the brunt of the fall. A strong net may also come in handy as a steadying staff in crossing a rapids.

More important is how and where the net is carried. Some are mounted on an elastic cord and carried over the shoulder. This elastic has the advantage that a fish can be netted without unslinging the cord. It also has a disadvantage. The net catches on a bush, the elastic stretches,

like the bands of a slingshot, the net lets go, and you've had it. Anyone who has been turned inside out by such a net handle hitting him in the middle of the back knows about such things.

A simple squeeze snap on the net handle is less nerve-racking. The net will still catch on everything in the neighborhood, but it won't slap you down each time.

The net can be carried several places. It should be handy when needed, and out of the way when not needed. When you are carrying a creel, it can be snapped on the ring which joins the shoulder strap and body strap behind the creel. When not wearing a fishing jacket or carrying a creel, I like to snap the net on a belt loop on the right back side. With a fishing jacket, a handy rig is a soft leather loop attached at the back of the collar. A net hung on this is completely out of the way, even of brush; and is still available.

A gaff, by the way, has no place on a trout stream. On light tackle, any trout in the gaff class will be completely tame before he permits himself to come in range of a fisherman. The only place where it might have any possible use in the trout-fishing realm would be on big lakers, and even there it should be used sparingly and with discrimination: merely hooked through his jaw rather than plunged crudely into his side. A big, two-handed net is more efficient and considerably neater.

Chapter 27

OTHER LANDS

Trout in one form or another are native in cold waters throughout the Northern Hemisphere, and of all this vast habitat the United States is blessed with the best. For nonmigratory trout the finest all-round area in the world radiates from Yellowstone Park in the states of Montana, Idaho, and Wyoming; and the best sea-run (steelhead) fishing is in our Northwest and Alaska. Norway has some excellent sea-run brown fishing, and there is good local trout fishing in many places in Asia and Europe, but I personally am not impressed with the latter. Too much of the fishing in Europe is reserved for the privileged only, and I am spoiled by our freedoms. One experience on the Traun River in Austria was enough for me. I was literally the only fisherman permitted on an entire stretch of river. The locals who should have been fishing merely watched the massacre—not with envy because they and their forefathers had never known anything else, but possibly with regret when I caught Fat Friedrich or some other hand-fet pet. Both the trout and grayling were gullible rather than discerning, and I was as uncomfortable as though I had my hand in the poor box. Besides that, the otherwise beautiful river was filthy with human refuse. It was a worthwhile experience only in strengthening my already great appreciation of American values.

No trout is native to the Southern Hemisphere, but browns from Europe and rainbows and brookies from the United States have been established there for roughly a century; so they are as good as native. Two areas in particular down under offer rich possibilities to trout fishermen: New Zealand and parts of South America. There have been many articles written praising these areas and perhaps even exaggerating their virtues, with the result that some

people who make the trip to these distant lands arrive with the wrong impression. This helps no one, neither the visitors nor those who cater to such fishermen. Although these are large areas each with a variety of trout waters, there are essential differences which could be of importance to anyone planning such a distant trout-fishing trip.

New Zealand

New Zealand is as lovely as anyone has painted it. Nowhere are there more unspoiled lakes and streams, generally as crystal-clear as water can be. And nowhere are there more hospitable people than the Kiwis, as New Zealanders call themselves. And of course language is no barrier; New Zealand speaks the Queen's English even though you might run across a few strange linguistic twists.

Trout fishing in New Zealand is generally high on quality, not so on quantity. It excels for fly fishermen, but the casual fisherman can also find a place there.

Two major islands make up New Zealand, and the casual fisherman should look only to North Island. He can go there with no tackle and no experience and stand a good chance of getting a five- to ten-pound trout by trolling such lakes as Tarawera, Rotorua, and Taupo. The season for this is summer (our winter); the legal open season on the first two lakes runs from October through June, while Taupo and some others are open year-round. One negative aspect of such trolling is that the trout may be deep enough to require leaded line, in which case the sport can be measured solely by the final results of boating a big trout.

For the experienced fisherman as well, there is

Geoff Thomas and Jean Holland landing a nice rainbow. Lake Tarawera, North Island, New Zealand.

Jean Holland with a fat rainbow from Lake Tarawera, North Island, New Zealand.

fine fly fishing on North Island. Again, the emphasis is on large trout, not a lot of trout, and some of the best fishing of this sort takes place during the winter months (April through August) when the spawners are running in rivers such as the Tangariro out of Lake Taupo. This fishing calls for high-density lines and the ability to lay out a fair amount. These big spawning rainbows remain in the rivers all winter, and the fishing in the lower Tangariro for instance picks up again in December as the rainbows are dropping back into Lake Taupo.

Fly fishing only is permitted on the Tangariro, as it is on many of New Zealand's best streams. There is often good fly fishing on North Island lakes as well. The best time is summer (December to March) and the radius of three hundred yards around a stream mouth is generally reserved for fly fishing. In addition there are many smaller rivers and streams on North Island which provide both wet-fly and dry-fly fishing, but the island is noted more for the former. Also on North Island there is some sea-run brown trout and salmon fishing, but I know nothing about it.

Southland, as it is called, is something else! It is the more scenic of the two islands, and there is no place comparable to it for the dedicated dry-fly fisherman. Where a four- or five-pound

trout on a dry fly is a lifetime's dream elsewhere, it is the reasonable expectation in Southland. The fishing is done both in clear lakes and in lovely little streams, or burns, and the choice time of year is during the summer months of December, January, and February. My only visit there was supposedly too late, mid-March, but there was nothing wrong with the fishing even then, and it was of a type at which I am most proficient: spotting big fish in clear water, stalking them, and presenting a dry fly with finesse. To make it better, I didn't exactly charm them out onto the bank. I attribute this to the fact that most of them were so old that they were as wise as the oldest fisherman; they couldn't have been that big without being old! I fished only two places, with Fred Gill on Lake Mavora and with Murray Knowles on a beautiful little stream called Iris Burn emptying into Lake Manapouri, and every trout I saw was big! I mean every trout and I mean big! And they were all willing to rise. It was totally fascinating. Next time we are going to arrive much earlier and stay much later.

In fact, anyone considering fishing New Zealand or South America should plan an extended trip if possible. The big expense is the trip there and back. The cost of more time on location is minimal by comparison. Even the casual fisher-

Lake Manapouri, South Island, New Zealand.

man cannot reasonably expect to hire a guide by the hour and get anything. He must give any guide a full day or two at least or he is wasting his time and money. It will take the serious fisherman much longer just to locate water which satisfies him.

South America

Having spent many months trout fishing in South America and having covered most of the rivers and a number of lakes on both sides of the Andes, I know that this subject covers a multitude of conditions and situations. Therefore, it is perhaps best to speak primarily in generalities and to point out the differences between South America and New Zealand for anyone choosing between one or the other.

First, and no small matter, New Zealand is not only English-speaking but it is organized. The visitor can find out anything about fishing by simply writing the Tourist and Publicity Department, Private Bag, Rotorua, New Zealand. There is no such reliable central source of information in either Chile or the Argentine that I ever discovered, although the airlines servicing them

The Chilean fishing rod, monofilament wrapped around a can and a spoon cast David's-sling fashion, . . .

. . . produces results.

may be of assistance. For my own part, I have found my way around simply by being hard-headed. And, of course, though the language is Spanish, there are many English-speaking people (except in the more remote regions).

New Zealand fishermen are accomplished to a high degree, as one might guess from the "fly-fishing only" restrictions. Anything goes in South America, and there are few fishermen by our standards in Chile. One of the most common outfits consists of a large can with a stick wedged across the inside and monofilament wrapped around the outside. It is no more nor less than a large spinning reel. The left hand holds the stick within and the right hand twirls a spoon in David's-sling fashion to make the cast. The retrieve is made by rewinding the lines around the can, a procedure which gives the spoon a good spurting action. Such *caña chilena* fisherman are good, but this is a somewhat different atmosphere from fly-fishing only. In the Argentine there are a number of accomplished

trout fishermen, especially in the San Martín de los Andes and San Carlos de Bariloche regions. Some of these can be persuaded to guide. One of the best to my knowledge is Laddie Buchanan in Bariloche.

The important thing is the nature of the fishing itself. In contrast to New Zealand, anyone can reasonably expect to catch numerous fish. They will be, on the average, large by our domestic standards, usually from a foot to sixteen inches, and truly big ones can be taken at times.

Chile is the best choice for the casual fisherman. In Chapter 18, the section on floating briefly describes the common method of fishing in the beautiful Lakes District of Chile. A good choice for such a float trip is the Toltén River. No one here needs prior experience with trout for success.

There are many bountiful rivers throughout this district down to Puerto Montt, where the roads end. Anywhere that a fisherman can find

This rainbow, hooked in the smooth water of a lake outlet, headed for fast water before being landed.

Sea-trout fishing. Río Grande, Tierra del Fuego, Argentina.

access he can expect good fishing on streamers. The same is true for the competent fisherman on the Argentine side on most rivers all the way from San Martín to Tierra del Fuego.

In addition, South America offers two special forms of fishing not available to us in the States. One is the "boca." A boca is simply a natural outlet of a lake, and we have hardly such a thing left in the United States due to dams. Among the few left is the outlet of Yellowstone Lake, and there were perhaps hundreds of tons of trout taken off Fishing Bridge during the many years that such fishing was permitted. There are also a few natural outlets in wilderness areas.

Most fishermen search for inlets to lakes, probably with the idea that the inflowing water brings food to attract trout. This is true after a rain, but normally it is the other way around. The greatest amount of food is grown in the quieter waters of the lake and is carried out into the stream below. Therefore, the area where the lake water commences to accelerate at the outlet makes an ideal feeding location. Depending upon the velocity of the water, the feeding trout arrange themselves, often in a semicircle, around the mouth of the outlet.

South American lakes for the most part still have their natural outlets. If the season is such that trout from lakes are preparing to run, of course the vicinity of an inlet is the place to fish; otherwise, the outlet, or boca, provides the most abundant fishing. Fly fishermen in the Argentine are quite aware of this situation, so available bocas have their share of fishermen, but in Chile this is less likely to be the case.

The other unusual trout fishing in South America is for sea-run browns. When I first visited Chile many years ago (in March of 1952, to be precise), I settled at the Petrohué River at the southern end of the Lakes District where the fishing was good for typical rainbow and brown trout; then I hooked and eventually landed something else! It was a seven-pounder as bright as a new dime and as wild as a fresh Atlantic salmon. I decided first that it had to be sea-run and, after considerable deliberation, that it was a brown. Of course I spoke of it to everyone, but no one knew of such a thing. I was sufficiently confident that I immediately published a magazine article referring to my find, but still no one would confirm it. This haunted me for years until I had to go back and prove the fact without doubt, which I did; then I couldn't keep from returning to enjoy it some more.

There are sea-run browns on the Chilean side all the way from the Lakes District to the end of

Huge sea-run brown trout. Río Grande, Tierra del Fuego, Argentina.

the continent, but, to bring this to a quick conclusion, there are two outstanding and very different South American sea-trout rivers. One of these, which is the less available of the two unfortunately, is the grand El Serrano, or Mountaineer. It is located in southern Chile, the closest town being Punta Arenas. El Serrano is a large and clear river which meanders through a plain under majestic snow-capped peaks in a setting that is among the most delightful I have ever seen. And in season it affords fine sea-trout fishing. My visits there have been in March since browns run in autumn, and at the time most of the fish I caught were bright.

The other top sea-trout river is the Río Grande on the island of Tierra del Fuego. It heads up on the Chilean side of the island, but the readily available fishing is on the Argentine side. This is a less lovely river than El Serrano. It meanders more, has cutting banks, and is somewhat silty. The fishing is slow, requiring miles of casting and a long line, but it is worth it

One of trout fishing's attributes is that it is relative. A twelve-incher in some circumstances can appear as large as a twelve-pounder in big water.

as an illustration or two in this book will indicate. When my friend Mike Konak and I last fished it, we used a variety of streamers with success. Over the period of eight days we averaged only one good fish per day, but they were good fish. They ran from about 8 pounds to 16 pounds 5 ounces, that one taking an Ambassador about two inches in length.

That is an enormous trout, but trout fishing is entirely relative to the water and conditions being fished. I have known times when a 16-incher looked just as big as a 16-pounder.

Chapter 28

THE EVENING HATCH

There's a time of day close to the heart of every man who has floated a fly. It's the time when the deer leaves his bed and the rabbit his form. It's the time when all is calm, and the cool mists begin to rise; the crickets and katydids commence to tune their fiddles, and the bull bats zoom and roar in their power dives. In short, it's the time when the May flies dance.

Certainly there are many people who enjoy this time of day, no matter where they are, but I doubt if anyone gets so much out of it as the trout fisherman along his favorite stream. This is the time when all the trout go on a feeding spree; when there is so much to see and hear that less fortunate people know nothing about.

Who else but the fellow who hunts and fishes knows about the strange courtship dance of the woodcock? The fisherman along an eastern meadow stream in spring hears him often at twilight. He hears the raucous buzz, like the sound of a high-voltage spark, and he can visualize the cock timberdoodle strutting about with tail spread, wings drooping, and his head twisting with each buzz. Later comes the telltale whistle of wings as he spirals up in his courtship flight; then the clear music, like the tinkling of little bells, as he cups his wings and tumbles back to earth. It's difficult to believe at first that a woodcock could create such musical sounds. The "owl snipe" is an odd little fellow.

The fisherman may also hear the distant-thunder drumming of the partridge, and he wishes him well in siring a large family. He's a grand bird, and autumn would never be the same without him.

The evening fisherman sees the muskrat, the mink, the coon, and the playful otter; then, if the rise is a good one, he sees the first bats in their crazy pattern of flight as they pursue the insect feast, and he will know that they operate by the original radar, forming mental pictures of their surroundings through echo alone. Or an owl might sweep eerily overhead, and the fisherman realizes that it has adapted to fly silently upon its prey by means of its finely fringed wing feathers. He knows of the strange—and often very compatible—relationship between parasite and host, and he experiences the unexplained power of instinct on all sides; then he wonders why some "nature" writers resort to their own feeble imaginations and attribute human qualities to their animals. All he needs to do is look about him to witness events far more wondrous than anything man could imagine.

Possibly the most wonderful event of all for the evening fisherman is the dance of the May flies. This is the time of action; for when a heavy hatch is on, all the fish in the stream gorge themselves on the rising nymphs, the floating duns, the egg-laying spinners, and the spent flies whose brief moment is ended. The Latin name for May flies is *Ephemerida* which stems from the same root as our word *ephemeral*, meaning short-lived. May flies may crawl about in the seclusion of mud, moss, or tiny caverns among the rocks and gravel of a stream bottom for as long as two years, but as winged insects they enjoy only a short spell of glory, sometimes but a few hours and at the most a couple of days. Toward evening thousands of nymphs of the same species, as if by some mysterious signal, abandon their secret ways in the shadowy depths and rise carelessly to the surface, oblivious to danger. Each floats momentarily while the nymph case splits down the back, then steps out of his coarse shell as a delicate and graceful May fly, complete with gossamer wings, gently curving body, and long sweeping tails. After a short ride while the wings dry, these dull-colored duns fly ashore and rest again until they shed once more. This time they emerge bright and shiny and are known as spinners. The male spinners gather in a swarm over the water, each species with its own peculiar form of flight. In a typical May-fly dance, the male spinners fly directly up in the air for twenty to thirty feet, then drop back down again tail first, thousands of them making up a vast cloud of insects. The females fly out from shore to join the males; then, with their heavy egg sacs, descend to the surface to spawn. Soon they drop to the water spent, with wings outspread, and it's all over.

Some species of May flies hatch, dance, and die the same evening. Others may go into their dance a day later, and the largest species waits until about forty-eight hours after hatching to return to the water from which they came.

Other species of aquatic insects are also inclined to hatch in the evening hours of spring and summer. Most noticeable of these are the mothlike caddis flies which race upstream over the water's surface, land for a short ride, and race up again. Others, less obvious because of their size, but possibly most numerous of all, are the swarming midges. Sometimes a fisherman will walk into a milling cloud of them and find himself literally covered with the tiny things. Luckily they don't bite like their near relatives, the mosquitoes, black flies, and punkies, or "no-see-ums."

The trout go wild when there is so much insect food at hand, and at times the water surface fairly boils. The swifts and the swallows, and later the bats, get their share too. The only thing around the stream busier than these feeding fish and birds is the fisherman. He's frantically tying on new patterns of flies attempting to match the insect hatch and get in on the fun. The trout are rising everywhere, and he knows that this magic hour is short. He must crowd so much into so lit-

This unusual picture of two at a time at the start of the evening hatch is a fine example of the unselfish attitude fostered by the non-competitive sport of fishing. The man at the left, although he has a big one of his own far from landed, is suddenly more concerned with the fortune of his partner whose trout is acting up dangerously.

Mayflies, the inspiration for the majority of our trout-fly patterns, make up the mainstay of trout diet the world around. Although consumed by the millions as nymphs, they are most evident to us during their brief adult life, some species hatching, dancing, spawning, and returning to the water dead all in one evening. This activity brings on the finest hour the trout fisherman can know, the evening hatch.

tle time. When he finally does succeed in choosing the correct fly, it is almost too dark to see it floating on the water. There are so many trout splashing that he can't tell for sure whether or not one has taken his tiny artificial from among the naturals. Finally, in desperation, he takes off the imitation and tries to replace it with a large white fly, which at least he can see on the water, but it is so late that he must hold it against the light of the sky to tie it on the leader. Then it's all over; and it has been a grand day. Maybe he has taken a trout or two, and maybe he hasn't, but it has been an experience that he would not have missed.

Time goes by, but fishermen don't change. I suppose they have been the same since the beginning of time. In reading the "Treatyse of fysshynge wyth an angle," written over 450 years ago, I ran across a passage which fits the fisherman of today as well as it did the one of medieval England. Changed to modern spelling it reads as follows:

> But if there be none (trout) in the water where he shall angle; yet, at the least, he shall have his wholesome walk, and (be) merry at his own ease, and also (smell) many a sweet ear of divers herbs and flowers that shall make him right hungry and well disposed in his body; he shall hear the melodies melodious of the harmony of birds; he shall see also young swannies and cygnets following their elders—ducks, coots, herons and many other fowls with their broods—which (to) me seems better than all the noise of hounds and blasts of horns and other games that falconers and hunters can make; and, if the angler takes the fish, hardly then is there no man merrier than he in his spirits.

It's no different today. When the evening hatch is over and the day is done, the fisherman doesn't always have a heavy creel to show for it, but he's richer inside. He's had the scolding chickadee or the clownish water ouzel for company, and he's witnessed the miracle of the dance of the May flies. Nothing else is necessary for a delightful day. But, if he does take a trout, "hardly then is there no man merrier than he in his spirits."